ILLUSIONS OF
CAMELOT

ILLUSIONS OF
CAMELOT

A MEMOIR BY PETER BOAL

BEAUFORT BOOKS

ILLUSIONS OF CAMELOT

Hardcover: 9780825309830
Ebook: 9780825308628

For inquiries about volume orders, please contact:
Beaufort Books, 27 West 20th Street, Suite 1103, New York, NY 10011
sales@beaufortbooks.com

Published in the United States by Beaufort Books
www.beaufortbooks.com

Distributed by Midpoint Trade Books
a division of Independent Publisher Group
https://www.ipgbook.com/

Book designed by Mark Karis
Cover photograph of Peter Boal © Steven Caras, all rights reserved.
Letter to the editor used with permission from *The New Yorker* © Condé Nast

Printed in the United States of America

CONTENTS

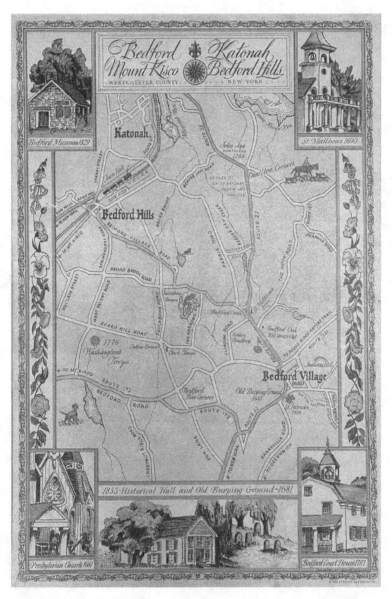

Map of Bedford in 1955 *(image courtesy of the author)*

BEDFORD IN SHORT

Bedford was a generational town. If your mother, uncle or great-grandparents were born in Bedford, you let people know. The Jays, Wallers and Woods boasted several generations, but Wall Street and Hollywood money were moving in, along with a few self-made celebrities: Tallulah Bankhead came first, then Patricia Neal, followed by Carl Icahn, Glenn Close, Ralph Lauren, Martha Stewart and Donald Trump. It wasn't just the proximity to New York City or the golf courses or bridle trails; it was the feeling of exemption. Residents retreated to their multi-acre estates with horses, highballs, golden retrievers and Land Rovers to forget all of the angst and agitation of the outside world. The homogeneity was not only comforting but desired.

The men, all schooled at Ivies, traveled home together on Metro North from law firms and brokerage firms to waiting wives. The wives were equally well educated but allowed marriages to trump professions. These well-coiffed matrons were power brokers of a different sort, guiding day laborers to plant lush gardens and championing local causes with zeal while Black and Irish women pressed their husbands' shirts, raised their unruly and ambitious children, and created perfect family dinners. Kids learned early on in private schools about SATs, BMWs and IPOs while building impressive applications for Andover, Choate and Exeter through summer volunteering. Kids and their parents shared the singular goal of repeating the cycle and adding another generation to the Bedford line. Migration to certain Connecticut towns was also acceptable.

Shared affluence was part of it, but that could be found on Park Avenue, Sutton Place or in Greenwich. It was the security that drew people to Bedford. Homeowners never locked their doors. There was no reason to. Everywhere you went, you saw yourself or someone just like you. Sure, there were people who didn't resemble you, but they worked for someone who looked like you. The town was built on shared sensibilities and trust. Florists left blooming flowers outside their shops at night. Fresh bottled milk and L.L Bean packages sat on porches beside teak furniture, cache pots, galoshes and a neighbor's homemade jam. Few houses had alarm systems unless you count the family Lab.

My Bedford was an odd place to come of age. In many ways, it was as wonderful as a warm embrace. My memories are vivid, especially the rolling green pastures of Sunny Field Farm, the snorts of passing horses on otherwise quiet dirt roads, and a town center that held dear its colonial past through the preservation of churches, a library, courthouse and one room schoolhouse. Bedford could be or could seem idyllic, but there were unwritten rules. Residents learned which rules applied, and which could be broken without consequence. These rules weren't taught in a traditional sense; they were learned, often indirectly, or simply understood. The butcher at Stewart's Market would set aside the best cuts for certain customers; the kennels would stay open late on Sundays if the ferry from Nantucket was delayed; the police would allow certain drivers to proceed with a simple warning despite clear violations; and the real estate agents would keep the neighborhood wealthy and white.

Rules amount to systems and systems need to be scrutinized. Though this book is written through the eyes of a child, awareness of what's right and what's wrong is an integral part of coming of age. The writing and the reading of this book brought a town's systemic forces and failures to light, revealing roots of oppression, latent and overt discrimination, protection of privilege, and perpetuation of wealth. Bedford was by no means alone in its flaws. Similar stories and situations exist in any number of communities. In truth, systemic failures are ever-present throughout histories and regions. We continue to be affected by them as we hold these systems up to the light to see what's really beneath the surface. Some hold justice and virtue at their core, while others are rife with harm and detriment. Bedford held both. Within these pages, this small town provides the opening scene and the early education of my story.

The citizens of Bedford in the late 1900s leaned in, wanting to uphold an earned, desired, and enviable lifestyle. As the town leaned in, the rest of the world was left out and I found myself in the middle.

Mr. and Mrs. R. Bradlee Boal

announce the birth

of a son

Peter Cadbury

October 18th, 1965

PROLOGUE

THE OAK

There are oak trees in North America that are supposedly fifteen hundred years old, and legend tells of a Norway spruce on a wind-swept shore of Sweden said to be more than 9,000 years old. The Bedford Oak, sprightly by comparison at 600, still manages to impress.

It stands along Route 22 like a bloated gargoyle or an imposing bouncer, a stone's throw from the Bedford Golf and Tennis Club and about a mile from the Rippowam-Cisqua School. During the course of its centuries of existence, it has witnessed Native Americans cede to white men and horses to automobiles. Horses still amble by, with riders taking note of the grand tree, but hundreds of cars and trucks roar past every day without even a hint of reverence. The span of branches is incredible, sprawling 150 feet in every direction from the massive trunk. One of the larger lower branches was given a humiliating but necessary crutch at some point during the 1990s by the Friends of the Bedford Oak. Friends indeed!

The Oak is estimated to have taken seed around 1405, long before Route 22, Aspetong Road, Christopher Columbus or Amerigo Vespucci existed. In 1680 the Oak and its surrounding land was purchased for fourteen pounds, sixteen shillings and a pile of blankets and wampum from seven Native American Chiefs. The purchasers were British settlers who traveled from nearby Stamford along a path now known as Long Ridge Road.

The Oak remained unscathed, along with one lonely house huddled on the perimeter of the village green, when most of the town was lost to a fire in 1770. Tree and town were once part of the State of Connecticut until political barter reassigned the town to the State of New York. Today the town proudly maintains its New England heritage and look. Alsace-Lorraine and Bedford: indifferent to the redrawing of political lines, choosing and honoring heritage instead.

The Oak is an unimaginable spread of twisted limbs, each with its own intended direction, yet swayed by and dependent on a neighbor. The families of Bedford are as intertwined as this panoply of branches; some have stretched and grown through winters and winds for hundreds of years, while others, with equally grand intentions, snapped before springtime, never to see the next summer. These discarded twigs land on the soft ground below and do not play a role in the grand story.

On the 18th of October in 1965, in the early dawn hours, my mother and father left their small home on Tarleton Road to speed to the Northern Westchester Hospital in neighboring Mt. Kisco. Hours later, I exercised my newborn lungs to let the world and the town know, like a fresh sprout on the great Bedford Oak, a new story had begun.

LUCKY WINNERS: Christopher Hughes, 8, of Rome Avenue, Bedford Hills, and Peter Boals, 2, of Guard Hill Road, Bedford, demonstrate new bicycles won at the annual children's picnics held by the Bedford police this week. The boys are shown with Police Chief Donald Hayes, left, and Policeman Samuel VanDorn, chairman of the event. Officer VanDorn said about 800 children turned up for the three picnics held at the parks in Bedford Village, Bedford Hills and Katonah. The crowd consumed nearly 400 pounds of hot dogs, 800 containers of ice cream. Winner of a third bicycle was Susan McManus, 16, of Peapond Road, Katonah. The bicycles were donated for the drawing by Barkers Department Store.

Staff photos by Meyer

Article from *The Patent Trader*

1

BICYCLE

My first memory was from the summer of 1968. It wasn't good.
I was two and a half.

Our family attended the Police and Fireman's Fair in Mt.
Kisco, the slightly larger town just west of Bedford. At the center
of town, on a traffic island in front of the American Legion,
stood the statue of Chief Kisco. Ironically, the Chief looks across
the road at another statue, this one of Christopher Columbus.
Muscular and proud, with tall feathers sprouting from his
headdress, the Chief looked like he had presided from that spot
forever, but locals know he tended to disappear each June when
high school seniors wrestled him from his base and transported
him to unintended and often inappropriate locations. In '66, he
was found splayed out on a seesaw at Leonard Park. The class of
'62 left him peering through the windows of Abel's department
store at alluring female mannequins. One Christmas the Chief
made a surprise and unwelcome appearance with the wise men

at the creche outside of St. Francis of Assisi, and after he was found face down on the pavement outside of Kelty's tavern, he was firmly bolted to the cement and pranks were limited to the humiliating adornment of bras, caps and boas.

In truth, Chief Kisco was a fictional character. The word "Kisko" originated from the Munsee word "asiiskuw," meaning mud. A deed from 1700 offers the misspelling or respelling, "cisqua." A postmaster respelled it again in 1850 as "Kisko," which stuck like mud. Chief Kisko was one of many casts scooped up by a landscape architect who needed an impressive ornament to top a grand fountain. In 1907 the Chief was donated to the town for citizens (other than poorly behaved high school seniors) to admire.

To call Mt. Kisco a town would be untrue in 1968. The hamlet was half Bedford, half New Castle until 1978, when cessation of such intermingling occurred. Still, for all intents and purposes, it was regarded as a neighboring town and had a markedly different vibe. Where Bedford was pastoral, Mt. Kisco was functional, with car dealers, furniture stores, shoe stores, a hospital, high school and affordable housing for workers from both towns. It also offered the nearest stop on the Harlem line for Metro North, making the gravitational pull on Bedford strong.

The Fair was an annual event that raised funds and bolstered appreciation for our local firemen and policemen. (In 1968, there were no women on either force.) It was a typical August Saturday. Kids and overwrought parents spent the afternoon milling around the stations sitting in squad cars, ringing the bell on the fire engine and licking rapidly melting ice cream cones. The servicemen were wonderfully inclusive, but as the afternoon wore on, the mercury edged up, and the enthusiasm drained. Fingers were sticky, couples were bickering, and the dalmatian had already been sent to the kennel. I know families wanted to leave. I'm sure my parents wanted to leave, but they couldn't. Upon entry, every child was offered a two-dollar raffle ticket, making them eligible to win a brand-new bicycle. Winner needed to be present to claim the prize.

The bicycle was purple and steel with a banana-shaped seat that sparkled and endless long handlebars like ape hangers on a Harley. Add grape-colored grips and bright red reflectors, and every kid was hooked. My mother read the description to Jenny and me while we lapped our dripping cones.

"Brand-new 1968 Schwinn Fastback Stingray with pedal brakes and purple power. Both safe and speedy, this classy ride will make some lucky child, age 6 to 8, very happy!"

"I'm two," I said.

"I'm four," Jenny said triumphantly.

"That's right, but guess what? One day, you'll both be six and besides, the likelihood of either of you winning this bicycle is slim. We bought the tickets to support our local police and fire fighters. The bike probably will go to some child who needs it. You both have tricycles. We'll be very happy for the lucky winner."

"I won't."

"Oh, Pete-bear, yes you will, now lick that one drip that's just about to reach your hand."

Dad took me to play games, which I wasn't particularly good at and, in the end, Dad played the games instead. He seemed to know everyone at the event as he moved from group to group, brandishing his young son and a cold beer. As I toddled alongside, or in his strong arms, I watched him interact with kids of all ages and make grown-ups laugh. He seemed to know everyone's name, what they did, where they lived and where they worked. People were happy in his company, and so was I.

At four o'clock, the bell on the tower rang, and the fire chief simultaneously rang the one on the engine. Raffle time. Kids crowded towards the truck where a small platform, had been constructed for this moment. Parents rummaged in purses and wallets for tickets, and the fire chief stepped onto the platform accompanied by the mayor of New Castle and a few local politicians.

Speeches followed for what seemed an eternity, with polite applause from the gathered adults and moans from the children. Finally, the bicycle was rolled forward by one of the policemen. A girl from Fox Lane Middle School with a staggering amount of community service hours was asked to draw the winning ticket. The policeman carefully lowered the microphone to her height. She stepped forward confidently, slid on a pair of wire-rimmed glasses and, revealing a mouth full of braces, read, "The winner of the brand-new Schwinn Fastback Stingray is ... " She paused. She was good at this. Parents clutched kids. "Seven ... four ... two ... nine ... that's seven, four, two, nine!"

A mom from the crowd let out a shriek. It was my mom.

"That's me ... I mean ... that's us. That's you, Pete!" The crowd was mostly cheering though there was a definite undertone of groaning, and a few kids just flew off the deep end wailing as they were dragged away. I was plopped down on the platform with my mother right beside as a fireman escorted me to my new bike. If I wasn't shocked, I would have smiled. I was certainly smiling on the inside.

As the beaming fire chief held me on my bike with a lollipop shoved in my mouth, flashes popped. Another round with the mayor and some other kid, then the girl with all of the metal in her mouth. Mom could be heard dictating my name, age and address to the reporter from the *Patent Trader*. I was a winner, and the large purple bike seemed like the ultimate prize.

As the excitement ebbed, a policeman asked, "So, kid, you gonna ride that bike home?"

Everyone laughed. I couldn't see the humor.

"I suspect his sister will be riding this one first. I imagine we'll just give the bike to her," said my dad, looking around at all of the nodding heads.

I don't think I said anything, but I must have looked up at my dad with big, watery eyes.

"It's a girl's bike, Pete. You can tell by the color and the seat. Not to worry, when the time comes, we'll get a perfect bike for you."

Between the lollipop and the very edge of tears, I said nothing, but my two-and-a-half-year-old mind was racing. This bike was the perfect bike. It didn't look like a girl's bike to me; it looked like my bike—my new purple-powered policeman's raffle bike.

Dad's prediction came true. Jenny rode the bicycle a few years later with training wheels stretching sideways to keep her on balance as she trundled around our driveway. By the time I was old enough to claim my rightful prize, I had a new Schwinn Racer with red and white stripes and a life lesson that some of the greatest wins in life should never be taken for granted because just as quickly, they can disappear. It was a rough start, but I got over it.

THE N

ROGER STONE'S TRICKS

I read with great interest Tyler Foggatt's reporting on Roger Stone's teen-age electioneering days in Westchester County (The Talk of the Town, March 18th). I knew Roger in school—when he was the president of the student council at John Jay High School, I was the president of the student council at the middle school. In 1971, a year after Stone graduated, I started examining a Westchester County legislature race for a social-studies project, and discovered that Stone appeared to be organizing churches as part of a smear campaign against the incumbent, R. Bradlee Boal, a potential violation of the Johnson Amendment, which prohibits nonprofit organizations from endorsing or opposing political candidates. (Stone later told the Washington *Post* that his candidate, a Republican named John Hicks-Beach, was the "dumbest politician" he had ever worked for.) To my knowledge, my amateur reporting was the first investigation into Stone's involvement in shady campaign activities, though certainly not the last.
Dean Corren
Burlington, Vt.

2

ILLUSIONS OF CAMELOT

Mom's 1953 MG convertible cruised along at about three miles an hour. Dad was behind the wheel, smiling. He kept his kid-like grin throughout his short life, and the moments when he was truly happy were infectious. Mom was in the passenger seat, leaning forward with arched back, looking like Jacqueline Kennedy. She wore a bright green-and-white print dress with bare arms that offered true stamina for waving to the cheering masses lining the parade route. These were the days before seat belts, and Jenny and I were not only unbuckled but also perched on the edge of the back seats with legs dangling over the trunk. We followed our mother's cue, waving left and right and proudly showing what teeth we had. Banners that read, "Vote for Brad Boal" were plastered on all four sides of the MG. I was four and my sister was six.

Dad was running for county legislator at the time. He won by a sizable margin—I'd like to think it was my wave or the adoration I unwittingly and genuinely bestowed on the candidate. Jenny and I had worked the campaign office, too. Licking envelopes was our forte, but we also helped by handing out buttons on street corners that read "B for Bedford: B for Boal!" In truth, my contribution was at best inconsequential. My dad was elected because he was an honorable and honest liberal Republican lawyer who helped run John Lindsay's mayoral campaign, believed in equal rights and higher minimum wage, and was pro-choice.

Not long after our triumphant drive down Route 22, my parents hosted a massive political fundraiser at our house on Guard Hill Road. In a town of about 4,000 residents, an impressive 500 guests arrived to support local Republicans. Incumbent State Senator Roy M. Goodman was guest of honor, and the rest of the guest list was no less impressive. Bedford was strongly Republican in 1970 and probably still is. The term "upper middle class" was just a humble word choice for the country club set that resided there. My mother was one of the few Democrats in town and remained steadfast in her liberal beliefs. Originally from England, she refused to become a U.S. citizen until President Nixon was out of office. Luckily, she and Dad saw eye to eye on politics. She and Nixon did not.

Though our house on Guard Hill Road was much bigger than our family of four needed or could afford, it was perfect for a Republican fundraiser. Guests wandered through the entire house, though most congregated in the oak-paneled living room around the Steinway grand. My parents hired a local jazz pianist for the night. The kitchen swarmed with caterers who rushed trays of hors d'oeuvres to the butler's pantry for smartly dressed servers to pass. The rest of the house offered twelve bathrooms, six bedrooms, two dressings rooms, a billiard room, wine cellar, phone booth, ladies' powder suite, men's room, key room, flower arranging room, two sleeping porches and ten fireplaces.

The grounds were sprawling yet manicured like something Jay Gatsby might have owned. There was a seldom-used grass tennis court and an Olympic-sized swimming pool complete with high dive, low dive and high slide. Well beyond the pool was an outdoor ballroom with a dance floor of alternating black-and-white marble squares. Ancient pines surrounded this vast checkerboard, looking on like wary chaperones. The marble could be flooded with water in winter to create an ice skating rink. When old Mrs. Wallace, who still lived on Tarleton Road, heard my parents had purchased the Smith estate, she recalled an August night in the late 1800s when she was a debutante. With tears in her eyes, she described her arrival in a horse-drawn carriage, "like Cinderella herself" at the elegant outdoor ballroom, to dance under the stars to the melodies of a small chamber orchestra. "So many invitations to dance, I couldn't say 'no'. My feet still hurt! But it was so sublime."

The house had known more glamorous days under its previous owners. It was Bernard and Gertrude Smith who transformed the place from humble farmhouse to grand estate near the turn of the century. Bernard made his vast fortune through the steel industry, assembling an extensive compound of acreage and buildings. It included an eight-car garage, Gertrude's stone stables and kennels, a lavish two-story pool house, a log cabin and a sizable mansion. By the time the Boals arrived, the eight-car garage had been purchased and renovated into a home for the Carsons, and the Nolans had converted the kennels and the stable into a sprawling home. My parents bought the main house. Jenny and I never fully understood why they took on this behemoth, but after seeing it for the first time, they returned to the property that evening, found an open door and ran the length of the house upstairs and down before collapsing in laughter.

Behind our house, across a perfect rectangle of lawn and beyond a three-foot stone wall, was the pool house. When we sold the property in 1983, our twenty-eight acres were subdivided with the Polks laying out a considerable sum for the pool house despite some crumbling from neglect. Built mostly of local granite, the pool house had a towering great room with an imposing hearth, a full servants' kitchen, a bedroom, ladies' changing room with bath, and a men's changing room with an adjoining bathroom complete with six urinals. Two large stone terraces afforded a view over the pool, sunken garden and fields beyond. A flagstone-covered porch lay in the center of it all, adorned with three sets of French double doors. My dad's two rusted tractors occupied the porch like two prized Ferraris.

On summer weekends, the tractors were rolled out and put to work grooming acres of lawn. Dad took great care in the cutting of the lawn because the dining room's enormous picture window looked onto an endless rectangular courtyard that stretched to the pool's edge. His tractor lines were impeccable. Though I was enlisted to cut much of the acreage at a young age, I wasn't allowed to cut the center courtyard until I was twelve. Before our late August GOP fundraiser, Dad took extra time to mow the courtyard, finally parking the tractor at dusk with just enough time to shower and dress before the guests arrived. Grass clippings would have to be collected another day.

The house teemed with energy as my mother lit long cream-colored tapers and caterers buzzed around the kitchen. Jenny and I were recruited to serve hors d'oeuvres, each entrusted with large, silver-plated trays full of cheese puffs, pigs in a blanket and deviled eggs topped with cayenne pepper and chives. Navigating through 500 tipsy Republicans and their clouds of cigarette and pipe smoke was not easy for an inexperienced server of four-and-a-half. After several runs through the dining room and foyer, I returned to the kitchen to reload with deviled eggs. I was relieved to find Mrs. Hattie, our nanny and housekeeper, who was keeping a watchful eye on her kitchen. She crouched down to my height and steadied my tray while reminding me not to forget to serve guests in the living room as well as those in the dining room.

"How am I going to get to the living room with all of those hungry people in the dining room?" I asked.

"I tell you how, little helper, you gonna cut straight across the courtyard and come in through the backdoor." One of her old worn hands pointed the way while the other smoothed my already slicked hair.

"Mrs. Hattie, how'd you get so smart?"

"Same way you got so handsome, we were just born that way. Now go on or those eggs are gonna be chickens soon if you don't hurry up."

"Okay, Mrs. Hattie, and now I'm going to run like a chicken all the way to the living room!"

"With that big old tray? No sir, you gonna walk." I got a kiss on the head and a pat on the butt.

My mom had dressed me in a ridiculous-looking little green jumpsuit with a baby chick embroidered on the right thigh. As I trotted across the freshly cut lawn, heads were turning in the dining room. Millicent Boggart called to the guests, "Would you look at that darling boy? Oh, Lyndall, he is such a gem!" Just then, with all eyes on the little trotter, I stepped on a crabapple, slipped and tumbled. Eggs flew, and the tray landed upside down. The crowd in the dining room gasped to see if tears or blood would follow. Instead, I quickly flipped the tray and picked up one of the eggs. It was covered in fresh grass clippings, which I tried to shake off. That grass was stuck. Blowing didn't work either, so I tried wiping the grassy part of the egg on the side of the tray. Seeing that the grass clippings were really indistinguishable from the chives, I made the executive decision to just soldier on, replace the eggs on the tray and serve. As I collected eggs, I could hear peals of laughter coming from the guests. Someone must have told a joke.

Mrs. Hattie was right—everyone in the living room took an egg, but none of the people in the dining room wanted one. By the time I made it back to the kitchen, I found Mrs. Hattie and explained, "Not too many people like the eggs. Can I have pigs in a blanket next? People like those."

The campaigns became more brutal as my dad pushed his way up the ladder of local politics. With the impending legalization of abortion, reproductive rights were a polarizing issue in election years. Though Bedford and surrounding towns were largely Presbyterian, Catholics were strong in number and influence, and a robust Right to Life Party took root within the Church.

The Cross, a Westchester-based weekly newspaper, covered topics of interest for Catholics in the community. Endorsements of John Hicks-Beach, the Right to Life Party's candidate for State Legislator, were seen frequently alongside factually inaccurate stories of botched abortions, resulting in damage or death to young mothers. To the great ire of the Right to Life

Party, Hicks-Beach was not gaining in the polls, and *The Cross* changed tactics, choosing to start a smear campaign against Democrat Hammy Fischer and the frontrunner: Republican R. Bradlee Boal.

At first, the inaccuracies were almost amusing with titles like, "Rubber on the end of every pencil? Brad Boal wants all first graders to learn about contraception."

We delighted in a story suggesting Lyndall Boal had been an advocate of free love since her summer at Woodstock. My mother asked, "What was Woodstock?"

My parents drew the line when an article was published alleging Jenny and I had traveled to a Catholic seminary near Albany to harass a Father Callahan, who was known for his tirades against the sin of abortion. Jenny and I were four and six at the time. What did we do, throw water balloons? Legal action was threatened, and a minuscule correction was added to a subsequent issue.

A few days prior to the election, a scathing editorial appeared in *The Cross*, chronicling Brad Boal's long history of public intoxication and reckless driving. This time there were painful threads of truth. The editorial read: "It's not just the unborn children Brad Boal will murder; he threatens the lives of his own son and daughter every time this irresponsible drunkard gets behind the wheel of the family car."

On Sunday nights, Dad would drive to Leonardo's Pizza in Mt. Kisco to pick up our dinner after downing three or four or five drinks. Bourbon on the rocks was his drink of choice following the afternoon beers. Battles raged as Mom tried to dissuade him from driving. Jenny and I begged him to let us go with him, thinking we could grab the wheel or keep him focused.

My dad crashed three of our cars on Route 172, colliding with a telephone pole and escaping with blood and bruises. Each time, the passenger seat was crunched like an accordion. The doctors at Northern Westchester Hospital were obligated to report the excessive amounts of alcohol in his bloodstream. The police report was listed each week in the *Patent Trader*, and minimal sleuthing could uncover the names involved in the crash.

Dad came home early from work on the day the editorial was published. The phone had been ringing incessantly. Apparently, *The Cross*, with its circulation of a mere 3,000 Westchester residents, found a wider audience on that day. Dick Pearl, Dad's campaign manager, urged him to issue a statement disputing the allegations, but Dad refused to do so, knowing that delving into the secret of his alcoholism would not end well. He holed up in his bedroom throughout the afternoon and evening, canceling last-minute appearances at the Bedford Town Hall and Leonard Park.

Mom told us about the article and asked us not to go to his room, but when she and Jenny went to draw a bath, I went to my dad.

He was in bed with the lights off. The fading daylight allowed me to see a pile of newspapers on the floor, an empty glass and a near-empty bottle of bourbon.

Before I got to the bed, I heard, "Don't come in here."

"Dad, it's me."

"Pete, go back downstairs, I don't want you to see me like this." He was slurring his words as he often did.

I kept walking to the bed and sat beside the man that I loved so much. "Dad, it's okay. It's not true, none of it."

He looked up with tears covering his face. I had never seen

my dad cry. The image was haunting. In a moment our roles were reversed.

"Dad, we love you so much." I was starting to cry, too. The smell of bourbon was so familiar. To this day, it reminds me of my father, like a favorite cologne. He leaned forward and hugged me with crushing force. The crying became heaving, and I could barely discern my dad's words: "I love you too. I would never hurt you or your sister, never."

Dad lost that election to Hammy Fischer and bowed out of local politics for a while. We never spoke of that evening but continued to wrestle as a family with a disease that affected all of us, never winning. Eventually, the family divided. I did my best to look after Dad, driving him home, arguing with him, removing stashed bottles, lending money, making excuses and failing with him against the death grip of his alcoholism. Everyone who loved him did the same. Anorexic, swollen, jaundiced and alone at fifty-two, his liver blew the whistle on the short life of a great man and the battle was lost.

Me, Mrs. Hattie and Jenny, Oakville, Ontario 1968 *(image courtesy of the author)*

3

THE NEGOTIATOR

"Lord, child, look what you've done!" Mrs. Hattie's voice bellowed across the kitchen. She got up from the table all at once. Her chair flew backwards across the floor and tipped on its side with a crash.

"You get over here, now!" She was headed straight for Jenny, whose frightened wide eyes were already starting to fill with tears. "Get over here, you bad girl. You come on!" Jenny cringed like a frightened animal.

Mrs. Hattie had her by the waist with one hand raised when my mother's voice interrupted her reprimand.

"Don't you touch her, Mrs. Hattie. Don't you dare touch my daughter!"

Jenny took advantage of the momentary hesitation and bolted from the kitchen. Her frantic steps sounded like a nervous heart as they raced up the stairs followed by the predictable slam of her bedroom door. Mrs. Hattie did not allow door slamming.

The two women stood motionless facing each other across the kitchen table, unsure who would speak next. My mom was a few inches taller, but Mrs. Hattie looked like she was about to grow. I kept my eyes on my drawing, wishing I were anywhere but there.

"Mrs. Boals, you know I spent all day making sense of this here project table, and your daughter come on home and made a royal mess of the whole damn thing. I told her to keep that table neat from now on, and she disobeyed me. I told her." Her finger repeatedly pointed at the crime scene.

Jenny's distant sobbing could be heard in the background.

I looked at the project table. It was a complete mess. Several hundred crayons lay in a heap in the center of the table, except for a few dozen that had rolled onto the floor. Mrs. Hattie and I had spent all afternoon separating the burnt siennas from the strawberry fields and the ochres from the golds. Each shade was placed in a clear glass jam jar, which Mrs. Hattie had carefully hand labeled, asking me to read every letter of the color so as to avoid misspellings. She was always trying to put method to the madness of our home.

"You do not ever hit my children. Ever. Do you understand me?"

Now how am I supposed to raise these children if I can't discipline them? Hmm?" Mrs. Hattie was mashing crayons back into jars as she spoke. "You tell me that, just let them run all over and do as they please? I mean." She shook her head slowly from side to side.

"Mrs. Hattie, let me be clear here, you are helping to raise my children." Mom picked up the fallen chair and slammed it back in its place. I jumped. "I am raising my children."

Mrs. Hattie turned to walk away. Under her breath, she muttered, "No you're not."

Words seemed to fail mom in this moment, but her finger was raised and she was turning crimson. Before she could speak, Mrs. Hattie blurted out, "Ah, ah, ah…don't you say anything to me. I am going to my room."

Not entirely sure mom heard this because she followed with, "Hattie Lindsay, when Brad gets home, he and I would like a word with you." Her voice was both measured and trembling. She was still red.

At the door to the kitchen, Mrs. Hattie turned around with her chin held high and said, "You and Mr. Boals can save your breath because I am not talking to anyone in this family except Peter." Up the stairs she went, and another door was slammed.

I didn't move from the kitchen table and sat looking at my drawing of an eagle. Mom asked if I was all right, and I nodded still looking at my drawing. She headed up the stairs to talk to Jenny, whose persistent sobbing could still be heard. Alone in the kitchen, I returned to the project table to start re-sorting crayons: reds with reds and golds with golds. There was a long period of silence.

About an hour later, I heard the familiar sound of Dad's Jeep pulling into the driveway. I met him at the door.

Rex, our dog, insisted on the first greeting, then I got mine, "Hey, kiddo, how was hi-ho today?"

"Dad, Jenny dumped all of the crayons in a pile, and Mom had a fight with Mrs. Hattie, and I drew a bird."

"That's great about the bird, Pete, but you better tell me a little bit more about this fight."

"Mrs. Hattie knocked over a chair and told Mom she needs

to be able to spank us. Mrs. Hattie went to her room, slammed her door, and Jenny's still crying … here's my bird."

Dad dropped his briefcase and called, "Lyndall? I'm home, can you come down here for a minute?"

Mom and Dad retreated to the living room, which was about a half mile from Mrs. Hattie's room. Through the closed door, I could hear their hushed voices. I knew I shouldn't go in, but I wanted to see my dad, so I peeked through the door. Dad told me it wasn't a good time and that I should watch some television. I considered checking on Jenny but decided against it. Instead I opted to pay Mrs. Hattie a visit since we often watched television together at night in her room. When I got to the top of the stairs, I saw her door was shut. Instead of knocking, I curled up on the top step outside of her room and waited.

After a while, I heard Mom and Dad approaching. Mom led the way, and when she spotted me, she whispered, "Oh, Pete, I didn't know you were here. You're as quiet as a mouse. Could you do me a favor and check on your sister to see if she's all right? Tell her we're going to make popcorn and watch *The Waltons*. Will you do that for me, Pete? Run along."

I went towards Jenny's room but had no intention of missing the conversation that was about to happen and hid in the alcove. Mom knocked gently on the door, calling, "Mrs. Hattie, it's Lyndall, can we talk?" Silence.

Dad's turn. "Mrs. Hattie, this is Brad, we want to talk to you for a minute." Still no response, though I thought I heard a sort of "hmpf." Dad decided to proceed anyway, speaking from the dark hallway. "Mrs. Hattie … it sounds like there was some sort of misunderstanding, and we want to talk about it … Lyndall says she overreacted and that you're doing a wonderful job with the children." More silence. Whispering, mostly from Mom. "It's not that Lyndall overreacted, but she may have misunderstood ..."

Mrs. Hattie's voice could be heard clearly through her closed door, "Mr. Boals, I will not talk to anyone in this family except Peter. You send him my way when you all have something to say, you hear?" Silence followed.

My parents retreated to the living room. I opened Jenny's door and slipped into her room, despite her objection to my presence, and closed the door behind me. Though my sister clearly did not want to talk to me, I stayed in her room tucked up on her window seat, looking out at the rhododendrons. Her clock ticked.

I heard Mom and Dad's footsteps approaching. There was a timid knock on the door, "Hi, guys, we want to talk to you both. Can we come in?" Mom asked. They were already in.

I waited for Jenny to answer, but she didn't, so I said, "Sure." Jenny glared at me and then rolled her eyes.

Mom sat on the edge of Jenny's bed, and Dad turned the desk chair around, standing behind it.

"Listen, you both know what happened with Mrs. Hattie tonight. Jenny, Mrs. Hattie was wrong to scold you like that, and it will never happen again, I can promise you that. Your father and I will make that very clear to Mrs. Hattie. You did nothing wrong. Mrs. Hattie needs to understand our family's system of right and wrong, regardless of how she may have been raised or how she may have raised her children."

"Did Mrs. Hattie beat her children?" Jenny asked.

"Jenny! I didn't say that, and I have no idea. We would be wrong to assume she did. I'm just saying she may have had different practices under what were likely very different circumstances. Times change, and people change. Your father and I do not believe in spanking or physical abuse of any kind."

"What's a circus stand?" I asked.

"Circumstance, lovey."

Dad redirected, "Now we need to move forward, and Mrs. Hattie has made it pretty clear she only wants to speak to you, Pete."

"Me? Why me?"

"Because you're her little favorite, that's why," Jenny muttered shaking her head at me. Of course, it was true, I was Mrs. Hattie's favorite, partly because Jenny could be so obnoxious as she was currently demonstrating. In truth, Mrs. Hattie and I shared a bond, one that ran deep, as unlikely as that may sound between a four-year-old and a seventy four-year-old. It was a bond of love, trust and friendship forged while carefully spelling the colors of crayons and existing side by side every day. "So, are we going to fire Mrs. Hattie?"

"Jenny, dear, please. We would not do that to Mrs. Hattie or to our family. Do you know how many times she has been there for us? Do you remember Mrs. Carter, who worked here before Mrs. Hattie?" Jenny looked confused, wondering whether she was supposed to answer or not. "Well, I do, she used to pee in the bushes. Do you want me to call her? I came home one day and saw you spit in the fireplace, and when I asked you why you were spitting in the fireplace, you said, 'that's what Mrs. Carter does.' No, we are not getting rid of Mrs. Hattie. She is a part of this family, and she loves you two very much. And besides, she pees in the toilet!"

"I love Mrs. Hattie," I offered.

"We all do, Pete," Mom said. Jenny didn't look so sure.

"And her pork chops are out of this world," Dad added. Mom shot him a look.

"What do I to say to her?" I asked.

Dad chimed in. "This is what you need to tell her." The list was long, and Dad counted fingers as he spoke. "Your mother apologizes, Jenny apologizes, the project table was a real mess and needed Mrs. Hattie's unique sense of order. She's like a mother to all of us and a real part of our family. And we want her to stay with us as long as she will have us, and then we'll take good care of her long after that. And tell her she won't have to clean up after Henry if she doesn't want to."

It was getting late, and I was getting tired, but this breakdown in our "family" needed to be addressed that night. My parents reviewed the list of terms with me several times and asked me if I wanted the list written down as a reminder. Reading was not yet a strength of mine, so I declined, and off I went to Mrs. Hattie's door.

I raised my fist to knock but decided to turn back to look at my parents for approval first. They were at the bottom of the stairs nodding vigorously, so I banged on the door.

"Who is it?" Mrs. Hattie's voice called.

"It's me, Mrs. Hattie, can I come in?"

"Yes, child, let me get the door. Of course you can come in."

The door opened. Mrs. Hattie stood before me with open open arms. Her hair was different. The chestnut curls were gone and a spray of kinky gray and white strands burst from her head.

"Oh, child! You look like you seen a ghost. I mean! You mean to tell me all these years, and you never never seen Mrs. Hattie without her wig on. Child, it's still Mrs. Hattie, come on over here and give me a hug. I need a special hug from my little man." I obeyed. The hug made tensions melt away, and somehow seeing Mrs. Hattie's natural hair felt like I was being entrusted with a secret. The trust felt like a gift, and the bond between us grew deeper.

I thought I would start with the terms, but when I tried to speak, Mrs. Hattie put her worn hand on my lips. She settled onto her bed and invited me to cuddle up next to her, which was one of my favorite places in the whole world. I snuggled, head in breast, and listened to the radio for what seemed like an eternity. Mrs. Hattie was petting my hair and humming while Nat King Cole sang along with her on the radio. Time stopped, and tension disappeared.

"So, you got something to say, Sugar, or you just come for the music?"

"Uh-huh," I had to think for a moment before the list of terms came back to me. "You don't have to take care of Henry anymore." Mrs. Hattie laughed so hard I jumped.

"Well, if that isn't the good Lord himself right here in this room. Amen. Go on child, this is getting good."

"And you treat us really good."

"Wait a minute there ... what did you say?" Mrs. Hattie raised an eyebrow.

"You treat us really ... well?"

"Better, now go on."

"You did a great job on the project table, which needs your unique sense of order."

"Now that sounds like your mother talking, but it's true. Of course I couldn't have done it without my little helper."

I looked up at Mrs. Hattie, smiling, "That's true, too. We both have a unique sense of order, don't we? Jenny's sorry, and

Dad's sorry, and Mom's sorry, too, and they want you to stay with us forever, and you don't ever have to take care of the dog again."

"Well, sir. You remembered all that? You're a pretty good negotiator. Let me see. I need you to go back out there and tell the rest of the family my terms. Yes, sir. First of all, Jenny needs to come in here right now. I'll even put my wig on for her, because she already looked a little scared, and I'm gonna need a great big hug from her. Tell your father he's done nothing wrong, and he has nothing to apologize for. He is a good man, and you can tell that dog of yours he better stay out of my way from now on, yes sir! He makes a big old mess, and I'm gonna just walk on by. You got all that?"

"Yup, I'll tell them. What about Mom? She's sorry too."

"Oh, did I forget her? Hmm. Tell her I'll deal with her tomorrow, but for tonight, she needs to go to her room."

"Really?"

"No, sir. You tell her she better get in here with the others, I may just be needing a hug from her too."

Mrs. Kammuck's first grade class, Rippowam *(image courtesy of the author)*

4

THEY CALL IT MACARONI

Where kindergarten may have been a bit traumatizing, first grade was confidence-building. Credit goes to Mrs. Kammuck who seemed to single me out on day one.

Mrs. Kammuck was new to Bedford, having just moved from Ann Arbor, Michigan. The jury was still out on her. We were her first class. She got good marks from the start by installing a huge fish tank in the corner of the classroom with a soft blue light with all kinds of exotic-looking fish and flora inside. Pepper Crofoot, our art teacher, offered Mrs. Hammock and her husband temporary digs in a rented suite of rooms over the garage. Apparently, her walls were still bare because she informed the class that she'd be looking closely at what we were making and selecting her favorite works for her new home. Everything would need to be signed since she only collected signed pieces of art. When my giant mural of a pony was picked, I was thrilled, though still not sure if the mural was any good or if Mrs. Kammuck was aiming to empower a shy boy with potential.

The year was 1972, and a heated and lopsided presidential election consumed the nation. Mrs. Kammuck's first grade class was not exempt from banter and debate.

Seated on the round blue carpet in the center of the classroom, we discussed the election. Mrs. Kammuck wanted to know what was being talked about in each of our households.

"McGovern's gonna raise our taxes, and it'll be hard to have a second home in Nantucket or Martha's Vineyard," Bing offered.

"Who would want a second home in the Vineyard?" Timmy asked. There was a ripple of appreciative laughter.

"Shut up, Carson my uncle has a place in the Vineyard."

"Now boys …"

"McGovern doesn't have respect for our military," added Kate. "He would take soldiers out of Vietnam and let the Commies rule." Mrs. Kammuck started to respond, but Jasper interjected.

"My mom said McGovern wants to kill fetuses."

Now Mrs. Kammuck was quick to jump in, realizing her political dialogue was not going as planned. "Jasper, he may be for a woman's right to choose, but to say …"

Eric interrupted, "He's from South Dakota, right? His dad was paid with potatoes or something like that, and McGovern didn't go to Harvard or Yale. I thought all presidents went to Harvard or Yale. I mean what is this country coming to?" Everyone laughed.

Mrs. Kammuck smiled along and shook her head. When the room settled, she weighed in.

"Look, politics is a difficult subject to discuss, and a first grade classroom may not be the place to do so, but I believe the better informed you are about candidates and political issues, the better decisions you will make as future voters. You might not even have the same opinions as your parents. Eric, you are correct, Senator McGovern did not attend Harvard or Yale." Eric stood up with his arms spread like Caesar entering the forum. Mock applause followed, "but neither did President Nixon." Eric was seated and a bit nonplussed. "Now here's something George McGovern did that may be of interest to all of you. He helped to lower the voting age from twenty-one to eighteen, meaning all of you will be able to vote in a decade or so." Angus raised his hand to ask a question.

Jasper blurted out, "Thanks George, but we're voting Nixon!" More laughter.

Mrs. Kammuck ignored Jasper and the laughter and called on Angus.

"What's a decade?" he asked.

Jeff's hand flew up. Jeff seemed to know everything. Mrs. Kammuck nodded in his direction. "Decade: d-e-c-a-d-e noun meaning ten years of time or 120 months or 3,650 days from the Latin root 'deca' meaning ten." That was Jeff. He always won the school spelling bees.

"Thank you, Jeff. Anybody know what a straw poll is?" asked Mrs. Kammuck. Silence. Even Jeff looked miffed. "It's like a vote, but it doesn't count. It's a way of seeing how people are feeling before they vote. I'd like to do one now." A feeling of dread crept over me. On she went, "Even though the voting age isn't six or seven or eight, let's see a show of hands for whose parents are voting for President Nixon." As I wondered whether to lie or not, all hands shot skyward, and all eyes scanned the room for dissenters. There was one, and he was blushing.

"And how about McGovern?" Now, a bit trapped and outed, my hand inched upwards.

"That makes two of us," said Mrs. Kammuck with her hand held high. "Based on this straw poll, Peter, I think we might lose." I had a new hero.

The year went well. Mrs. Kammuck kept lifting me up until I didn't need it. I found my strengths, friends and self, excelling academically, in track and field and even socially.

She was a most creative teacher, constantly introducing new lessons and projects that we looked forward to each day, learning through art, building and interaction. Activities were so enjoyable, we hardly realized we were back from recess.

Sometime in the spring, Mrs. Kammuck entered the classroom with two brown paper grocery bags from the A&P. As she placed the bags on her desk, we gathered around, excited to see what snacks were being offered. She seemed to enjoy the anticipation. First, she pulled out a box of macaroni, then another, followed by sixteen more—one for each student in the class. We were perplexed by the abundance of uncooked pasta.

"Today we are learning about architecture with a particular focus on tall structures."

"Excuse me, Mrs. Kammuck?" Beau spoke without having raised his hand. "Those aren't Lincoln Logs or Legos … that's pasta!" He snickered and scanned the room for approval. Mrs. Kammuck followed with one of her favorite expressions, tipping her head to the side and pressing her lips together as if to say, "You don't say, stupid."

"Thank you, Beau, for that astute observation. Now, will you please tell the class what 'astute' means." Beau paused and squirmed on the blue carpet while looking at the floor. "Astute, Mr. Crawford, means smart. Smart can either mean intelligent or rude, try to be one and not the other in my classroom, thank you." There was an awkward and prolonged silence before she continued, "You will also find nine pieces of cardboard and nine tubes of glue in the art corner. This week we're constructing macaroni towers in order to better understand architecture and the principles of balance, support and structure. You'll be working in pairs, which I've written on the blackboard. To make this fun, the team who builds the tower with the strongest construction and most appealing design gets to be honorary class president for the remainder of the year with rights to feed the fish every Monday." A delighted gasp from the first graders. "Questions? Please ask. I'm here to help. Let's build!"

Kids scrambled. You could feel the excitement in the classroom. I was paired with Bing. We found a corner with a low project table. Armed with our two boxes of macaroni, Elmer's glue, cardboard from the Village Cleaners and a dangerous amount of ambition, we set out to win.

"Build a base first," I offered as we spilled macaroni onto the floor.

"We gotta go up first. Risk equals reward, Boal. Look at Beau and Timmy's, theirs' is already as tall as a pencil!" Bing pointed out the high-rise in the opposite corner of the classroom. At that exact moment, it toppled to the side looking like a twisted slug.

"Build a base, trust me, we'll get height later." We built a base, but it was sloppy because we were already dreaming about height and trophies and winner's status.

Like the political discussion in the fall, this activity didn't go quite as planned. Mrs. Kammuck didn't have a lot of experience with kids in Bedford. Things were different here. By Wednesday, you could feel the influence of parents. Kate's dad was an architect, and his expertise seeped into her design. Eric was her partner, but he wasn't even allowed to hold the glue. Noodles interlocked in serpentine threads, which mapped out squares, with each new level receding into a slightly smaller square until a pyramid to rival Giza started to emerge.

Sariah's mom was a landscape architect. She and Tina created an Asian-influenced design with noodles standing on end like small decorative grasses in the wind. A noodle stream meandered past an impressive pagoda. Carrie's dad was a night club promoter. She and her sisters had traveled the globe with him, attending the openings of the latest trendy haunts. She was always talking about the skyscrapers in Chicago, Hong Kong and Berlin. She and Cindy cut their cardboard into eight equal rectangles and constructed a seven-story tower with an impressive rooftop club, complete with macaroni lounge chairs, ottomans and a wave-shaped bar. Skip and Jasper built a geodesic dome while Bing and I raced Beau and Timmy to complete Manhattan's tallest skyscraper.

The adrenaline rush was addictive and horrible. Bing and I couldn't stop or talk and spent far more time craning necks to see the competition than we did studying our base and structure. We would delight in their missteps, returning to our triumph, adding noodles hastily to an impossibly tall tower before the glue had even dried. I hardly slept all week, and when I did, I dreamed of building.

As the school day came to a close on Thursday, Mrs. Kammuck made the rounds. She seemed impressed and a bit surprised by most of the entries. She offered encouragement about those buildings that hadn't come together yet, asking the disgruntled teams what lessons might have been learned in the process. She identified four pairs who were in the lead, noting that tomorrow marked the final day of construction and the designation of awards. Bing and I were in the top four, but so were Beau and Timmy.

Kids headed home for the day as parents stopped by the classroom, collecting belongings and complimenting structures. Lots of pointers were communicated, and one dad started adding noodles until Mrs. Kammuck dissuaded him from doing so.

I was walking home, so no one was there to pick me up. I took advantage of the opportunity and kept piling on more macaroni. I could hardly reach the top of our tower, so I decided to relocate the structure to the floor to gain greater access for the next day's additions. I dragged the cardboard base carefully to the edge of the table and lined up a thin, hardcover book with the edge, then slowly inched the towering structure onto the book.

I lowered the book to the floor and began to slide the cardboard to the linoleum when the building top started to bend perilously forward. In a panic, I let the cardboard land on the floor and grabbed the top of the tower which came off in my grip. I held the top of the tower tightly as the bottom half collapsed and landed with a plop on the linoleum. I started to tremble and sweat with anxiety boiling deep inside. I dropped the noodles, grabbed my coat and bag and headed for sign-out, knowing tears were not far away.

I did cry on the walk home, turning my head to the side as each car passed on the dirt road. I thought about blaming the janitor. That could work. I would act surprised when I entered the classroom. I would be given some kind of consolation prize. Then I felt worse for having entertained a lie at the janitor's expense. Mrs. Kammuck might think it was Beau, on whom she always kept a watchful and wary eye. But it wasn't Beau, or the janitor, it was me and my foolishness, quest for glory, and ineptitude.

Trying to slip into the house undetected, I came face to face with Mrs. Hattie. I told her I wasn't feeling well and headed for my room. If Henry hadn't pooped in the guest room, she would have known I was lying, but she was preoccupied and in a foul mood. When my mom came to my room before dinner to check on me, I burst into tears.

"I wanted to win so … badly. We had the tallest building. The structure was better than Timmy and Beau's, and we were going to win." I was shaking. "I feel sick, Mom. I can't go to school tomorrow … I can't." I couldn't stop crying. Rex was nuzzling his nose into my leg. My father was now in the doorway, which made me feel worse.

"Brad, please, let me handle this." My mom waved my dad away. He gave a wink from the door and retreated.

After a long hug, the crying quieted, and my mom revealed her plan.

"You need to go to school tomorrow, Pete Bear. Running away or hiding from defeat or disappointment won't serve you well in life." My breathing was starting to fracture into gasps again. "Look, Pete, Mrs. Vail is dropping Angus off early tomorrow morning because she has another chemo treatment. Bless her, I don't know how she does it. I'll take you and Angus to school then. The school's open at seven, so we'll head to your classroom, and I'll take the remnants of that tower with me. You never need to see it again. I'll call Mrs. Kammuck tonight and explain what's happened. She thinks the world of you, Pete, and, like your mother, she will want to protect you from this hurt. I'll call Bing's mother, too, though I do not like that woman. This whole thing seems to have gotten out of control, and I'm going to put a stop to it. I want you to wash your face, and when you don't look like you've been crying, come downstairs and eat some dinner. Then let's tuck you in for a much-needed sleep. It will all be better in the morning, I promise."

I was so relieved Mom would make it all go away. Her solution was massively flawed, but it also represented the fierce devotion and love my mother felt for me, and I welcomed it.

In the morning Angus and I stormed the classroom. Angus seemed oblivious to the trauma and loved the idea of a commando raid. Mom stuffed the remnants of the tower in an L.L. Bean bookbag and then took us to the school library, where the few early arrivals with two working parents would congregate.

At eight-thirty we were all in Mrs. Kammuck's class, again waiting for the bell to start the school day. Kids were anxious to hit the glue and pasta for the final day of construction, but Mrs. Kammuck had a different plan.

"Good morning, students. How are you today? I know we were planning to build again today, but we have a new plan." There were plenty of perplexed looks, and my eyes were wide. Bing was whispering to Ian. "Last night we had a mishap, and one of the structures tumbled onto the floor." She paused and scanned the room. Everyone was looking for their structure. "I can't say how it happened; it might have been human error, it might have been one of you, or the janitor, or even your favorite teacher, Mrs. Kammuck. But it happened. So those of you who still have structures should sign them. I was truly impressed by all of them and probably couldn't have chosen a winner anyway. At day's end, they all go home. Fish feeding will be done on the usual rotation, and to show how impressed I was by your efforts, we will be heading outside for the entire morning period to work on human structures and support. We will be doing headstands, handstands, armchairs and human pyramids and before lunch, we will be doing trust falls." Cheers from the entire class. Macaroni forgotten. Some cartwheels were seen in the hallway, and a blissful bonding morning with Mrs. Kammuck's first grade class followed.

A few hours later, I stood on the roof of the maintenance shed with my back facing twelve friends below. With arms crossed over my chest. I closed my eyes and fell backwards like a plank as Mrs. Kammuck had instructed us to do. I landed softly in twenty-four arms with a newfound understanding of risk, trust and community.

Homegoing Celebration

For

Vivian Wilson

Sunrise:	*Sunset:*
December 28, 1923	*September 28, 2011*

Monday, October 3, 2011

11:00 am

Bethel Baptist Church

37 Maple Avenue

Mount Kisco, NY 10549

Rev. A. Denise Gomez, Pastor

Program from Mrs. Wilson's memorial service *(image courtesy of the author)*

5

LOSING MY RELIGION

Though I was a birthright Quaker, religion was somewhat absent from my upbringing. Mom was born in London, England, February 19, 1936, as Lyndall Elizabeth Cadbury. The Cadburys were Quakers. Her father was the third George Cadbury of the chocolate-making family. His grandfather, the original George, is credited with having invented milk chocolate. On the other side of the family, Great-Granny Pearce at four-foot-eleven was a suffragette who once chained herself to the gates of Parliament to advocate for women's right to vote. As a bobby carted her off to the paddy wagon, she poked him in the bum with her hat pin, earning herself a two-week stay in Holloway Gaol. Upon release, she penned an article about the experience, which, in turn, earned her employment with the Evening News, becoming London's first full-time female journalist. My grandparents, George and Barbara Cadbury, chose social causes over chocolate as their mission. In the wake of World War II, the family crossed the Atlantic to the prairies of Saskatchewan. Barbara's memory of a firebomb rolling into their London living room prompted her to say, "I want to live in a place where bombs don't fall."

We attended Quaker meeting once a year when I was a child. The peace in the room was unlike our home, where arguments were common between parents and between siblings. The architecture of the Friends Meetinghouse was unadorned and pure, like an interior from an Andrew Wyeth or an Edward Hopper. Worn wood and worn faces were the only distractions available to a small child. I succumbed to the tranquility and silence that enveloped the room, entering something close to a religious meditation.

I might have been religious, but my mother started telling me at a young age we did not believe in God; instead, we believed in all of the things that God stood for. She elaborated, explaining how we would strive to be good to others, help those less fortunate and generally lead a life of high moral standard, not because He or She required it with the looming threat of eternal damnation, but because it was the right thing to do. The reward was not an all-white interior, but the satisfaction of knowing we had chosen the right course consistently throughout our lives.

I wasn't sold on our heathen lifestyle. While touring an English chapel when I was six, my parents lost me for a moment only to find me on my knees in front of an altar on the side of the church. Asked what I was doing, I told my parents I thought someone needed to pray for our family, and since no one else seemed to be doing so, I saw fit to take it on myself.

My mother suggested Jenny and I could choose our own religious paths, but there was a subtle bias running through our upbringing. She often told the story of her own introduction to religion. Granny Cadbury thought her two girls ought to have a basic understanding of the stories of the Old Testament, since other children in school seemed to have a good familiarity with them. She found a children's Bible and turned to the tale of Noah's ark, thinking the animals might provide the perfect entree. By the time the flood hit, little Carol screamed in indignation, "Why did God kill all those people? That's horrible, I think God should be killed!" Away went the children's Bible, and another course was chosen.

Carol later became known by her full name of Caroline, but the name change and a few years of maturity did not change her religious views. A postcard arrived at the Cadburys' home from a summer camp attended by the sisters. It was written by my mother. It read, "Caroline has said there is no God. I have hit all I can. Please come immediately."

Mrs. Hattie carried her religion with her every day.

She worked a long day and didn't hesitate to remind us of just how long that day was. Every morning at seven-thirty, the back stairs would creak under her heavy footsteps. She emerged dressed in her starched white uniform, the one my parents implored her not to wear. But she insisted, countering, "Mrs. Boals, I wore one my whole life. Don't see a reason to stop now. I'm still cleaning. What would I wear, my church clothes?" At five forty-five, after cooking our dinner, she'd haul herself back up to her room to change. She ate dinner with us every night, but when the New York Mets played, she'd tell us she was "coming down with something" and take her dinner to her room.

Her lunch break always coincided with *Search for Tomorrow*. "Now you run on, Sweetie, Mrs. Hattie's got to watch her story." When she wasn't watching her story, she was like a machine:

washing, folding, ironing, making beds, doing the mending, vacuuming, dusting and cooking. But even without cleaning up after Henry, she was losing the battle to keep a 12,000 square-foot house clean while taking care of two small children.

One day she emptied a pail full of tarnished silverware on the counter next to the sink, causing a deafening clatter. Platex Living gloves, Noxon, clean rags and a felt cloth were at the ready, preparing to wage war against the intimidating silver army. Three rings and two dozen bracelets were shed and placed on the windowsill. I knew not to interrupt the process of cleaning the silver and sat a safe distance from the sink at the kitchen table pretending to read my book. The more Mrs. Hattie polished, the more she grunted. Each piece was doused with silver polish and hand rubbed with a fierce brutality before being wiped to gleaming perfection. Cleaned pieces were placed gently on the other side of the sink, but as the hours passed, forks and knives were slammed onto the counter with great dramatic effect. The silver seemed to be winning the battle.

When I heard Mom's Volvo roll into the driveway just before five, I ran to warn her about the storm brewing in the kitchen. Too late.

"Hi, everyone, Mommy's home. Hello, Mrs. Hattie. Oh, how nice, we'll have clean silver for a change."

The pause was a little too long before Mrs. Hattie responded, "For a change. For a change? Pray tell, what in God's name does that mean, Mrs. Boals? You know I clean this here silver every month *and* the candle sticks *and* the serving trays *and* all those silly old shakers and bowls that's never even been used. Do you know I have been doing this all day and I'm about to drop, Mrs.

Boals?" She mopped her brow, though no sweat was there.

Mom started to speak but didn't succeed because Mrs. Hattie wasn't done.

"It's too much. I need some help around here with this kitchen. In fact, I need some help with this whole darn house."

"Here, Mrs. Hattie, let me help you."

"You? You're crazier than I thought. You just come home from work, and the kids need help their homework. I can't do that. You know that. Mrs. Boals, we need another cleaning lady, or I'm just gonna have to find me a job that wont kill me."

"Oh, I see."

The next week Vivian Wilson arrived in our home. Mrs. Hattie welcomed her with a small amount of disdain and an even larger amount of silver.

The two had a pecking order, and Mrs. Hattie was clearly at the top. She lived with us from Monday to Friday and therefore regarded our house as hers. Mrs. Wilson was a day worker, and at five sharp, Mrs. Hattie let Mrs. Wilson know she needed the kitchen because the "family" needed their dinner, and Mr. Wilson probably wanted his too. For the next hour or so, tantalizing smells of pork chops, curried lamb, buttery vegetables, or sweet potatoes doused with brown sugar wafted through the house.

Mrs. Hattie naturally and unflinchingly assumed the role of matriarch or patriarch. The ritual of dinner started with her asking Jenny and me if we had washed our hands, to which Jenny would always report that she had, and I would report I had not. I know Jenny lied about the hand washing sometimes, but regardless, I was the one who was sent to the sink to wash my hands for an entire minute. Our "family" also included a college student named Joe, who lived with us and helped work the grounds. Everyone would await my return ... fifty-eight ... fifty-nine ... sixty.

Mrs. Hattie sat at the head of the table opposite my mother, since Dad wouldn't arrive home from the city until close to nine. Prior to every meal, without fail, Mrs. Hattie bowed her head, closed her eyes, clasped her rough hands and prayed in silence, saying only "amen" in a whisper after a few moments. We ignored this private meditation and started passing and pouring.

"Why does Mrs. Hattie always pray?" I asked one night after dinner.

My mother explained, "Religion is very important to Mrs. Hattie. She once told me it was a comfort to her in times of hardship. You may not know she had her first child at thirteen and married unsuccessfully at fifteen." Her five children were estranged except for a daughter named Butch, who lived across the hall from her mother in Mount Vernon.

On most weekends, our house was empty. For the better part of a decade, my mother and sister would travel to warmer climates in the winter months so Jenny's pedigreed ponies could compete in a circuit of equestrian shows. My father would dispatch to Winston Salem, North Carolina, for meetings with his client, R.J. Reynolds Tobacco, or he'd head off to far away destinations because of his responsibilities as treasurer of the International Planned Parenthood Federation.

What to do with the son? There were weekend stays with friends in Bedford, which included Sunday morning visits to the St. Matthew's Episcopal Church. Clad in a madras blazer and some measure of lime green, I looked the part but always felt like an impostor because I didn't believe in God. Besides, the frequency of need went beyond the social acceptance, and there were many weekends when I found myself headed home with Mrs. Hattie or Mrs. Wilson.

I don't remember going to church with Mrs. Hattie, but I do remember driving to Mount Vernon on Friday nights with my mother to take Mrs. Hattie home. Mount Vernon was a densely-populated, mostly Black suburb next to Pelham. As I looked out the window with wide eyes, I could see a neighborhood that no longer resembled the one I lived in. Economic disparity and a racial wealth gap was evident. Despite the frequent sounds of sirens, there were no visible crimes, just more graffiti, fewer gardens and more people on the streets with nowhere to go. As we approached Mrs. Hattie's apartment building, we'd see Butch on the stoop. Butch was like nothing Bedford ever saw or knew. She had the voice of a man and might have even been one for all I knew. Spikes of semi-relaxed hair in several unnatural colors flew back from her face. She was often in a tank top regardless of the weather and always looked pregnant, though logic told me she was too old for that. Butch sat on the top step surrounded by a posse of men drinking Miller beer. She'd spot our car and waddle down the steps to greet me. She doted on me, calling me "Sugar." She'd walk right up to the car, beer in hand, to embrace me. The beer never left her hand, and I wondered if she might not be able to release it because each of her nails was at least an inch long. She'd see me looking at them and ask, "You like my nails?" as one hook-like nail approached my chin, "Or do they scare ya?" Then she'd threaten me with a claw and roar with deep laughter. All the men would laugh, too. Butch liked to put on a show, but it always ended with an embrace. I got used to my welcome and eventually looked forward to my curb-side banter with Butch.

Mrs. Hattie was quick to rescue me, asking if I would help carry her bag up the steps to her second floor apartment. Butch followed close behind.

Weekends with Mrs. Wilson included a Sunday morning trip to church. Bethel Baptist was on Kisco Avenue behind the center of town. You could feel the excitement from Mrs. Wilson the moment we got up. She barked orders to her husband, Waylan, who despite a flurry of preparations, inevitably chose not to go to church. Smoking had taken a toll on Mr. Wilson, and he was left with a tracheotomy and no desire to go out in public unless it was required. He and the Lord seemed to have worked something out with prayer at the oversized Zenith television in the living room.

I was dressed in the starched jacket and tie that my mother had sent. Hair was combed and slicked. There was an endless stream of, "Oh, aren't you handsome? Waylan, will you look at Peter? So handsome. I am so proud, so proud!"

We'd arrive early and, once outside the church, were deep in the social world of Kisco Avenue, the crowded street behind the train station where most of the Black people in Mt. Kisco lived. Members of the congregation spilled onto the narrow sidewalk, and the buzz of conversation and laughter could be heard a block away.

"Mrs. Fox, you remember Peter, don't you?" Mrs. Fox was a little shorter and a little rounder than Mrs. Wilson with a big bosom.

"Of course, I do. Would you look at him? Vivian, I mean." She pinched my pink cheek. Everyone remembered me because I was there so often. Decades later, Black women would smile at me on the streets of Mt. Kisco and say they remembered me from church. "Weren't you the boy that come to church with Vivian?"

I would end up sitting with Mrs. Fox or any number of other carefully coiffed matrons because Mrs. Wilson sang in the choir and stood at the front of the church. I dreaded leaving her side, but Mrs. Fox was cut from the same cloth and did her best to make me comfortable. The service started quietly with the preacher finding a rousing phrase and repeating it with more passion. The passion became infectious as different members of the congregation called out, "Yes, Jesus." and "He is here!" The congregation would hum and sing and sway, and when the preacher asked everyone to reach out and tell the person next to them how much they loved them, Dozens of hands reached towards me to offer a greeting. At first I was taken aback, wishing Mrs. Wilson was not in the choir, but seated beside me. In that moment, I also recognized the warmth and generosity of these strangers, as they accepted me into their sacred space. More Sundays brought more familiarity. A few of the friendships forged in Bethel Baptist Church endured for years to come.

One Sunday the sermon inspired a member of the congregation to act out, falling onto the floor sweating and shaking. The stricken was a woman in her forties dressed to the nines in black taffeta and heels. She was pulled into a chair, steadied and spoken to, as sweat dripped down her rouged cheeks. Mrs. Fox clutched my trembling left knee while she hummed. The power of the Lord—which was not in my house nor in St. Matthew's Episcopal Church in Bedford Village nor in the whitewashed walls of the Friends Meeting House in Katonah—was clearly manifested in the writhing body on the floor of Bethel Baptist. The spirit of the Lord had taken root with a vengeance.

I thought I might walk back into that same environment

more than thirty years later for Mrs. Wilson's funeral, but the church was nearly empty. Nine of us were scattered across the pews. Mrs. Wilson's one surviving son sat with his wife and their grown daughter. Her other son, Herman, the fashion designer, had been her favorite. Herman always mentioned his mother's sense of style as inspiration. But AIDS swooped into Herman's life and snuffed it out, leaving an empty hole in his mother's heart. There was one other woman seated near the family, but no one seemed to know her. Mom and I sat near the rear with three seedy-looking men from the funeral parlor, who sat quietly in the back row waiting to complete the day's work. The choir was a disaster. Five singers moved painfully through hymns, rarely singing on key. Apparently, the good singers weren't available that day. How robust that choir was in my childhood.

Mrs. Wilson's niece delivered the sermon. She spoke of how Mrs. Wilson had lost her sight a few years prior. I hadn't known. She spoke of how she lost her mind and her health and how hard it was for her. I hadn't spoken to her in five or six years. She must have left this world long before her death, a defiant heart refusing to stop when there was nothing left to live for.

After the service we assembled on the sidewalk in the harsh winter sunlight and spoke with Mrs. Wilson's family. My mother had kept in touch with Waylan Jr. for the past several years, sending checks and helping with insurance and health care costs. Mrs. Wilson had worked for our family for thirty years after Mrs. Hattie had welcomed her with a massive heap of tarnished silver. Active enough to run, play tennis, or just talk, she became my friend on day one. While I ate, she ironed, and the television helped the afternoon hours pass. At fourteen, I left home to move into my own apartment, blissfully free from my family, but Mrs. Wilson insisted on traveling to New York City on Metro North every Monday to wash, iron and clean for me. She kept coming after I married and even cared for my first child. The bond was deep.

I wanted to tell her son and granddaughter, whom I had played with on occasion as a child, all that she had meant to me, but even at forty-five years old, I couldn't get the words out over the lump in my throat and instead cried like a small child with a skinned knee.

I did visit Mrs. Wilson in a retirement home she moved to in Peekskill, New York, about five years prior. I had been warned she had dementia. The visit was difficult, and Mrs. Wilson didn't comprehend much. When I saw her withered frame sitting on her bed in the shared room, I touched her shoulder, putting my face in front of hers and asked if she remembered me. She looked up with anger in her eye and said, "Don't you ask me that, of course I remember you."

I brought her a few small gifts, one of which was a chocolate bar. She ate about half of it before a healthcare worker checked in on us and snatched the bar away. A struggle ensued between Mrs. Wilson and the nurse, and I tried to intervene, but the nurse reminded me Vivian was a diabetic and couldn't have chocolate. I didn't know.

She wanted to walk the halls with me and brought her purse, which was loaded with those possessions she cared about most. She kept trying to enter the elevator, but a tracking alarm on her wrist prevented her from doing so without a harsh sound. She protested, telling the workers that she had to get the fifth floor where she lived. They reminded her that her room was on the third floor and the building was only three stories tall.

They weren't rude about it, they just told her she had already made it to the top floor. I could tell this was their line every day. After about an hour of a painful visit, I kissed her for the last time and left.

Before getting in the elevator, I stopped by the nurse's station to apologize for bringing the chocolate bar. I thanked the two women for their good care. I also wanted them to know Mrs. Wilson lived most of her life in apartment #502 on the fifth floor of her building in Mt. Kisco with a small balcony overlooking the train tracks and a large Zenith in the living room. She had lived there for almost fifty years with her husband, and later by herself, until one day that she didn't remember, when she was taken somewhere unfamiliar. I wanted them to know all of her attempts to board the elevator were just her way of trying to go home. She got there in the end.

Henry and me *(image courtesy of the author)*

6

HENRY

We were regulars at the Bedford Village Public Library. Jenny was a star reader, moving through a dozen books every summer, from JRR Tolkien to Judy Bloom. I was more of a story-time kid, listening to Mrs. Eggleston's animated readings of *Yurtle the Turtle* and *Blueberries for Sal*. After the last page was read and the book was closed, I was ready to go home, but my mom and I invariably had to wait for Jenny to choose a new Nancy Drew story. Mrs. Eggleston and my mother seemed to enjoy the chat time while we waited. I did not.

"Lyndall, does your family want a dog?"

This caught my attention. We did not need a new dog, but my mother was an avid dog lover, and this was by no means an appropriate question for her to field. Mrs. Eggleston took the momentary pause as encouragement and continued.

"I'm only asking because the Polks took in a sweet little puppy last week, and they are really hoping to find a good home for him. The poor thing is locked in their kitchen, and the Polk kids are scared to death of him. He's a little whippet who was thrown from a moving car in a leaf bag. Just horrible. How people could do such a thing, I will never know!"

My mother gasped. The hand was on the heart.

Emboldened by my mother's dramatic gesture, Mrs. Eggleston continued, "His leg is shattered and splinted, and he sounds as if he's in real pain. I've seen him, and he's just as sweet as can be. Don't you have a dog already? Perhaps he wants a playmate?"

"Oh, dear, that just breaks my heart."

I sensed trouble and moved closer. "We really don't need another dog, do we Pete? Rex is all we can handle, and he's getting older, so I don't know how he would do with a new puppy bouncing around." Mom glanced over her shoulder to see how Jenny was doing. She was now seated on the floor in the middle of a pile of Nancy Drew books. "Did you say he was thrown from a car? That's really beyond cruel, isn't it? Don't the Polks live right next to the library? Perhaps we should just have a quick look at the little pup?"

I cleared my throat, "Mom, I need to get home, I have a ton of homework."

"Pete, lovey, they're right next door; let's just see if they're home, and besides Jenny's not ready to go yet. Honestly, lovey, how much homework can you have? You're only in pre-school." She glanced at Mrs. Eggleston and laughed.

Mrs. Eggleston interjected, "Let me give Marilyn a ring now. Why don't we just see if she's home."

Before I knew it, Mom and I were standing in a war zone formerly known as the Polks' kitchen. Three small children with mucus all over their faces cowered at the top of the stairs behind a child's safety gate, crying and hugging each other. Mrs. Polk stood pressed against the kitchen table, nervously promoting the skinny white dog, which was tied to a leg of the stove. Wee-wee pads were everywhere. The animal, which the Polk kids had named Henry, was bug-eyed, underweight and shaking like a leaf either from fear, cold or both.

Suddenly, Mom was on all fours crawling towards the animal. She held a dog treat given to her by Mrs. Polk in her outstretched hand. Henry cowered, gobbled, wagged and licked. He was ours, no turning back now.

As we left with Henry on a leash, a new dog bowl and replacement bandages, I noticed the Polk kids had left their roost at the top of the stairs. I wondered for a moment if they were just there for effect. Regardless, it worked, and off we went to collect Jenny, the bookworm, and to introduce Henry to Rex and the rest of the family.

Henry was bad news from the start. It wasn't long before my mom started referring to him as the devil incarnate. His leg was shattered in several places, and he needed to be carried everywhere: to his food, to his bed, to the bush, etc. After several visits to local vets and many bills, it was determined that his multiple breaks could only be treated by the Veterinary Hospital for Special Surgery in Manhattan. After treatment Henry was prescribed two months of physical therapy appointments three times a week in Manhattan. These included massage, water therapy and psychological evaluations plus freshly prepared nutrient-rich meals. He was issued a patient identification card for the Hospital's Canine Therapy Unit that read, "Henry Boal, white male, unneutered, age unknown. Bedford, NY."

"Sounds like a Republican," Dad said.

In time Henry healed, but only with a significant depletion of my parents' savings account, so much so that they declined to have Henry neutered before he left the hospital. Besides, his pet psychologist determined the operation might further erode Henry's confidence.

And so he found his place in our home, defining his relationship with each of us, one by one. Rex was first. Rex was a true hero in our family. He'd tolerated plenty of toddler fingers up his nose and in his ears and, at the age of nine, sensed a rival in the house and put him in his place early on. The scoundrel was really no match for the prince, and Henry left Rex alone, choosing his battles wisely. For the most part, he ignored Rex, while Rex kept a watchful and leery eye on the newcomer.

Jenny and I fell for Henry's charms immediately. He would go weak in our presence, and we would dote while he would purr. We were famous for coming to his defense when there was a trial.

The adults were a bit more complicated for Henry. Mrs. Wilson just laughed. She would call out, "Oh, Lord," and "No, Sir," when she came across an errant poop or a shredded pillow. Mrs. Wilson later told us that the only times Mr. Wilson would brighten up during his final months of battling cancer were when she would say, "You won't believe what that dog did today ..."

With twenty-eight acres of land, we never walked our dogs. We just opened the door and let them go. A loud holler and back they'd come. Henry was quite the independent young male and frequently wouldn't come when called. He had a weakness for our neighbor Luly Carson's latest plantings, ripping them out by the roots and shoveling potting soil across her travertine walkways. He had a knack for getting out just before we left on a trip, running to the dirt under the arborvitae hedges just beyond the back porch. My mother followed in hot pursuit while Henry started to howl. We couldn't see anything except shaking hedges. Henry whined desperately as if he were being beaten. Jenny and I called for an end to the cruelty with more and more urgency. "I haven't even touched him, dammit!" All the while, during my mom's frantic struggle to put an end to the charade, Henry twisted his pure white coat into the mud, somehow managing to drag my mom in as well. We'd listen with horror as their battle raged until finally my mother, like the larger sumo wrestler, emerged victorious and muddy, dragging a filthy and whimpering Henry back to the house. Jenny was near tears, I was in total disbelief, and Dad and Joe were unsuccessfully trying to stifle their laughter. Rex sat in the kitchen, eyes closed.

One Saturday morning, Mom and I were driving through downtown Bedford, which consisted of no more than the convergence of three roads with no traffic lights, few cars and fewer pedestrians. All of a sudden, we came to a complete halt. Not since the gas crisis of the previous year had I seen this many cars lined up on Route 22. No one was moving, and I realized I was going to be late for my piano lesson with Mrs. Lobbin. Mom was not one to sit and wait, and after commiserating with a few nearby motorists, she headed towards the village green to see what had brought the town to a standstill. I followed. After passing several dozen cars and trucks, we could hear shouting and laughter. The crowd was mostly day laborers and nannies. Mrs. Fox spotted me and rushed over to say hello. A police car was in the middle of the circle of onlookers with lights flashing. We stepped into the circle and found the problem. It was Henry, on an escapade a few miles from our home.

In the middle of the intersection of Bedford Center Road

and Route 22, Henry was bottom to bottom with a female Irish setter. His elongated penis was lodged inside her with no signs of coming out. He and the frightened Irish setter were whirling in circles first clockwise then counterclockwise with a distraught Officer Malkin and a few other men repeatedly and unsuccessfully trying to grab Henry by the neck. His collar had slipped off and lay on the ground nearby. Mrs. Fox tried to cover my eyes.

Suddenly my mother's voice could be heard above all others. "HENRY!"

Everyone turned to see the source. All froze including Henry and his cohort. Henry spoke next, trying to drop to the ground but unable to do so in the rear because of his attachment. He offered a wild victim's whine. Someone yelled, "Mama's here. Party's over now." The crowd laughed.

My mother was either red from embarrassment or rage. She marched over to Henry, grabbing him first by the ear and then the leg. She called to Officer Malkin, "Stewart, pick her up and help me." The officer was as taken aback as the rest of onlookers but obeyed orders, and the canine couple was hoisted, still connected by Henry's erection, and carried trembling and thrashing to our car. The crowd started to applaud with plenty of cheering and laughter.

Someone shouted, "Don't get caught with your pants down, you dog."

And another, "Yeah, and watch out for the bitch, too!"

With this, my mom wrestled an arm free and held up her middle finger to the crowd as she walked away. A chorus of laughter and taunting faded in the distance as our awkward procession moved towards the Volvo.

I could hear Mrs. Fox's voice in the distance saying, "Lord, have mercy on that child."

When Officer Malkin and my mother tried to lower both dogs onto the back seat, they separated with a loud pop. The Irish setter bolted, and Henry would have too, but my mom wasn't going to let him off so easily with this one.

With Henry barking incessantly inside the car, my mother thanked Officer Malkin for his help.

"Mrs. Boal, I'm afraid I'll have to issue you a citation for failure to control a pet in public. I should give you a disorderly conduct citation as well, but given the circumstances, I'm going to let that one go. It really wasn't intentional on your part, but it is your responsibility to see that your dog is under control at all times. We do have a leash law in Bedford, which I trust you know about. In fact, I believe your husband wrote it, didn't he?" Mom threw her hands up in the air. "If this happens again, we'll have to fine you."

"You must be kidding me, really? I do not think Brad wrote Bedford's leash law. Oh, this is ridiculous, just give me the ticket, we're late as it is."

Henry didn't get much better as he aged; in fact, he got worse. Mrs. Hattie spent more time trying to hit him than she did cleaning our house or caring for Jenny and me.

Some years later, when I was in the seventh grade, Henry would sneak into Rippowam School through the fire escape doors as kids were sneaking out. He would trot down the corridor, stopping at each classroom door to stand on his two hind legs and peer through the window looking for me. You could hear him coming as classroom by classroom would erupt into chatter. When he'd reach my classroom door, which was inevitably during Mr. Clark's history class, he would drop to the floor and whine until Mr. Clark would send me out of class.

"Boal, it's your damned dog again. Get that animal out of this school. This had better be the last time, Boal." Mr. Clark was a total control freak, and he had lost control of the class again as Henry wailed in the hallway.

Once I stepped outside the door, Henry was a lamb with tail wagging. We'd walk down the hall back to the fire exit. After a few moments of love and petting, he'd trot off down Clinton to Guard Hill and return home. Mission accomplished.

He lived to sixteen years of age, torturing my mother, Mrs. Hattie and Luly Carson until the end. There was no illness or accident, just one last wild adventure. An officer picked him up ten miles north in Katonah after he went missing for almost a week. He was barking outside the yard of a Westie's home. She was in heat, and the old guy was looking for some action. By the time my mom collected him in the pound and took him to the vet, he was without collar, filthy and exhausted, with organs failing (except one) due to dehydration and malnutrition. Henry was put to sleep.

Jenny and I were too old to cry, but we did anyway. Mom did not.

Days later a summons arrived in the mail requiring the owner of Henry Boal of Bedford to appear in Westchester County Court. The summons specified that we were to answer the following charges: INABILITY TO CONTROL A DOMESTIC ANIMAL RESULTING IN DISORDERLY CONDUCT AND UNNECESSARY TRAFFIC, the hamlet of Katonah, town of Bedford, Officer Stewart Malkin. Henry had done it again.

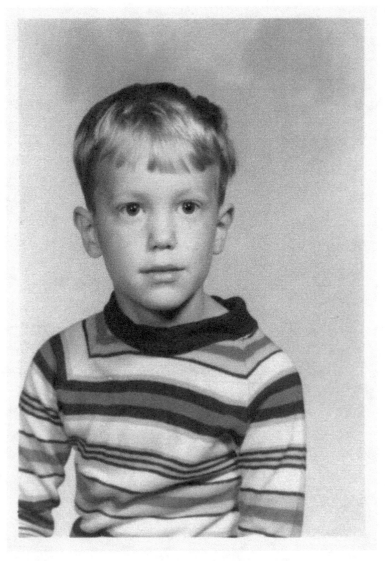

My kindergarten photo *(image courtesy of the author)*

7

RIGBY

Rigby Allen and I were inseparable all through kindergarten and first grade. As if that wasn't enough, we'd see each other every weekend as well. He lived about a mile up the road in a grand Victorian perched on a hill across the street from the Canfield mansion with his mother, father and two sisters, Aerin and Penny, who everyone called Pea. Sometimes Rigby mentioned Aerin's older brother, Wally, who had died before Rigby was born. I sensed that I wasn't supposed to ask for details, and Rigby didn't offer much, except that there had been an accident, and his parents didn't want him to mention Wally's name.

I slept over at Rigby's house all the time, and he at mine. We took him skiing when he was only six. Mom said he peed in his pants during the long drive to Vermont while Jenny and I slept. After the incident Mom always said, "Six is just too young to be away from your parents, remember what happened to poor Rigby. He was such a good sport about that."

Rigby was born in May and I was born the previous October, so I always felt older and more mature, if a seven-year-old can really be mature.

Mr. and Mrs. Allen were a few years younger than my parents, or at least they seemed younger to me. She was tiny with olive skin and thick black hair, while Mr. Allen was tall and rugged with a broad smile. Aerin, the oldest of the three kids, was gorgeous, especially to a first grader. Her suntanned friends filled the varsity ranks at Rippowam. They doted on Rigby and me, making us sugary desserts, piling ice cream on top and treating us like we mattered.

The Allens left their bedroom doors open all the time. One night as I got ready for bed, I was on my way to the bathroom off the hallway outside of Rigby's room to brush my teeth. The door to Mr. and Mrs. Allen's bedroom was wide open, and I saw the back of a woman completely naked stepping into a nightgown. At first I thought it was Aerin, but then realized that it was Mrs. Allen. I scurried into the bathroom, closed the door tightly and did not emerge for a long time, ashamed I had looked. A few days later, the exact same thing happened in the same place, but the body belonged to Mr. Allen. Guilty again.

I slept on the floor next to Rigby's bed. In the morning, I jumped in bed beside him, and we lay on our backs talking and laughing until Mrs. Allen called to us from downstairs "Rigby, Pete, pancakes are on the counter. Dad's at the Club playing all eighteen, Aerin's sleeping upstairs, and I'm taking Pea to the store with me." Mrs. Allen managed Fits, a popular shoe store in New Canaan, and often had to fill in on the weekends. "You two are on your own until one."

"Okay, Mom."

A minute later their enormous front door slammed shut, and the screen door creaked closed. As the Jeep pulled out of the driveway onto the dirt road, Rigby jumped out of his bed and bounded over to his bookcase. He dragged a book out from underneath a pile of oversized game boxes on the bottom shelf.

A flying jump landed Rigby back in the bed, "I found this in the attic; it was Wally's." He showed me the cover: *Blushes, Crushes, and More Normal Stuff.* "It's awesome."

Out of the bed again, he closed his door tightly and returned. We started flipping through pages full of cartoon pictures of boys and girls transforming from tight little bodies to hairy fleshy ones. Patches of hair sprouted from the girls' private parts and underneath their arms. This was all new information for us. Peals of nervous laughter accompanied each page turn. The boys in the book were worse than the girls, with fur on their chests, chins, backs and even on their butts. We almost put the book away when diagrams of blood and tubes began to make us queasy.

One picture of a fleshy girl with some kind of cut between her legs and blood on a washcloth was a cue for me to close the book and ask about the pancakes.

"No, wait," said Rigby, "I have to show you the good part." He flipped to a well-worn page near the back of the book. The chapter title was one word, but it was so long that neither of us could read it. Rigby thought it was a fancy way of spelling "fucking." We laughed nervously. The first picture showed a smiling man and woman lying on their backs in a double bed with the covers pulled up to their hairy armpits. They were looking at each other and holding hands on top of the covers. Each wore a wedding ring and neither wore a shirt. We turned the page and discovered a full-fledged erection pointed at the girl's hairy area.

Total silence. One of us was brave enough to turn the page. The picture on the next page showed the massive erection entering the hairy area. There was a close up and a full body shot that showed both the man and woman smiling.

"You and I could try that." Rigby giggled, looking away from the book to see my reaction. I actually did not think we could do that for anatomic reasons, and I had no intention of trying. Rigby was giggling uncontrollably but managed to get out, "I don't have any underwear on. Look!" He lifted up the sheets to reveal a tiny erection.

Speechless for a moment, I finally said, "Rigby, we would have to be married to do that ... and besides, that's only for a man and a woman, it doesn't work for two men ... or boys." I was freaking out and climbed out of the bed. I fumbled with my pants, catching my foot in the leg and tumbling onto the carpet.

"What are you doing?" Rigby inquired as he watched me throwing clothes and shoes on in record time. "I was only kidding."

"I have to go now. I'm walking home."

I grabbed my toothbrush and ran down the stairs while pulling my shirt over my head. As I rounded the corner into the kitchen on my way to the backdoor, I ran directly into Aerin, who was wearing only a long gray shirt. "Whoa! Hey, there, Petey, I see a whole plate of pancakes with your name on it. You hungry?"

"No, thank you, I have to go home now. I have a ton of homework."

"I think school's out for the summer kiddo, but sure. Careful walking on the road. Hey, cutie, what was going on up there? I heard massive amounts of giggling from you two. RIGBY! Get down here and say goodbye to your friend!"

"We already said goodbye. I'll see you, Aerin, thanks for having me over."

I ran the whole way home without stopping and stayed in my room for the rest of the day.

8

LOUISA CARSON

I don't think my parents ever set foot in Louisa Carson's house despite the fact that she lived a few hundred yards to the west of us and we shared a driveway.

Louisa, known to all her friends as Luly, could be seen on most sunny days in the spring and fall sitting in her garden chair next to a small transistor radio with a tri-fold piece of aluminum foil held under her collarbone to maximize the effect of the afternoon sun on her neck and face, which were already the color of an old saddle.

Luly never worked, though she volunteered twice weekly at the Northern Westchester Hospital, chaired the events committee for Caramoor and served as an honorary member of the Bedford Blooms Club. She was also somewhat famous in town for having repeatedly and successfully chaired Let 'Em Ripp!—the Rippowam-Cisqua School's annual fall fundraising gala. Luly came up with the title herself.

A year before we bought the Smith estate, Luly lost her husband, Robert Ericksen. He blacked out in the bathtub one night and drowned, leaving Luly a widow with four children between the ages of five and ten.

How she found and married Art Carson so quickly, we never knew. Art stepped right into high Bedford living with aplomb. He was a decent golfer who dressed the part, mixed the drinks and shook a lot of hands. Art was a commodities broker on Wall Street, and between long commutes to the city, business trips on the weekends and a second life at the Yale Club in New York City, wasn't around all that much. Most of the men in town weren't. It was the women, like Luly, who ruled the Bedford operations.

The Carsons occupied what was once the Smith's eight-car garage. However, there was no trace of a car park in their home, with glossy hunter green walls, heavy layers of yellow chintz, polished mahogany and plenty of heirloom silver. The house looked like all of the others in Bedford, though maybe a bit smaller.

On the south and west sides of the Carson's home, beautifully shaded courtyards had been created with water features to distract from the Guard Hill traffic. The north side held their front door, which looked onto asphalt and plenty of it. The asphalt stretched right to our back door, where our three rusty cars sat, garage-less, for the Carsons and their guests to behold.

Soon after we moved in, Luly sent Art over dressed in all kinds of colors with a gold ascot bulging at the neck. He presented a bottle of brandy and a jar of homemade blackberry jam. Mom answered the door, thanking him effusively for the gifts until Art said, "We also wondered if you might want to consider parking your cars in the front loop of your driveway? We so often sit in the rear courtyard and prefer the tranquility without the comings and goings of vehicles." There was a brief and awkward pause before Art concluded, "It's just a thought. Enjoy the brandy. Maybe once you're settled in, we can have you over for cocktails? I make a mean Martini."

There was a bit more chatter, but only out of obligation. Cocktails never happened.

On three occasions over the next few months, we accidentally left a car in neutral. An imperceptible slope of the shared driveway rolled cars quietly backwards towards the Carsons'. They never hit anything, except for one hideous green pot of geraniums; they just drifted gently backwards settling in front of the Carson's door. Luly would rise early to get her pruning done before putting her kids on the school bus. Whenever one of our fleet was there to greet her, we could hear the muffled swearing and then the sound of Luly's clogs marching across the shared driveway to pound on our backdoor. Mrs. Hattie would march with similar purpose up the back stairs to her room and close the door before Luly reached her destination. Mrs. Hattie would certainly have been a match for Louisa Carson, but she also knew how and when to choose her battles and left this one to my mother, who was obligated to answer the door with an artificial pleasantry. Dad and Joe would hide themselves just around the corner, snickering like two badly behaved schoolboys.

After the third car rolled over the property line, Luly built a wall. It was a well-crafted stone wall like so many others in Bedford, standing about three-feet high like a proud fortress. Luly placed two enormous stone chicken planters from Perennial Gardens on top. Their backs and heads were hollowed out for earth. Something fern-like sprouted out of their backs while colorful impatiens sprung from their heads. Luly placed them facing one another on opposite sides of the entry in the middle of the wall. They looked like Hatfield and McCoy glaring at one another, so after a few days, she turned them to face us. There they sat like weather-beaten gargoyles with ridiculous Mardi Gras headdresses atop their sallow expressions.

No more than three weeks after the mortar from the new wall was dry, Joe rolled into our driveway and jumped out, leaving his venerable Country Squire in neutral. Just as Mrs. Hattie was setting lunch on the kitchen table, a blood-curdling scream came from outside followed by a loud crash. Mom, Dad, Jenny, Joe and I ran outside to see what had caused the commotion while Mrs. Hattie toddled up the stairs to the safety of her room. Across the driveway, Luly stood barefoot with tiny paper towel rolls between her toes, wearing a pink bikini top, white tennis skirt and an imposing blue sun visor under her helmet of dark curls. Her hands were clasped to the side of her head as she looked down at a pile of shattered stone, earth, and impatiens. The remaining stone chicken looked more irate than ever.

The five of us stood still, not knowing whether to run to Luly to see if she was all right or to burst into laughter over the death of the angry chicken. Joe chose the latter, stifling his cackling as he tiptoed back to the house. The rattle of Mrs. Hattie's window could be heard as she hoisted it up to hear what was coming next.

Luly helped the rest of us decide what we should do next. She looked up at the remaining four and bellowed, "Bradlee

Boal, you will be hearin' directly from my law-yer! Do not come near me. Do not move this here vehicle. This ol' jalopy stays right where it is until the police arrive, y'all hear me?"

We all nodded in unison. Then, in a deep guttural yell that might have been heard as far away as the Yale Club on Vanderbilt Avenue in New York City, Luly shouted, "Arthur!"

9

THE TWINS

My parents believed in the merits of a strong public education system and planned on Jenny and me being part of one. The Bedford Village Elementary School was two miles from our house, right in the heart of town. Jenny attended kindergarten and first grade there and had plenty of friends and a lot of fun. When I was ready to enter kindergarten and Jenny the second grade, Westchester County began a redistricting plan for the area with the opening of the newly constructed West Patent Elementary School located off of McLain Street on the border of Mt. Kisco. It was not only new in architecture but also in concept, with round tables, no doors, few walls and a new democracy of learning.

My kindergarten year with Miss Vogel was fine. Jenny also made the switch without incident, but the following year did not start well for either of us. Jenny was put in the dreaded Dr. Hollingsworth's class. There was rampant speculation on what exactly Hollingsworth was a doctor of. Calvin Pearl said he was a failed podiatrist and gave him the nickname Doc Hollow Warts. When one kid in his class misbehaved, which was a daily occurrence in the third grade, Hollow Warts punished the entire class, forcing everyone to sit silently at their desks copying pages from the *Encyclopedia Britannica* during bus calls. In the final minute before bus departure, Hollow Warts would release the panicked kids, who would race down the hall in a mad dash to catch their bus. With my backpack and coat spread across two bus seats, I stood behind the bus driver imploring him to wait for my sister.

"Rules are rules, kid, if she isn't here at three o'clock sharp, she missed the bus. Nothin' I can do about it. Complain to the district."

This bus issue wasn't helping what was already turning out to be a stressful year. The school had decided that, based on my triumphs in kindergarten, I was eligible to be placed in a combined first and second grade, which would in turn result in me skipping to third grade the following year. I knew no one in my new class. Entering my learning area—classrooms were not part of the new democracy of learning at West Patent Elementary, but learning areas were—it didn't take long to realize I was the shortest in the group. A smiling Mrs. Edgecombe asked us to call her Linda. Linda then asked us to find our name on a chair placed upside down on one of three round tables. Why should the janitorial staff have to put all of the chairs back on the floor with the new democracy of learning? After walking three full circles, I started on a fourth with the dread of failure coming on fast. The titans claimed almost all of the chairs, and the few remaining did not have my name on them. One Marcie, one Timmy, one Kim-Sook, but no Peter. There was no chair for me, just an accusation from Linda that I was probably in the wrong room, which I wasn't. Eventually a chair was found, but I never really recovered.

I think Jenny would have been fine for another year in West Patent. Hollow Warts was reprimanded for his misinterpretation of school etiquette, and kids were allowed to board the bus on time. I, on the other hand, shook like a leaf each morning before heading off to school.

Mom panicked and pulled us both out of West Patent, trotting us over to Rippowam to see if late enrollment was an option. Rippowam started five days after the public schools to avoid the Labor Day weekend crush on the Nantucket Ferry. If we made the switch, we could still start classes on the first day of school. All they would need was a hefty deposit. Jenny went right into the third grade without a friend in sight. Since Rippowam observed a December 1st age cut-off for boys, I went back into kindergarten for the second time, setting my public-school plan back by two years.

Despite the adjustment, Rippowam was a perfect fit for me. On day one, I was still trembly from the trauma of West Patent, but a warm hug from Mrs. Whitty and special attention from Mrs. Pierce went a long way.

Jenny's year at Ripp was miserable. Her class was notorious as one of the meanest and most problematic in the school's history, perhaps because seven children in Jenny's grade lost a parent within a year. Four of the seven were twins, and to add insult to injury, Jenny lived next door to one set of twins: Migs and Babe Ericksen. Migs was short for Margaret, and Babe was actually Penelope, but since she was the smaller of the two and the second born, everyone called her Babe. They kept their father's last name even after Luly married Art.

Babe and Migs were bullies, and Jenny Boal fell right into their web.

Smart, tiny and friendless, Jenny didn't know anyone in the third grade at Ripp, and everyone seemed to know everyone else. Tears, teacher conferences, parents in denial and a bad choice without a solution left Jenny to brave her way through probably the worst nine months of her life. During the course of the year, my parents campaigned the Bedford public school system and eventually won permission for Jenny to return to Bedford Village Elementary for fourth and fifth grade, which she did, somewhat scarred, damaged and relieved to be on the other side of misery.

Tim Ericksen and I were great friends. Being in the same class and living right next door to each other helped. We were content to while away the afterschool hours playing with Matchbox cars in the labyrinth of tracks our fingers had made in the dirt behind our houses. Migs and Babe would seek us out. I suspect they befriended me either to further torture my sister, who was holed up in our house, or to torture their younger brother, which also delighted them.

They had a system down where Babe would play the nice one and Migs the more obtuse and abusive. Babe was a shade prettier and Migs's voice a shade deeper. In the end, both could throw some pretty hard punches. Timmy would either groan or run when they approached.

"Hi, Peter," Migs called, and to Timmy, "Hey, retard."

"How's your sister?" Babe asked me.

"She's fine," I answered, still looking at the dirt.

"Where is she? How come she doesn't ever come outside?" Babe persisted.

Migs answered before I could, "Remember Babe, she doesn't come out because she's scared of us." She would let out a deep laugh.

"Does she have any friends? I never see her with any friends, she's always alone and looks like she might cry. Does she cry a lot at home?" Babe actually sounded concerned.

I was starting to squirm and told Timmy I had to get home. Timmy followed me back to my house.

Migs called after us, "Tell your sister we'll see her tomorrow."

"And not to forget her Kleenex!" Babe called. The two were laughing again.

I started to avoid the twins at school, but they sought me out. Migs always put her arm around me in the hallways between classes and stood closer to me than I wanted. Babe sat next to me on the bus. When I'd get home and Mrs. Hattie would empty my school bag, I'd realize Babe had slipped a hot dog or a chewed piece of gum inside my bag. I never told Mrs. Hattie who'd done it for fear of a showdown.

There were times when the twins were actually fun to be around, but these were rare. Timmy tended to panic in their presence and would often have to run to his mother for help, which the twins would tease him about ad nauseam. It was when Luly was out of the house that the twins were at their most dangerous.

One afternoon Timmy and I played lacrosse in the driveway. Luly's Mercedes drove through our game. She rolled down the window to tell us that she was off to the club and would be back in time for dinner. "Peter, you are most welcome to join us if you'd like. We always want a gentleman at the table."

"Thank you, Mrs. Carson. I have to have dinner with my family."

"Lobster Thermidor if you change your mind. Twins are inside doin' their studies. Bye boys!"

Catch continued until Migs appeared holding something behind her back. She smelled her little brother's fear, enjoying it as she walked towards us. Suddenly she pointed a long wooden rifle at Timmy's face. He screamed and wouldn't stop as he ran behind a nearby oak. Babe could be heard laughing as she sauntered out of the garage with a matching rifle.

Migs was in hysterics. Babe spoke first, "Hey, chicken shit, we're not going to shoot you guys." Timmy's muffled sobbing could be heard behind the oak.

"Yet," Migs blurted out. More laughter followed.

"We thought you guys might like to see the new BB guns Mother and Art gave us for our birthday. We were thinking of taking them out back and looking for squirrels. You all want to come along?" Babe offered.

"Migs, you scared the fucking shit out of me!" Timmy had not fully recovered. He was still behind the tree panting, and I was still frozen in the middle of the driveway with an armed twin on either side. "We're not going out back with you two and those guns. Just go away and leave us alone," Timmy shouted from behind the tree.

Migs lifted up her rifle and aimed it at the oak. She started clucking like a chicken and then fired a shot that hit the tree with a thud. Timmy started to cry.

Babe pointed her gun at me, telling me not to move. I obeyed. She headed to the tree with her rifle raised and motioned for Migs to head that way too. They circled the great oak, closing in on their little brother. "Get over here, retard, and stand with your friend." Timmy's crying had turned to a whimper while a mixture of mucus and tears dripped from his chin. He backed up, eyeing the two barrels while Babe prodded and Migs aimed at his face.

"Y'all gonna do what we say, right boys?" Migs asked, basking in her power.

We both nodded, but apparently that wasn't enough and Migs asked, "What did you say?"

"Yes," I said, "we'll do what you say."

Timmy started a high-pitched hysterical scream, and I wondered whether Mrs. Hattie would hear him. It wouldn't be the first time we had heard Timmy scream. "Leave us alone, Migs, just leave us the fuck alone. Mommy! Help me, Mommy!"

"Mom's at the club, retard, so you can shut up," Babe said, stabbing Timmy with the butt of her rifle.

"We just want you to do one thing for us, and then you guys can go," Migs said. We were too scared to speak. Timmy's tears were back full force. I had the feeling that the twins hadn't figured out what that one thing was and were improvising with their newfound power.

"Turn around!" Migs barked. We did. Not seeing, not knowing what was coming next, I started to cry too, realizing I was about to be shot by twin one or twin two in the back of the head.

"Pants down, retards!" Babe shouted. We jumped at the crack of her voice. Timmy and I looked at each other for a moment as if we didn't understand how to do this.

"I said pants down, little fuckers!" Babe smacked Timmy in the side of the head with the rifle, shouting, "Now!"

We fumbled with our belts and zippers and lowered our khakis to our ankles.

"Boxers, too!" Babe shouted. Only in Bedford do all second graders wear boxers. Timmy's cheek was now bleeding, and I didn't want to be next, so I slipped my boxers down. Timmy followed, gasping for breath between sobs. I started to wonder what the twins' plan was, nervous that the point of the rifle might do more than hit us on the side of the head.

Behind us we could hear the whispers of the two girls and the laughter that followed. Babe spoke next. She poked Timmy in the bare ass with her rifle as she did. "Okay, guys, you did what we said. Now all you have to do is count slowly to three and then you can go."

Timmy shouted, "one, two, three," and reached for his pants, but the rifle swung at his head again, making loud contact. He almost fell over with his ankles bound by the khakis.

"Not so fast, little fucker, I said *slowly*," Migs continued, "Now, count when we tell you to, got it, retard?"

We nodded. There was a moment of silence, and then we heard the triggers cock one by one. They were planning to shoot us at point blank range. Migs' deep voice said, "Count now, boys, real slow."

"One … two …"

We didn't make it to three, when a BB fired into my ass from three feet away. I hollered, but my scream was not heard, because Timmy's was much louder. He wheeled around and grabbed Migs by her hair and started ripping it out in clumps. Babe was trying to pull him off without much success. I yanked my boxers and pants over my knees as I ran back to my house. Luly's Mercedes could be seen pulling in the driveway as I stumbled onto our porch. I slipped into our house unnoticed and stayed in my room until Mrs. Hattie rang the bell for dinner.

10

REBEL WITHOUT A CAUSE

I was a rule follower. I did what I was told—in school, at home, at friends' houses. It seemed so much easier. Later in life, I realized I wanted to avoid confrontation, and rule-following helped, so I don't know why every now and then, I needed to rebel for no good reason: a rebel without a cause.

When I was about eight, I would wait hours in my bed until I was sure all members of the household had fallen asleep. I knew everyone's bedtime rituals. Jenny's room shared a wall with mine. After completing homework, she would read until my mom came in to say goodnight, then her light would go out. Mom was great at the goodnights. She would peek in the door in her long Lanz nightgown covered by her floor-length robe with two sheepskin slippers poking out beneath. In her most soothing voice, she would wish us a good night's sleep and give us a kiss and a reassuring rub on the shoulder. She would return to the living room, pour herself an orange juice and gin and finish an article in *The New Yorker* before heading up to bed herself. I suspect it was her most cherished moment of the day. Dad would either be passed out in his blue armchair in the living room by the dwindling fire with the needle on the record player skipping, long after Carly Simon had stopped singing, or he would be deep in an alcohol-doused slumber in his bed. After dishes were cleaned and put away, Mrs. Hattie retreated to her room, removed her wig and turned on the television, not to be seen again until early the next morning.

I had two vices: an old pack of Parliaments and bourbon. The cigarettes had been left behind after one of the crowded Republican fundraisers. They lived unnoticed in a small Russian lacquer box on the long teak coffee table in the living room. Mrs. Hattie found them after the party and asked my dad if she should pitch them. R.J. Reynolds Tobacco was one of my dad's biggest clients and seeing as Parliament was a brand he represented and defended, he suggested we keep them.

"Mrs. Hattie, you know I detest smoking, but if someone's going to smoke in this house, it better be a brand I represent." She chuckled. Mrs. Hattie and my dad didn't see each other often, but the bond between them was clear. "Since I'm banning Marlboros from this house, we better keep an alternative on hand, don't you think?"

"I haven't touched one in some forty years and I can't stand them. Can't get the smell out. I'll put them right here in this box, Mr. Boals. You don't think we should worry about the children getting them?"

"Have you met the children, Mrs. Hattie?"

"Oh, Mr. Boals, I mean. What are you talking about? I raised those two."

"My point exactly, now good night, Mrs. Hattie."

"Yes sir, good night, Mr. Boals."

One summer night, after everyone in the house was asleep, I headed downstairs for the living room. I had a choice of three staircases for my descent. One took me right past my parents' bedroom door. The other was closest to Jenny's room, and the third went past Mrs. Hattie's room. I chose the latter. Moving down the upstairs hall on carpeting was quick and soundless. Mrs. Hattie's stairs posed a greater challenge. Her room was in the original part of the house, which was built in the late 1700s, long before Bernard and Gertrude Smith extended it into a sprawling mansion. The original wing was wonderfully lopsided and creaky with low ceilings and abundant woodwork. I took about ten minutes to descend the stairs, checking each step with a gentle push of the toe to test for groans in the wood. The tiger maple bannister was no help. Once on the ground floor, I moved nimbly down the length of the house to the living room, making sure my dad was no longer slumped in his chair. Lifting the black-and-red lacquer lid, I slid a Parliament out of the pack and grabbed a book of matches.

I was a most cautious thief, careful to leave no evidence of my crime, so I headed outdoors. As I mentioned, our house was large, and I had seven doors to choose from. Once safely outside, I trotted across the main courtyard, up three steps and across the second courtyard to a long, curved stone bench on the far side of the pool house at least a thousand yards from our house and well out of sight. Pajamas came off and were folded and placed on the bench. Clad only in my boxers, I moved far away from my pajamas at the other end of the bench. I placed the white cigarette in my mouth as I'd seen so many of our guests do. I struck the match and placed it just under the far end while inhaling deeply. At first, I coughed, but with repeated attempts, I was able to smoke about half of the cigarette. Plumes of smoke circled into the chilly night air. I put the butt out on the underside of the stone bench, threw the half cigarette over the wall into the bushes, slipped back into my pajamas, and raced back to the house. Once matches were returned to the living room, I retraced my steps, tiptoed back up Mrs. Hattie's stairs and climbed into bed with my heart racing.

I committed the same crime several more times before deciding to try a new one. Long after all were in bed and asleep, I took the identical route with all of the same precautions. Once at the bottom of Mrs. Hattie's stairs, I took a left and stepped into the kitchen. The cool linoleum tiles felt good on bare feet. I went to the table and picked up one of our old wooden chairs. These chairs were passed down from my dad's mother, whom none of us had met since she died when Dad was only seventeen. Grandma Thane had stenciled the backs of each ebony-colored chair with regal wings and tiny leaves of gold. Seven were still standing, though from time to time, they needed glue. One never recovered after Mrs. Hattie broke it years ago during the crayon incident. I carried one of the secure chairs to the butler's pantry and placed it underneath the liquor cabinet, which was not quite reachable for a small eight-year-old.

Once safely balanced atop the chair, I opened the cabinet and grabbed the bottle closest to me. I unscrewed the cap and took a deep inhale. Jim Beam Bourbon, my father's favorite. The smell was so potent, it felt like I had already swallowed. Though harsh, the smell triggered instant affection for my dad. I tipped the bottle up and took a swig. Before swallowing, I quickly screwed the cap back on and replaced the bottle. Gulp. The burn was intense and unpleasant. I grabbed the back of the old chair, realizing I was on the verge of gagging or vomiting. Instead, I let out a cough, which I tried to stifle by gripping the chair back even harder. The explosion of the cough was followed by the rattle of a wooden leg rolling across linoleum and then a loud crash as I went to the floor with three quarters of a chair shooting across the pantry and hitting the sideboard with a crunch.

As quickly as I could, I located the leg, sat on the floor and stuffed the runaway back into its hole. When the chair was reassembled, I started towards the kitchen table, when I heard Mrs. Hattie's voice.

"Child, what in the name of the Lord are you doing down here with that old chair?"

Mrs. Hattie was wigless which added to my surprise.

"I knew one chair was broken, and I thought I could fix it."

"Uh huh, is that so. At one o'clock in the morning?" Somehow her voice was harsh, and yet she was whispering. "Look here, you're a bad liar. You don't ever need to lie to Mrs. Hattie, you don't ever need to be doing what you're doing. You need something to drink? You have water by your bed. You need something to eat? Mrs. Hattie closed this kitchen hours ago. You don't need anything down here or anywhere else after lights go out in this house. You understand me?"

"Yes, Mrs. Hattie. I'm sorry, and I won't lie again, I promise." A first tear was headed down my cheek with the second in hot pursuit.

"Lord, child, don't cry ... besides, those tears smell like liquor."

I froze, wiped my tears, closed my mouth and backed up a step.

"Listen, here. I'm not mad, maybe just a little disappointed. You're almost a man now."

"I'm eight."

"Stop interrupting me, please." A brief pause followed. "Well, someday soon, but not tomorrow, you'll be a man. Nobody's gonna tell you what you can and can't do. You're gonna be in a position to make your own rules. You'll choose when you go to bed, whether or not you brush your teeth and whether you have one glass of milk, or a glass of wine or six cans of beer. And when you make these decisions, you're gonna know what's right and what's wrong. Even at eight, you already know, don't you? Even at eight."

"Yes, I do."

"And listen here, you are no ordinary eight-year-old because you've seen a lot. Both you and your sister seen a lot right here in this house. I know you know your sweet father drink way too much, which is why we help him and we pray for him. You don't want to be like that when you're grown and besides, your father's going to need you."

She hugged me and kept talking, "Mrs. Hattie knows everything that goes on in this house, and she's done a thing or two in her time as well." In this moment, we grew even closer.

She pulled back from our hug and looked me in the eye. "I'll do two things for you, and I only want one in return. I'm gonna tell your parents I broke another chair. Lord knows, I'm the one who's got to fix it anyways, and I'm gonna give you a tip. Next time you sneak downstairs use the ones by Jennifer's room, they creak a whole lot less than mine."

"What's the one thing I have to do for you?"

"Don't sneak downstairs again until you're eighteen."

Four cousins dressed for "Charleston Night" aboard the QE2, 1975
(image courtesy of the author)

11

QUEEN ELIZABETH, THE SCOTCH AND THE HIGH SEAS

As they entered their seventies, George and Barbara Cadbury realized they were all traveled out. Jet lag was no longer for them. The amount of world travel the two had undertaken over many decades of public service was impressive to say the least. My grandfather, an economist, headed the Technical Assistance Administration for the United Nations for six years and chaired the International Planned Parenthood Federation for many more, resulting in my grandparents living in the U.K., Canada, New York, Ceylon, Jamaica and Barbados, with extended stays in Burma, Malaysia, Hong Kong, Indonesia, Thailand, Singapore, Haiti and Puerto Rico.

Though George held the official jobs, Barbara wasn't one to sit by and clutch an arm or oversee afternoon tea service.

Upon the urging of her friend Norman Manley, she ran and was elected President of the Jamaica Family Planning Association. She also helped to found five Planned Parenthood Centers in five nations and was a sought-after keynote speaker on family planning around the globe.

World War II sent Barbara back and forth across the Atlantic, spurred by the phony war of 1938 and the real one in 1939, during which her husband remained on British soil to serve as a volunteer firefighter. The small girls and their mother were touted in the Birmingham newspaper for their bravery crossing back and forth across the Atlantic with the ever-present threat of German U-boats and Axis airstrikes. On one crossing, they shared a boat with fleeing members of the Ballets Russes. Little Lyndall prompted a chance encounter with danseur noble Anton Dolin, as she almost tumbled off a deck chair. Granny liked to refer to him by his given name of Patrick Kay.

Still crossing the Atlantic at least twice a year between daughters and grandchildren, the Cadburys opted for travel by sea, often booking passage on a streamer or cargo ship, nabbing one of a half-dozen staterooms and dining with captain and crew. Twice they transported the entire clan on the Queen Elizabeth II between New York and Southampton.

How thrilled we were to spend five days on the luxury liner. After check-in and family photo, the ship's horn deafened as we waved to throngs of strangers from the top deck. Suitcases and duffles were thrown onto beds and placed on luggage racks, and off we went to explore the seven stories and endless acreage of our ship. Though my parents traveled with us, on both occasions they brought Joe to watch and entertain the four cousins. But there was no catching us, as we sprinted from shuffleboard deck to hair salon, from pool to pool and dining room to bowling alley. This was kid paradise, and we all knew it.

The four cousins were as thick as thieves. Mom and Aunt Caroline timed our arrival into the world perfectly with Jessica appearing five months after Jenny, and Nick just five days behind me. Nick's birth forced Granny and Grandfather to the skies in order to be with each daughter for the arrival of the grandsons. The four of us were a perfect team and spent every summer together on one side of the Atlantic or the other.

Dinner was at six in the Coronia Restaurant. We were seated next to the adults but had our own table, laid with a thick off-white tablecloth, rows of weighty silverware and all sizes of crystal glasses that sprayed prisms of rainbow light onto our table as the setting sun put on a show.

A tiny, stooped man with a wide grin named Paul introduced himself as our waiter for the evening and for the entire week. "Paul, may I ask, what is your surname?" Granny inquired.

"Paul Pacic, ma'am."

Granny, who could place anyone by their name, pegged Paul as Croatian, but questioned the given name.

Paul confessed in a slightly lowered voice, "Yes, I was born Zeljko, but management suggested Paul. Guests cannot say Zeljko."

"Zeljko is a mouthful!" exclaimed Granny, "but so is Bar-ba-ra, and heaven knows no one can say, or spell, Lyndall." She turned to my mother and patted her arm saying, "My mistake, dear."

"Zeljko Pacic," she pronounced and paused like a librarian from Zagreb considering an acclaimed author. "What did your chums call you?"

"Chums, ma'am?"

Granny burst out in a spontaneous laugh. "Chums,

ma'am—try saying that ten times over. What did your friends call you in school?"

"Pacito … ma'am." The grin grew just a little wider under his thick mustache, and we could all imagine the boy that was.

Another hearty chortle from Granny, delivered as only the British can. "What a delightful name! May we call you Pacito? We promise not to let management in on our secret." Pacito nodded, winked and scurried off with nine drink orders.

Pacito's accent was faint, though he could never quite master "Miss Jessica." It was more like "Miz Jethica," which sent us into giggles and endless coaching and correction. We settled on "Miz Jeth," which seemed not to address any of the problematic syllables. Why Pacito didn't retaliate by making us say Zeljko, I do not know. Might have been management's watchful eye.

Pacito seemed to serve only our two tables all night, and we kept him at a near sprint throughout our meal, needing more Shirley Temples, absolutely no pickles, french fries with extra ketchup, more napkins, lobsters out of shells, another request to preview the dessert tray and finally two baked Alaskas, flaming in cognac.

The dessert tray, wheeled around the dining hall all evening long like an old dowager, was truly a work of art with brightly colored cakes, thick creams and light parfaits. We made it our mission to try them all and required multiple viewings throughout our meal in order to make the right decisions. To our delight, as Pacito trundled the tray in our direction on a particularly stormy night, the massive lemon meringue tart became airborne and landed inches from Jenny's little blue espadrilles. Management's watchful eye was a bit closer, and Pacito was Paul for the remainder of the night.

Poor Joe was saddled with four very unruly children. We really mastered outsmarting him in no time. He could never seem to round all four up, with adjoining doors to suites, endless staircases and shortcuts that only fast-moving children could know about. Joe gave up and started pursuing a pretty woman more his age. We may have tortured the two of them, but no one's going to admit this.

Our favorite haunt was the gymnasium, partly because Joe never thought once to check there. In fact, no one visited the gymnasium during our five-day crossing. We delighted in hoisting and heaving the medicine ball and dangling from the chin-up bar. In the corner were two machines with pink canvas straps and a small standing platform. The platform doubled as a scale. Jenny and Jessica read the directions to the Firmline Exercise Shaker. As often happened, they selected their younger brothers for a trial run. Nick and I placed the straps under bums and attached them to the opposite side of the fat burner and leaned back as instructed. Jenny and Jess flipped the switches, and the straps flew from side to side in little frantic jerks, causing our butts and bodies to shake uncontrollably.

"Turn it off, Jess!" shouted Nick. She did. It was a bit shocking at first, but also hilariously funny. Nick was the heaviest of the four but couldn't have weighed more than sixty-five pounds. The vibrating strap sent us into spasms of movement and laughter. The boys strapped the girls in and let them have a go. We decided on a daily regimen, frequenting the empty gym each day after breakfast for more fat-burning sessions.

Bedtimes were soon abandoned with a one-hour time change each day. The adults gave up, and the children stayed up. After dinner, most first-class passengers headed for the Queen's Room on the quarter deck. After dinner drinks arrived accompanied by potato chips and peanuts. There was sherry for grown-ups and more Shirley Temples and chocolate milks for children, all served with tiny parasols. There was also an emcee in a tux who moved through a fairly stale stand-up comedy routine, working the room and winning favor. Honestly, there wasn't much else to do on the ship, and the mood in the room was jovial.

The jokes were a bit off-color by today's standard with references to blondes, golf games and mothers-in-law. He had an elegantly dressed sidekick with a plunging neckline, who helped people to the stage and showed prizes. We listened, and we didn't.

One night, Jenny and Jessica headed for the bath ("bawth" as Jessica said) while Joe put Nick to bed. I always enjoyed time with the adults. It wasn't the conversation or attention but just the proximity and maybe the potato chips. I was listening to the emcee more than to my parents and grandparents.

He asked his partner to hold up a bottle of Macallan Scotch Whiskey, which she did with great flair. I tapped my dad's leg, but he didn't seem to notice. The emcee was talking up the brand and promoting a visit and tour of Easter Elchies in Scotland to see and sample the drink.

"In fact, I'm going to be giving away some aged-to-perfection Macallan Scotch Whiskey on this very stage tonight." The emcee was capturing more attention with this announcement. I tapped Dad's leg again. Dad was telling a story and wasn't paying much attention to the leg taps or the impending give-away.

"Yes, one lucky man in the audience is going home with not one bottle of scotch, but … twelve bottles, all duty free, in fact, all free, and free to consume whenever you would like!"

The crowd was listening, but my family was not. Dad's story was far better than the ramblings of our emcee. Miss Elegant Assist was working the crowd with her bottle, stopping only at men and bending forward to show the label and her low-cut gown.

Barking into his microphone, "You strike me as a scotch-drinking crowd. Does anyone here drink scotch?" the emcee drew a late-night laugh, accompanied by several dozen hands.

Someone shouted, "I drink scotch, and I could use a refill!"

My mom leaned over and whispered, "Bed soon, Pete," before turning back to Dad's story. She would inject truths and clarifications along the way.

The emcee continued, "Sir, these prized bottles could be yours, or any other man's in this room."

"Ahoy, bloke, what about the women?" Granny belted from her lounge chair. Cheers and laughter followed.

"Women are welcome to join this little contest too, ma'am. But I don't think you'll qualify." My grandmother let out a harumph and turned back to my dad, who was closing in on the punchline. I inched closer to the stage.

"Yes, every man and maybe even some of the ladies here tonight have what I'm looking for, so most of you are eligible to win. I'm giving twelve bottles of scotch to the first man, or rather person …" He turned to the band, whose members were pretty checked out on the side of the stage. A light drum roll followed. "Twelve bottles of Macallan Scotch Whiskey go to the first man with …a hole in his sock."

I was off running through low round cocktail tables, leaping over extended legs with all of the agility a young track star could muster. In a flash, I was onstage standing next to the emcee, having shed my right Topsider, offering my naked heel to a startled audience. I had holes in all of my socks. At some point, Mom and Mrs. Hattie just gave up on the darning. Though I don't think my family had noticed my escape, Granny's chortle was rising over the stunned hush of the crowd as she pointed at her far-away grandson in disbelief.

"It would appear we have a winner. Let me ask you, what is your favorite type of Scotch Whiskey, young man?" Now my parents were watching with a hint of pride or shame.

Miss Elegant Assist arrived with a second mic and held it close to my face.

Unsure how to answer, I mumbled, "Johnny Walker." The crowd erupted. I looked at my mom who threw her hands up in the air.

"Wow, I did not see that one coming" He was having trouble holding it together as the crowd continued to laugh. He looked at his audience with eyebrows raised and pointed downward at his new sidekick. Then he knelt, placing a fatherly arm around me. "You should really try the Macallan, young man. I hear it's quite good. Let me ask you, are you traveling solo, or do you have a dad in the audience? I think I see your mom, is she the one blushing up on the landing?" My mom was nodding and blushing.

"My dad's right there next to her."

"And is he a teetotaler or a man of spirits?"

"Excuse me?"

"Kid, does your dad drink scotch like you?" I nodded a little too vigorously, causing the crowd to laugh again. "Do you think you might share one of your bottles with him?" I nodded again. Miss Elegant Assist was ushering me in the direction of my family while cradling the showcase bottle. I limped along, trying to wrestle my Topsider back onto my foot.

"Next we'll be giving away a sewing kit to the mother of that ragamuffin alcoholic!" The crowd was in stitches, and I was off to bed.

Backstage at The Nutcracker, photo by Martha Swope, 1975

12

THE NUTCRACKER

Ballet was introduced in small doses. My grandparents started the process by taking me to a matinee of *Swan Lake* at the O'Keefe Center in Toronto, performed by the National Ballet of Canada. Halfway through Act II, either due to excessive fidgeting or an all-out tantrum, we left. Granted, I was four-and-a-half.

Six months later came *The Nutcracker*. It wasn't bad. I made it through both acts and earned the right to return the following year. My parents were longtime subscribers to the New York City Ballet and were sincerely hoping their appreciation of ballet would find its way to their children. Jenny started accompanying my parents to the non-*Nutcracker* performances first, given her seniority and her superiority to me when it came to sitting still for two hours. I can't say I really cared. An evening at home spent in Mrs. Hattie's room was far better than an evening at the ballet.

Late one Thursday night, Jenny burst into my bedroom and announced, "I just saw the best ballet ever."

I sat up.

"It was called *The Concert*. There were butterflies everywhere and big plume-y blue hats and … Daddy, do you remember when that ballerina got trampled?"

By then Dad had joined Jenny by my bed. "Trampled, yes, and the other ballerina got clubbed by the little guy with the glasses."

They both laughed until Jenny finally said, "It was the just the best, and they aren't doing it next season, we checked. Maybe you'll get to see it one day. Good night."

My night was ruined. The next morning, I informed my parents of my desire to attend the ballet as often as possible. So, they bought a second subscription, and off I went to see the New York City Ballet on select Thursday evenings. Though it was years before I actually saw *The Concert*, I discovered a million other pleasures as I fell slowly and blissfully into the world of ballet with its world premieres, classics, neo-classics, cavaliers and ballerinas, all provided for the wide-eyed kid in the second ring.

During a performance of *Coppelia*, in the middle of the villagers' romp, I suddenly realized I wanted to try ballet lessons.

I tugged on my mom's sleeve and whispered, "I want to try that."

"Try what?"

"Ballet. Can I try ballet? I won the long jump and the high jump, and I came in third in the fifty-yard dash, so I'm guessing I would be …"

"Shhhh!" This was coming from the lady behind us.

My mom turned around to face the woman, "He's only seven!"

"Mom, I'm nine."

"Shhhh," this time from my mother.

At intermission, Mom agreed to call the New York City Ballet and ask for some direction. They suggested either looking for a local ballet school that taught introductory classical ballet for boys or attending a fall audition for the School of American Ballet (SAB).

After calls to Elizabeth Rockwell School of Dance, Stephie Nauson's Dance Center, and even the Boys and Girls Club, we realized no boys were studying classical ballet in Northern Westchester, so we headed for Lincoln Center to audition for SAB. I hadn't planned on auditioning but agreed to on one condition: I wouldn't wear tights.

At the end of a long windowless corridor on the third floor of the Juilliard School, a pack of nervous girls stretched while their mothers brushed their hair and tied colorful ribbons around their perfect buns. Once inside the glass and wood doors of the school, a swarm of kids and parents filled every available inch of space. A few straggly boys were in the mix too. We pushed our way to the registration desk and received a form and the number 106.

Groups of fifteen at a time were taken into Studio #1 for a twenty-minute audition. When my number was finally called, I followed a line of girls into the studio and took my appointed place at the barre. Everyone wore leotards and tights, and I wore jean cut-offs with my favorite blue-and-red striped polo shirt. Three women, two Russian and one American, walked from one nervous kid to the next, asking questions and pushing on legs, shoulders, hips, knees and feet.

As they approached me, the oldest may have smiled imperceptibly. She looked like a shriveled apple doll with piercing blue eyes that peeked out from wrinkled flesh with a tiny blond topknot fastened on the top of her head. The American woman stepped forward first with a large black book and pencil to ask my name and age, which I suspected she already knew. After my mumbled confirmation, she retreated to let the Russians run the show. The blond kept lifting my chin and pushing my shoulders down. She barked something at me while holding her hand out. I believe she spoke to me in English, but I only heard Russian and offered a feeble, "Sorry, what did you say?" She repeated the phrase with more force. Still no response, so the other Russian said exactly the same thing with the same thick accent. This time I thought I heard the word "leg" in the middle of a string of garbled consonants, so I lifted my leg slightly. Blond Topknot smiled at my translation skills and grabbed my leg hiking it much higher than I thought possible. Up it went, with sudden excited Russian chatter and scribbling in the black book. More smiles. The leg went in front of my nose and near my ear and behind my shoulder blades with all three saying, "Arabesque!"

Before moving on to the next kid, Topknot asked me to jump straight up in the air, pressed my feet into the shape of a croissant, put a final finger under my chin, gave a wink, and moved on to number 107.

Back at home that evening, we were gathered around the dinner table when the phone rang. Dad answered. It was Natasha Gleboff, one of the two Russians. Dad couldn't understand her accent and beckoned for my mother to come to the phone. The two stood with ears pressed to the receiver while the Russian voice droned on. I moved closer too.

"Mr. Boal, I am Natasha Gleboff, executive director of the

School of American Ballet, and I would like to talk to you about your son, Peter."

"What did he do?" my dad joked, but I think his humor was lost on Mrs. Gleboff.

"What did he do? He auditioned for our school today. You do know that Mr. Boal, don't you?"

"Yes, I do."

"And he did very well. We would like to accept him for the fall term with a full merit scholarship. Of course, he is behind for his age and must study three times a week in the A-1 level for ninety minutes on Mondays, Wednesdays and Saturdays in order to have a chance to become a professional dancer."

"Peter's only nine."

"That's correct, Mr. Boal, and he'll be ten next month, but I suppose you knew that too. Madame Tumkovsky would like a word with you now."

A new Russian voice could be heard, "He has good arabesque and big instep, and he is so handsome. He is so handsome." My mom was starting to laugh.

"Yes, that's because he takes after his father." Again, the humor was lost on the Russians, but my mother swatted my dad with a big grin on her face.

Mrs. Gleboff returned, "We will see Peter on Monday at five-thirty. He must wear black tights and a white tee shirt with white socks and black or white ballet slippers. Capezio will have everything. Good day, Mr. Boal."

Off I went the following Monday, somewhat mortified to be wearing my new tights but also excited to try something new. Much to my relief, two other boys were in my class along with about twenty girls. I struggled through day one with Miss

Reiman, who seemed to float between disbelief at how untalented her class was and self-pity over the long road she would have to walk once again with such a hopeless gaggle of pupils.

The last few minutes of class were devoted to learning the French terms for ballet steps. On my first day, Miss Reiman paused in front of me. During the silence, I offered, "I haven't learned any names yet."

"After ninety minutes, you haven't learned one step, really? I find that hard to believe. Are you deaf?"

I didn't respond. The class laughed, for which they were reprimanded. Miss Reiman returned to her meditation, looked me in the eye and said, "What's this?" She stood with her heels touching and her toes turned outward in a perfect 180-degree line and bent her knees.

I smiled because I knew the answer, blurting out, "It's a plié!"

"Nope, it's a demi-plié, get a book and learn the terms." On she went to the next victim.

As the weeks passed, I struggled but also progressed. Our other teacher, Madame Dudin, carried a stick and had a great helmet of hair that made her look like a first lady. I assumed the stick was for beating us, but the most it ever did was poke a knee or tap a thigh. She spent far more time with me than anyone else in the room and seemed immensely pleased with my every move. I began to realize that different people would enter the studio through the large black door, point me out, and then disappear. At first it was Miss Reiman with a younger man, then Mrs. Gleboff returned with the same man.

After class one day, the man approached me, introducing himself as David and explaining that he was the ballet master for the children in New York City Ballet's performances, and he wanted to work with me on the role of the prince for *The Nutcracker*. I told him I was in fourth grade, had a lot of homework, and that I was dancing the role of the skeleton in the school play, so I wasn't sure I could fit the role of the prince into my schedule. I asked him if I had to do it, to which he laughed and said to tell my parents he would be calling soon.

In the end, my parents convinced me learning the role of the prince was an incredible opportunity and one of which I should really take advantage. Twice weekly, David and I rehearsed the prince's pantomime from Act II. I was also introduced to my partner, Stephanie Selby, who would play the role of Clara, and to a photographer named Jill Krementz, who was working on a book about Stephanie called *A Very Young Dancer*. A great overbearing man named Mr. Kirstein also watched rehearsals. After two weeks of trying to learn steps and dance with Stephanie, David called my parents to report that I wasn't ready. The role of the prince would have to wait a year, but I would perform as one of the party guests.

I was excited to have a role in *The Nutcracker* and relieved to know I wouldn't have to take on the challenges of the prince's pantomime. My parents also realized we had a problem ahead.

They made the decision not to tell any of my friends at Rippowam I was taking ballet lessons, fearing my classmates would think it was not cool. Having been a semi-serious gymnast with the skills to prove it, we opted to tell my peers I was taking gymnastics lessons in New York City three days a week. Everyone bought into the lie, but now New York City Ballet's *Nutcracker*, a Bedford family favorite, was about to blow my cover.

My mom called Waldo Jones, principal of the Lower School, and set up a meeting.

We sat silently in the waiting room outside of Mrs. Jones's office. I hid my face in a copy of *Ranger Rick*, ashamed for many reasons. Sitting with a parent outside of the principal's office was never good for a fourth grader's social life. Talking to the principal about your ballet lessons didn't seem like much fun either. After a flustered mother emerged from the office with a fidgety kindergartener, we entered. Mrs. Jones greeted my mother and me by name, showing us to a pair of worn leather armchairs that faced her wooden desk. The room felt like a home with large lamps, plenty of framed photographs, drawings from students, and shelves brimming with brightly colored books.

"So, how can I help you two today?" Mrs. Jones asked.

"We have some very exciting news, at least we think it's exciting, and we're not sure how to tell Peter's classmates about it."

"Are you in the Westchester County Boy's Choir?" Where she got this, I do not know. My mom and I looked at each other for one stunned moment before my mom interjected,

"Oh, no, Pete's a terrible singer." This was news to me. I actually was in Miss Fiala's choir and thought I wasn't bad. "He's going to be in *The Nutcracker*. It's a very small part, but he'll have to miss some school, and we feel it's probably time to tell his class that he's taking ballet lessons."

Now it was Mrs. Jones who was confused, "Why is he taking ballet lessons? Isn't *The Nutcracker* a play?"

"Oh, no, it's a ballet. He'll be performing with the New York City Ballet at Lincoln Center. You must come see it. It's absolutely magical. We'll have to get you some tickets. You really must see it."

"Why thank you, Mrs. Boal, but that's not necessary. I'll get my own tickets, and Peter, we are going to tell every kid in your class what an honor this is that you have been selected for this part. We just might take the whole school to see you. Do you leave school early today for your gymnastics lessons because I think Thom Fennell and I might want to talk to your classmates this afternoon?"

I looked at my mom. She put her hand on my knee, "He's not taking gymnastic lessons, he takes ballet lessons. We just said he was taking gymnastic lessons because we were afraid of what the other kids would think if they knew he was studying ballet. You can understand why we did that, can't you?"

Mrs. Jones took off her gold-rimmed glasses and looked at my mother. "I see. Now whose bright idea was it to tell the whole school Peter was leaving early to take gymnastic lessons?" Waldo Jones had served as principal of the Lower School for close to two decades and was not above scolding parents. My mom started to answer, but Mrs. Jones wasn't really looking for a response.

"I don't need to tell either of you that the truth is always the best course of action. We are not responsible for reactions, but we can deal with them as they come if we need to. Hiding the fact that you are studying classical ballet indicates you think it's not something to be proud of, but it is. Let me talk to Mr. Fennel about how best to break the news this afternoon. Peter, can I ask you something?"

I nodded.

"Do you have plenty of friends?'

"I guess."

"And do your friends respect you?"

"I guess so."

"Peter, I have known you since kindergarten, and I happen

to know for a fact you are one of the most respected kids in this school, and I guarantee that won't change a bit once your friends know you are studying ballet and that you've landed a major role in *The Nutcracker*. If they like you today, they'll like you tomorrow. And if they don't, I'm not sure you really want them as friends in the first place."

My mother interjected, "It's not really a major role and ..."

"Mrs. Boal, I suspect any role in *The Nutcracker* is a major role. Let's just leave it at that." The glasses went back on. "Listen, Thom and I will handle this, and Peter, you focus on those tendus and pliés. You should be very proud of what you're doing. Rippowam is very proud of you. Now you had better get to your third period class, or you're likely to be sent back to the principal's office."

I stood up. "Thank you, Mrs. Jones. Bye, Mom."

I left the office just a little taller than when I entered.

Mother Goose

Cast of Mother Goose, author seated on floor in center *(image courtesy of the author)*

13

COACH

In a windowless subterranean studio under the New York State Theater, I pulled back an imaginary arrow and let it fly.

"Good!" exclaimed ballet master Tommy Abbott, sitting up in his chair. "I think you're ready. Tomorrow you rehearse with Mr. Robbins."

Students from the School of American Ballet are often chosen to dance children's roles with the New York City Ballet. *The Nutcracker* offered my first onstage opportunity, and my second part came the following spring. I was slated to play Cupid in Jerome Robbins's compilation of fairy tales called *Ma Mère l'Oye* or *Mother Goose Suite*. It was a role given to the tiniest boy who could follow directions. In 1976, that was me.

The following day, I reported to a much larger windowless studio on the fifth floor of the New York State Theater known as the Main Hall. The energy in the room was bristling with excitement and nervousness. About half of the dancers from the company were on hand, practicing pirouettes and securing pointe shoe ribbons. A small coterie of bustling ballet masters darted about the room while keeping a watchful eye on Mr. Robbins. Tommy tucked me and two other boys into a corner by the piano. My first rehearsal with the legendary choreographer was underway.

He wore white sneakers, brown khakis and a blue hooded sweatshirt, which showed both the dancer within and the widening girth of middle age. He was tanned and handsome, with a bit more hair in his meticulously trimmed white beard than on the top of his head. He puttered about the front of the studio fixing while deploying assistants to fix elsewhere. Despite a clear power structure, everyone called him Jerry.

Even a ten-year-old knows the difference between true benevolence and feigned benevolence. Jerry had the latter. It wasn't that he wasn't helpful or encouraging to those in the room, just begrudgingly so. One sensed his tolerance was as thin as spring ice. Soon pops of ire and annoyance filled the room and attention shifted to heightened nervousness and intensified focus. I started to wonder if Jerry needed one of my arrows. Cupid enters late in the ballet, so I used the time to review my minimal choreography in my head.

Tommy took each of us to our place for our entrance, ushering us into the space on our music. Sean was first. He was the messenger who galloped onto the stage atop his imaginary horse, delivered his message and then rode off with equal confidence, earning a smile and a nod from the front of the room.

Pint-sized Knowle was next. He played Hop O' My Thumb. Knowle couldn't quite follow directions as well as I could, but he was younger, smaller and absolutely adorable, like a tow-headed

Lilliputian. He battled birds, skipped with vigor and led his dopey big brothers through his dramatic tale. When Hop finally saved the day, landing on the tallest brother's shoulder, the entire company broke into applause and hoots of approval. The release of tension was much needed. Jerry responded with a hearty laugh and a hug for Knowle. Now I was nervous.

When I made my entrance, I tried to incorporate every correction Tommy had given me in the lower concourse. I cleared tall reeds held by corps de ballet dancers in order to make a navigable path for Prince Charming to follow. The path led to the sleeping princess. I could see Delia Peters, the Fairy Godmother, on the other side of the studio smiling at my success. I was pretty sure I was nailing it.

A whistle sounded in short, fractured notes like a code for distress. Jerry stopped the pianist and headed towards me. Not a sound could be heard except the squish of his tennis shoes as he made his way across the studio floor. Tommy hovered nervously, nodding constantly. "Not bad." Jerry's hand was on my shoulder. "What's your name?"

"Um … Peter Boal"

"Okay, Paul, good, remember, you're an Indian scout moving through the forest trying not to make a sound. The success of your mission depends on how quiet you can be." As he said this, he demonstrated his words perfectly. I wanted to ask if the scout was an American Indian or an Indian from India but decided to figure it out later. I also briefly considered correcting him on my name but thought better of that too. I was "Paul" to Jerry for the next twenty years.

"When you step, you want to be very careful not to snap a twig that might be underfoot. Does that make sense?"

It did. The image was so clear, so perfect, so completely defining of exactly how I would step in my imaginary forest. In that moment, at age ten, I found one of the most effective coaches I would ever work with, and thankfully I benefited from Jerry's coaching for years to come.

A decade after our first encounter in the Main Hall, I was in the company and cast in the title role of George Balanchine's *Prodigal Son*, a role that carried great weight with an illustrious list of interpreters, including Serge Lifar, Edward Villella, Rudolf Nureyev and Mikhail Baryshnikov. This was a startling honor for a young member of the corps de ballet. Putting my name on casting was a bold move made by Peter Martins. But in the wake of Balanchine's death, it wasn't clear who would coach me. Balanchine had always coached the prodigals himself. The night my name went up on the casting sheet, I watched Jerry approach Peter. Their conversations were not always amicable, but this one seemed to be, with Peter nodding to everything Jerry said. After Jerry walked away, Peter approached me and said, "He wants to coach you. I said 'yes.'"

Jerry was New York City Ballet's first Prodigal Son in 1948, having learned the role from Balanchine himself.

The following day we met in the practice room. A ballet mistress was there to assist, but Jerry asked her to leave. The first cast dancer was seated in the corner eager to hear what Jerry had to offer. He was asked to leave, too. The rehearsal pianist was asked to leave as well. Only the two of us remained.

"Let's see your first entrance. We don't need music; you'll get that later. Let's see what you got."

I retreated to the upper corner of the room, threw my arms open and ran across the floor to the opposite corner. I heard the familiar whistle, which always left me feeling like an errant puppy.

He walked towards me, cleared his throat and asked, "What did you have for breakfast this morning?" Jerry had studied acting with Sanford Meisner. I didn't know much about the Stanislavsky method, but I was about to learn.

Breakfast, hmm. Seemed like an odd question, but I wanted to answer honestly.

"I had an Egg McMuffin." Hearing the words come out of my mouth deepened my regret, but I had spoken the truth.

With rising anger Jerry shouted, "Not you. The character. What did the prodigal eat? What time did he wake up? What time does your father wake up on most days, and what time did he wake up today? Why is he up earlier than usual? Come on, you can do better." He continued to pepper me with questions about the rumors my friends and I had heard about the alluring Siren who lived in the land beyond, and in the end he reminded me never to walk into the studio again without having done my research for a role.

Once I understood the importance of inhabiting the character more deeply than inhabiting self, the real work began. The harshness evaporated. Jerry was an icon in many fields— ballet, Broadway, film—and I was just twenty with only a toe in the water as a dancer, actor and adult. And yet we were two casts, one former, one current, two prodigals, comparing notes, researching roles and defining portrayals, methods and motivations. His words, however gruff and prodding, pushed me into finding my voice as an artist.

Jerry was a coach like none other. He demonstrated with articulation that defied age. In his later years, the legs did less, but the eyes did more. The timing was impeccable and indisputable.

In 1985, with the help of original cast member Wilma Curley, Jerry revived *Moves*, an experimental work originally created for Jerome Robbins's Ballets USA in 1959. *Moves* was performed without music, relying solely on the stomps, slaps and footsteps of the cast to create meter. Jerry would reiterate the length of each silence, encouraging us to find a duration that would make an audience and even fellow cast members uncomfortable. With the right pause, the next movement startled. He granted us license to read the environment, suggesting each performance might allow for longer or shorter pauses. After each show, he emerged from the wings to weigh in, "Did you hear the coughing? Too slow, baby."

The stories of Jerry's anger are legendary. I stood by while he berated many dancers, ballet masters and pianists, sometimes interrupting to shift blame onto me or music or anything I could think of. The ire seemed to envelop and fuel him without any realization a line was about to be crossed. It was hard to watch the abuse, but with Jerry it was always about the work. It wasn't personal. His standard was so very high, and we were part of achieving that standard. Though patience was tested, I found his process both challenging and hugely rewarding. Collectively we reached an apex of artistry, athleticism and intellect.

After a particularly grueling rehearsal with a young soloist in the company, Jerry left the room. The dancer burst into tears. Moments later, I was in the hall with Jerry as the dancer turned the corner, still sobbing. Jerry looked at her and asked with genuine concern, "Oh, honey, what happened?" He approached her with a hug, wanting to help her cope with whatever circumstance may have caused such hurt. He couldn't connect the dots to his own abusive behavior minutes ago.

It would be unfair and incorrect to characterize Jerry purely as a taskmaster or a whip cracker. Yes, he was demanding, but his compliments were sincere and thoughtful. He nurtured many and helped those he worked with find their best selves. He had the unique ability to become kid-like in the studio, giggling with others and often laughing robustly at his own jokes. A dog bounding into a rehearsal erased all annoyance and filled him with boyish glee. He was certainly his own best audience for his comedic masterpiece, *The Concert*. How many times had he seen those gags and yet, when done correctly, fresh spontaneous laughter erupted from him as if it were a first telling.

My stories with Jerry took place during the last twenty years of his life. But his entire existence seemed to have been a tapestry of triumph and torture. The Oscars and Tonys and critical praise were never enough to keep the self-doubt at bay.

Two years before he passed, he started to create *Brandenburg*, his final work. I was paired with fellow principal Wendy Whelan. Parts of the creation process were inspired, watching Jerry discover fresh new talents in the corps like Christina Fernandez, Maria Kowroski, Benjamin Millepied and Christopher Wheeldon. Others were more painful as his doubt crept in. It seemed to be the ballet that wouldn't end. A tumble off of his bike left him without secure balance, which sapped his ability to demonstrate choreography. He was more scared than frustrated. As Jerry grew frail and could no longer move well or hold on to ideas, we offered everything we could. Peter Martins finally suggested a date for the premiere, and Jerry shrugged and agreed, though the piece had no ending and he was still unhappy with what he had made.

The premiere was greeted with a sincere ovation and strong

critical praise, but the accolades seemed to herald the last chapter of a remarkable career and not the arrival of a new gem.

Just after the final curtain call, Jerry was on stage calling for Wendy and me to try a different ending to our pas de deux. We obliged, but Jerry conceded it still wasn't right.

I remember many words, many moments, his belief in my ability and even his understanding of my mistakes. Despite his capacity for forgiveness towards others, he couldn't accept his own failures.

Opus 19/The Dreamer was the work that brought us into the studio together more than any other. I had seen the premiere with Mikhail Baryshnikov and Patricia McBride not long after my debut as Cupid in *Mother Goose*. I've heard Misha say he thought the work held elements of Jerry's own existence, with a protagonist haunted by demons or ghosts from his past. Jerry pushed me harder in *Opus* than in any other ballet. He seemed to demand inhuman effort.

I learned the work from ballet master Bart Cook before showing it to Jerry. My first rehearsal with Jerry was like an audition. He sat in the front of the room and watched without interruption or emotion before rising to say I wasn't ready. The moment was far more devastating than my interrupted first rehearsal as Cupid. As he started to leave, I called him back and requested another chance. No one really called Jerry back. I asked him to sit down. I saw an essential if not career-defining opportunity about to disappear from my reach forever. Though my second shot was met with approval, each subsequent performance was held to his high standard, with some hitting the mark and some less successful. I didn't always get it right, but on one occasion, after the curtain descended and page bows were done, Jerry found me in the wings with tears tumbling down his cheeks. He didn't say a word, he simply pulled my head forward to place a kiss on my forehead. A greater compliment I've never known.

January 4, 1978

Dear Mr. Boal:

Unfortunately, Governor Rockefeller left on a holiday vacation before he had the opportunity to sign this, thus the reason for the delay in returning it to you. My apologies for not getting it back to you in time to give it to your son, Peter, for Christmas.

With his best wishes for a very happy new year,

Sincerely,

Rebecca Byam

Rebecca Byam

Mr. R. Bradlee Boal
Cooper, Dunham, Clark, Griffin & Moran
30 Rockefeller Plaza
New York, New York
10020

Letter from Governor Rockefeller's office *(image courtesy of the author)*

14

BEYOND HAPPY

One day, Mom came home earlier than usual from her job at the hospital and found Jenny and me hoisting Mrs. Hattie out of her chair. Henry cowered for a moment in the corner at the sight of his nemesis rising slowly from her roost, but quickly realized she was no longer a credible threat. I had folded most of the laundry, and Jenny was putting away dishes before Mrs. Hattie summoned us to help her up.

"What's going on here?" asked my mom, placing purse, coat and mail onto the counter. "Everyone okay?" Henry looked imploringly at Mom then flopped onto the floor.

"Oh, Mrs. Boals … phew … we've been working. Yes, sir. I folded all the clothes, put away the dishes, and I'm about to start your dinner. Jennifer and Pete helped some too." Jenny's eyes were as big as marbles.

Though Jenny and I hadn't wanted to share the truth about our increasing workloads, Mom knew Mrs. Hattie was no longer able to keep up with all the chores she used to do, and child labor had helped close the gap. Mrs. Wilson, who was now working three days a week, was racing around the house with Mrs. Hattie delegating tasks to all three of us throughout the afternoon.

Later that night around the kitchen table, a difficult conversation ensued between my parents and Mrs. Hattie about her transition to retirement. She was almost eighty and accepted the fact that the time had come. My parents would give her half her salary for the rest of her life. The annual trip to Bermuda or the financial equivalent was offered every year as well, plus any healthcare costs that weren't covered by Medicare. Mrs. Hattie accepted, understanding and never doubting she would remain part of the family. She was loved, and she knew it. She did have a few demands, though.

"You'll still take me to Ho Yen on my birthday like you always do?"

"Of course, we will, Mrs. Hattie. We all love that place ... and you!" My mom did not love that place and forbade us to wear sweaters or wool there because the smell would simply not come out even after dry cleaning.

Mrs. Hattie was having a Proustian moment, "That jumbo shrimp, Lord have mercy, I do love that jumbo shrimp. And what's this about Peter being in the show. I'm gonna need to see that. What's it called?"

"*The Nutcracker*, why yes of course, he will be so pleased to have you in the audience, and Jenny's playing Mrs. Who in her middle-school play ..."

"I don't want to sit in the back. Get me some good seats. I need to see my baby."

Mom and Dad sprang into action, buying seats for *The*

Nutcracker the next day. Unfortunately, *The Nutcracker* was popular, and a block of prime seats was hard to find for a weekend matinee. Mom chose an expensive single seat right in the center of the first ring for Mrs. Hattie. This was actually the best seat in the entire theater. We purchased four in the second row on the aisle for the rest of us.

On the night of the performance, dinner was at Fiorello's at five. Though Fiorello's was literally just across the plaza from the New York State Theater, Mom wanted to allow for an extra hour for Mrs. Hattie to cross two streets. Somehow, we managed to have a near-perfect family dinner. Mrs. Hattie was dressed to the nines with her finest church clothes and a gray pillbox hat tipped towards the brow with a lace veil floating between hat and wig. All the silver bracelets were on her wrists and forearms, announcing her every move with a familiar clatter. Mom was relieved as our attentive waiter, named Dima, doted on Mrs. Hattie. Dad was enjoying the reunion after Mrs. Hattie's retirement, and Mrs. Hattie kept asking Jenny about Mrs. Who, sixth-grade stories and her newest pony. I took it all in. Mom kept an eye on her watch throughout the meal, knowing she needed to get me across the plaza for my make-up call and get the entire entourage there in time for curtain. She discreetly motioned to Dima for the bill.

"Mrs. Hattie, we should get a move on. The show starts in an hour, and I've got to run Peter to the stage entrance for his make-up call. We don't want to be late."

"What! That boy don't need no make-up. Skin's perfect. He's beautiful just the way he is." There was a pause as Mrs. Hattie scanned the table warily, "Wait, we are not leaving all this food. Where's that waiter, Donny?" Mrs. Hattie started to call loudly for Dima who was already trotting purposely across the restaurant towards her. Listen here, you need to wrap this up. Wrap it all up. Why are you still standing there?"

"Yes Ma'am, of course, right away." Dima was motioning for back up staff while nodding. "Would you like me to wrap the rest of your shrimp and pasta?"

"Yes sir, Donny, and put the zucchini in the there too. Wrap Jenny's leftover pizza and put it in a separate container and give me another piece of that key lime pie." My mother was speechless, Jenny was now laughing. Mrs. Hattie looked around the table perplexed by all of the reactions. "It's not for me," she said, looking up at Dima, whom she might have had just a little crush on, "It's for my daughter. Oh, I don't have a husband in case you're wondering." Did she bat her eyes? Dima nodded, not knowing quite what was expected from him at that moment. She turned to the other waiter who was scooping up Jenny's pizza, "Can you get that all in one doggy bag? And don't forget the bread and a few a those breadsticks too. Thank you so much. Young man, you are making this old woman very happy, very happy indeed, now run on because we've got a show to see, and this little man here's the star." She tried to smooth my hair to the side.

I was ushered across the street to the stage entrance to perform as a guest of the Stahlbaum's in the Act I Christmas party scene. By intermission, I would be back with Mrs. Hattie and my family in the audience. I wasn't present for the next part of this story but heard four different accounts.

Dima delivered Mrs. Hattie's order in a stack of boxes all neatly tied up in a plastic bag (this was at Mom's insistence for fear of Mrs. Hattie smelling like the Italian restaurant across the street while sitting in the first row of the first ring). Sheets of aluminum foil surrounded the stack with an elegant swan's neck emerging on one side and pluming silvery feathers cascading off the other.

Though my dad carted the foil creature across the street, Mrs. Hattie insisted on keeping the swan on her lap once seated in row A seat 111. Mom sank deep into row B, seat 115.

Dad described Mrs. Hattie as the Queen of England, looking over the front balcony at Buckingham Palace. Mom thought the Queen was far more reserved and humble than Mrs. Hattie was as that moment. Jenny said she seemed to be in her element, constantly fixing her hat and hoisting the swan to a more visible height. Mrs. Hattie said it was as if she was the show. "All eyes were on me. Must have been the lipstick."

A few minutes before the curtain rose, several ushers came to the end of the steps at the entrance to row A. A man in a black suit with a walkie-talkie approached the row and looked at all of the patrons seated in the area. You could tell he was a bodyguard. He kept eyeing the foil swan and eventually entered the row to ask Mrs. Hattie what she was carrying. After a few words, he nodded his approval and retreated. Mom thought the lingering smell of fried zucchini was enough to confirm Mrs. Hattie's claim of leftovers. As he shuffled out of the row, Mrs. Hattie turned to my dad who sat closest to her and said, "Don't worry Mr. Boals, I wasn't gonna let him take it. I told him I was taking it home to Butch, and I told him he didn't want to make Butch mad."

Just then a man in black tie and two women wearing thick strands of pearls approached the entrance to row A. They looked important. Mom recognized Happy Rockefeller, who was often in the news since her husband Nelson had been elected vice president. Abby Rockefeller followed Happy into the row with the vice president, and the bodyguard close behind.

Mom turned to Dad, "Tell me Happy Rockefeller is not sitting next to our fettuccine alfredo!"

Dad responded, "Don't worry, it's shrimp and pasta."

Nelson turned to my father. "Brad? Is that you? Are we going to see your son?" Dad worked in the same building. They were elevator acquaintances. With Dad on the 39th floor and Nelson on the 56th, they shared many stories in all senses of the word. Somehow, news of my role in *The Nutcracker* was a much-discussed topic at 30 Rockefeller Plaza. Nelson had also served as major funder and key planner for the building of Lincoln Center and the New York State Theater.

"Nelson, wonderful to see you. Let me introduce my wife, Lyndall, and my daughter, Jennifer, and I hope you'll introduce yourself to our friend Hattie Lindsay who's seated next to you." Happy was already making her way to the center of the row, nodding politely to all around her and taking her seat next to Mrs. Hattie or rather next to Mrs. Hattie's swan.

Leaning to the left, Mom could only hear snippets of the conversation between the two women. It started like this: "You're kidding me, Happy!?! What kind of name is that?"

Happy responded, "Well, Hattie … it would seem it's an awful lot like your name." Warm laughter followed. The two seemed to enjoy each other's company. The contents of the doggy bag were described in detail. Tales of my fullest diapers and earliest kicks were discussed. Mrs. Hattie pointed me out to Happy each time I entered the stage.

At intermission, Mrs. Hattie introduced me to her new friends, "The Rockefellers." The name rolled off her tongue as if she had practiced pronunciation often. Nelson leaned over to ask Mrs. Hattie how she liked the theater.

"Oh, it's nice, I like it very much … but I do not think there is enough space in these aisles, and I wish there was a place for bags or food. Whoever planned this theater didn't do a very good job." Mom cringed. Dad laughed. Nelson turned back to give my dad a quick wink. Mom sunk a little lower in her seat.

"But it doesn't bother me one bit, because I am so happy tonight." She turned to the vice president's wife and patted her on the leg, "In fact, I'm sitting right next to Happy herself, and that makes me beyond happy." Both ladies burst into laughter. It was a night to remember.

Me and Yuki entering Rippowam with CBS camera crew *(image courtesy of the author)*

15

MAY I PLEASE BE EXCUSED?

A representative from CBS News called to ask my parents if the station might film a segment about me for *Evening Magazine*. They were interested in the story of a twelve-year-old boy who wanted to be a ballet dancer, and particularly one who had the full support of both his mother and his father. Cameras followed me to Rippowam, filming my best friend Yuki and me entering the building, dissecting a frog in Biology class and hanging out with friends. Classes were filmed at the School of American Ballet as well as rehearsals and performances of *The Nutcracker*.

One night, we caused a small commotion in Grand Central Terminal as our camera crew filmed my father and me racing through the rush hour crowds to catch the 7:27 to Westchester. On a break from shooting, a fellow partner from my dad's firm saw us in the throngs of onlookers and asked what all the cameras were for. Dad's deadpan humor kicked in, and he responded, "It's for me. They're making a film about my daily commute." The friend laughed at the absurdity of the notion. Just then lights flashed on and the production manager yelled, "Cameras, rolling ... action!" Dad and I took off sprinting with two cameramen close behind as we crossed the main concourse, leaving Dad's friend to look on in disbelief.

There was plenty of filming at home too, with shots of me doing homework, talking on the phone, petting Rex, and having dinner with my family.

None of this fazed me except for dinner with my family. This was really the underbelly of our dysfunctional family dynamic, and the likelihood of us pulling off a "normal" family dinner was nearly impossible. When CBS came back into my life to do a follow-up segment twenty years after the original, they provided me with a transcript of all of the dialogue from the first take. The tension of our family dinner leaped from the typed pages, and the painful memories flooded back, making me squirm.

Dad was really never there, which was probably for the best. On most nights, he would arrive home near nine. Once I started commuting with him, I realized at least four bourbons were consumed before he walked through the back door at night. It's a miracle he only totaled three of our cars during our Bedford years. Mom would say, "It's once he pours that second drink, everything starts to unravel." She didn't know it was the fifth that pulled the thread. After wine or beer at lunch, he met Tyler Ingram's dad at the Harvard Club for two quick bourbons in the early afternoon following a squash game. Before we boarded the 7:27 or the 7:33, he'd purchase two more bourbon shots with a cup of ginger ale. Driving home from the North White Plains train station to Bedford, we'd stop in Armonk to purchase more booze. Because Dad was such a regular customer at Bedford Wines and Spirits, the liquor store in Armonk provided a perfect second site, a safe distance from the chattering tongues and watchful eyes of the Bedford set. It also stayed open until nine.

So, Dad and I would sit down to dinner together at around nine-fifteen. Conversation wasn't always coherent, but I was hungry for a relationship with my dad, since I had only known pieces of what that relationship could be while growing up.

Tuesday nights were different. There were no ballet classes on Tuesdays until I turned twelve, so for a few years, Tuesdays provided my only opportunity for a dinner with the rest of the family. The family included Mom, at the head of the table, Mrs. Hattie opposite her seated proudly in Dad's chair, Jenny on her left, and me to the right. Joe sat next to Jenny. He worked the grounds on weekends with Dad and me. In return, we not only gave him a home, but paid his way through college—a sweet deal. His brothers, Pete and Mark, lived in our pool house during the summers, and all three sisters took turns babysitting for us on weekends and during European vacations. Joe was from a rowdy family with seven kids on the other side of town. He had no means of paying for college.

Having Mrs. Hattie and Joe at the table made for some level of normalcy. Mrs. Hattie scared us into good table manners and polite conversation. Joe was always laughing at Mrs. Hattie's strict manner; luckily, she had a real soft spot for him.

"Wouldn't hurt you, Joseph, to put your napkin on your lap. How are these kids supposed to grow up with manners when you're sitting there with none? I mean!" Joe just laughed as he placed his napkin on his lap, and Mrs. Hattie chuckled under her breath. Their banter distracted from our missing dad and the tension between Jenny and Mom, which arrived and grew during Jenny's teenage years.

On Sunday nights, we were on our own with Mrs. Hattie in Mt. Vernon with Butch and Joe at home with his parents for their family dinner. I dreaded Sunday night dinners. As the day wore on, you could feel my mom's expectations looming. "I'm making a roast chicken tonight, and I picked up the freshest corn from Henker's market today. I also picked your father's tomatoes from the garden. They looked just perfect! It will be so nice to sit down, just the four of us." Uh-oh. Red flag.

You could also feel Dad's allergic reaction to Mom's expectation starting to swell. He medicated with bourbon throughout the afternoon, which was invariably accompanied by hushed warnings from Mom, "Oh, Brad, not another one, it's not even three o'clock. I'm preparing such a nice dinner, and you'll just ruin it like you did last week."

Dinner was served promptly at six. Mom rang the old cowbell Mrs. Hattie insisted on using because "this house is just too big." After grubby hands were washed, we assembled. Dad stood at the head of the table with the prized bird awaiting his carving knife. He would serve my mother, then Jenny. The usual chatter of "pass this," and "pass that" could be heard. Dad then served himself. As he carved for me, Mom interjected, "Brad, won't you please give Pete a nice portion this time; he's growing so." You could feel Dad recoil at the words. He would retaliate by placing the smallest serving of chicken on my plate.

Mom, watching like a hawk, was quick to reprimand, "Oh, Brad, I insist you give him some more. There's a whole chicken there, and he's hungry," to which I'd respond, "Mom, it's fine."

No one heard me; this was between Mom and Dad. Jenny's head was lowered, either focusing on the mashed potatoes or dreading what was next. "Lyndall, if he wants more after he's finished what I've served him, he can ask for more, and I'll give him more."

I persisted, "Yeah, Mom, that works. This looks great, let's eat."

With some measure of emotion now creeping into her voice, she'd make one last stand, "Brad, I simply don't understand why you do this every Sunday night ..."

Dad, not a man of many words, slammed down the carving knife and fork, causing Jenny to jump in her seat, took his plate and his iced bourbon and headed for the kitchen counter a safe twenty feet from the toxic table. He'd reset his place for dinner on the long counter and eat facing us, outside of our circle of conversation in his self-imposed exile.

On most Sundays, Mom would act like nothing had happened, sighing, looking dejectedly at her food, taking a deep breath and soldiering on with, "So tell me about your day" to either child. We could recall nothing about our day and could only think about the bizarre weekly outburst and the ritual baiting between our parents and the inevitable outcome. Even stranger, Dad would jump back into the conversation at certain points as if he were not twenty feet away standing at the kitchen counter. As soon as our food was consumed, Mom was clearing, needing to get to Mt. Vernon to pick Mrs. Hattie up and somewhat relieved to be on the other side of another Sunday night dinner.

Some Sundays, she'd burst into tears and leave the table. None of us knew what to do. Jenny and I would look at each other. Jenny too had tears in her eyes, but we'd stay and eat. Sometimes Dad would return to the table and talk to us.

I had the clever idea of asking my dad if he would let me carve the chicken one Sunday night. Mom started to object to seeing her ten-year-old wield a long carving knife, but she quickly caught on to the merits of my request. There were a few valuable lessons in carving from Dad for the next few weeks, which I welcomed, though his words weren't always easy to decipher. From that point forward, I carved and served, giving a healthy portion to myself and everyone else, and occasionally, we sat together for an entire Sunday night dinner.

Our family camping *(image courtesy of the author)*

16

SIERRA CLUB SAM

We were not campers. At most we'd make it through a few hours on the courtyard lawn in our flimsy tent, tossing and turning in too-tight sleeping bags before heading back to the comfort of our soft beds and down pillows. Mrs. Hattie would just watch from the window and shake her head.

But there was something about the Sierra Club that spoke to each of us. It must have been the calendar, which had a permanent home in our kitchen next to the beige wall phone. Mom had the weekly on her desk, and a few other copies moved about the house and appeared annually in Christmas stockings. Arresting images of snow leopards, falcons and redwoods repeatedly beckoned us to a world we didn't know, far beyond Bedford.

We also sent in a minimal annual donation, which earned us quarterly copies of *Sierra* magazine. On a rare weekend when all four of us were home, we gathered in the living room by the fire. Each read in silence, occasionally sharing highlights. Dad was working his way through the Sunday *Times* crossword.

"Four-letter word for preferred step of the pony or fox?"

"Trot," Jenny responded, while thumbing through *Sierra* magazine. "Can we try an Iditarod across the Yukon?"

"Trot works. Thanks. Last I checked, you kids never want to walk the dogs in the snow, or even in the sun for that matter, so we should probably pass on the frigid dog race to the North Pole." No argument from any of us. He had a point.

As Jenny continued to describe rafting trips, Arctic treks and mountain climbs, I laid down my latest copy of *Ranger Rick* and sidled up next to my big sister to add visuals to her descriptions. Mom's attention was mostly devoted to *The New Yorker* with her knees tucked up into the blue armchair under a long, quilted robe with a glass of sherry just to her right. She peered over reading glasses at her two children, content to see the family interacting so passively and pleasantly.

"What about this one?" Jenny continued, emboldened by the rapt attention of her brother. "Leave your world behind and sleep under the stars. Five families will spend two weeks camping, cooking, and climbing in the Sierra Nevada mountains surrounded by wildflowers and snow-capped peaks. Cross ravines and fish for dinner while learning about the extraordinary flora and fauna of one of California's most beautiful regions. Kids must be six or older."

"What are the dates? How old's Pete?" Dad was headed over to Jenny to learn more.

"Seriously, Dad? I'm ten."

"I knew that." I got a mild shove that felt more like a hug.

"June 24 through July 7. Fox Lane gets out on the 21st and Rippowam is always done sooner. Could we do it, Dad? The dates work." How Jenny knew both her school calendar and mine is beyond me.

Mom was surprised and encouraged by the excitement, taking her glasses off and sitting forward. "Does it say camping experience required because we have absolutely none."

Jenny read all of the requirements and the basic gear list. It seemed inexperienced campers were welcome. Kids looked to parents, who looked at each other. If the moment could have been bottled and saved each of us would have jumped at the chance. Both Jenny and I started chanting, "Please, please." As smiles crept onto our parents' faces, we knew we were California-bound.

"Let's do it!" Mom declared. "It sounds perfect. Brad, are you sure you can get away from work? Both Mrs. Hattie and Mrs. Wilson take their vacations then and the dogs will have to go to Craighead's." An enthusiastic nod from Dad let us know this was actually going to happen. Jenny ran to get pencil and paper to write down what we would need to buy and what we could rent. For a moment, we felt like a normal family brimming with happiness, excitement and admiration for each other.

June came quickly. After many gear checks and rechecks, itineraries were dispersed to grandparents, neighbors, secretaries and friends, and we boarded a Pan Am flight for San Francisco. Most of our gear had been shipped or rented from the Sierra Club. It was all neatly packed in a van that was waiting for us at the San Francisco International Airport along with Chad and Monica, two very toothy, long-haired Sierra Club employees with reflective sunglasses. It was a bit of a bait and switch, because Chad and Monica proved to be very likable and knowledgeable during the three-hour drive into the mountains, but once they unloaded people and gear at a trail head in what felt like the middle of nowhere, they climbed back in the van and disappeared, leaving an unwelcome cloud of road dirt.

"I'm Hal Christiansen. From Utah."

Mom let out a grunt, which may have referred to her backpack or the state of Utah. Both Hal and my dad looked her way, but nothing followed. "You must be Richard, and is this your lovely wife Lynn-doll?" Mom was really wrestling with the backpack now. Hal stepped forward bravely. "Lynn-doll, let me help you." Ignoring the offer, Mom swung the overstuffed bag in a great arc onto her shoulder, nearly taking out Hal, who dodged the pack like a boxer. He was failing to ingratiate himself to the Boals.

Dad responded, "Hello, Hal, it's actually Bradlee. Richard's the birth name, but somehow it makes me sound like a dick."

"Oh, Brad, stop it. Hello Hal, I'm LYN-DALL, and these are our two, Jennifer and Peter. Will you be hiking with us?"

"Yes. In fact, I'll be your team leader."

"Oh, I wasn't aware we had a team ... or a leader."

For the next thirty minutes, more conversations like this ensued, with more road dirt wafting over all of us as two other nervous families arrived, unloaded, sized each other up, and wondered if the promise of this trip was going to match the reality.

The last vehicle to arrive was a muddy Westfalia. A young woman stepped out of the passenger seat, her sandy-colored hair emerging from a green bandana and descending to the small of her back. Behind her was a sturdy blond toddler with food all over his mouth and shirt. For some reason, he worn a helmet with an American flag design. On the back of the helmet were the letters S A M.

"He is *not* six," my mother whispered to no one in a voice that might not be considered a whisper.

"Brad, that child is no more than three. Jenny, didn't it say children had to be six or older. Should I tell his mother?"

"Tell her what?" my dad asked with more than a hint of annoyance.

"That he's three!"

"I'm guessing she knows that, Lynn-doll." Dad walked away to talk to the dentist from Sacramento.

Mr. Christiansen blew forcefully into a whistle, causing Mom to jump. He asked all of us to put our backpacks on and prepare for the first leg of our adventure, which would be a short fifty-minute trek to our first camp. Mr. Christiansen, equipped with a wide-brimmed hat and a gnarled walking stick, led the way. His daughter Eloise was by his side, with wife Greta at the rear. It wasn't long before we all realized we had packed too much. But as the wildflowers surrounded us, the weight was forgotten. Eloise pointed to individual blooms as we walked, offering us names like columbine, blue toadflax and Indian paint brush. Low meadows gave way to round hills, and trees seemed to stretch from mossy mounds towards a clear cobalt sky. Around us, birds offered a raggedy and under-rehearsed chorus. Polite conversations drifted off as the alpine landscape cast a spell on the Christiansens and their flock.

As we stumbled into camp, letting backpacks drop with a thud, we were pleasantly surprised to see a few shelters and a distant outhouse.

"Don't get used to it." Greta told my mom. "It's all wilderness starting tomorrow. The plan is to break you in slowly."

"Oh, dear," Mom said as she surveyed the site. "Last outhouse, I suppose."

"Yup, afraid so. We'll be digging latrines tomorrow."

"Can't wait."

Once unpacked, we assembled around a raging fire. Hal and Eloise had prepared a feast of ribeyes, skillet potatoes and grilled vegetables. Wine was brought out for the adults with sodas and milk for the kids. Satiated and settled in, we were all content knowing we had made the right decision months ago in our respective living rooms across the country.

The Christiansens talked us through basics of safety, cleanliness, respect for the wilderness and for each other. Turns out we would be jumping into icy rivers and lakes and foregoing bathing for the next fortnight. Latrines were to be dug at each stop and filled with dirt before moving on. All garbage went back in the backpack and we'd be cooking dinners in teams.

Mr. Christiansen summoned the kids for a meeting near the s'mores set-up. He produced nine bright yellow whistles, just like the one he wore around his neck. One was given to each child, including Eloise, even though she was a few years older than any of the other children. We were told to blow the whistle only if we were lost or in danger. Before we could ask, Mr. Christiansen gave two examples of what danger might look like.

"If you're facing a bear or if you've fallen in a ravine, you blow, you understand?" He looked into each nervous child's eyes until getting a nod of agreement. "And I don't need to tell you about the boy who cried wolf, do I? You only blow this whistle when you are facing danger. Am I being clear?" All heads nodded.

Sam nodded too, but Sam was always nodding his head. His red, white, and blue helmet was always a little too loose, and by nodding his head, the helmet sloshed backwards and forwards in a way that Sam seemed to enjoy. Not more than a minute after our meeting disbanded, Sam started to blow his whistle loudly and incessantly. His parents seemed amused at first and then chose indifference. Mr. Christiansen took it upon himself to reiterate the rules to young Sam, but Sam tooted in his face. Mr. Christiansen retreated. All the birds left the area.

The meals were not bad. Adults were paired in teams of two. Spouses were never together, and new friendships were made over grills and skillets. Dad was up first along with Mrs. Delridge from Cincinnati. Turns out Mrs. Delridge, or Nan as Dad called her, ran a catering business back home. She put Dad in charge of napkins and seating and did all the rest. Dad took his job seriously, enlisting me to help him construct a long buffet table with nearby sticks and logs. Our rain shield served as a tablecloth, and the napkins, which were actually paper towels, were rolled into white cones resembling snow-covered conifers. Nan took her job seriously too. Delicious grilled peppers were sprinkled with crushed garlic. A mushroom frittata complemented fresh-caught trout topped with butter and dill and served over wild rice. The hungry group broke into applause for our first culinary duo. Even the Christiansens seemed impressed. Dad proudly took credit for the success, reminding people that Nan had helped. He also insisted on cleaning up.

Mom's night was less of a hit. She and Burt, the dentist from Sacramento, were assigned a rainy night in the second week. By then none of us knew which day of the week it was, but we were well aware the fresh food was gone and most of the spices had run out. The men had strung tarps over much of the cooking area. Some huddled in their tents but the majority of the group sat glumly around a fire that Burt struggled to keep alive. Sam's whistle had been taken away, but he had a new pastime, which involved shuffling his feet through the dirt around the camp site. Despite the rain, clouds of dirt were launched into the air by Sam's little brown hiking boots. Neither his parents nor Mr. Christiansen were able to dissuade Sam from kicking dirt. His parents had retreated to their tent. Mom tried ineffectively to fan the dirt away from the cooking area with a spatula.

Mom called to him in her pronounced whisper, "Sam, Sam, stop it! No more dirt." Upon hearing his name, Sam redirected and headed towards Mom and the food, shuffling as he went. Once under the tarp, he met with drier earth, which created bigger clouds and more success for Sam.

Several others in the group offered to pitch in, recognizing the delays and frustrations Mom and Burt were experiencing. The fire wouldn't boil the water, the pasta wasn't cooking and the backup breadsticks had to be brought out. Mom had diced some beef jerky to add to the pasta along with a powdery cheese sauce. Burt roasted some mushrooms, but the lid for the pepper fell into the skillet along with all the remaining pepper. Mom's one culinary rule was you can fix everything with salt. This proved untrue.

There was no applause that night.

The latrines were challenging to dig, but we all pitched in. Once dug, a pop-up toilet seat was set over the hole and a black tarpaulin was strung from the surrounding trees with a small overlap on one side that served as an entrance. We all watched from our tents each morning to see when the black tent was vacant, and we could take our turn. Mom was up early in order to get in and out before the rest. Sam woke early too. He had developed an interest in Mom. Whenever she entered the latrine,

Sam would pop out of his tent, grab a long stick and circle the site, shuffling as he went. Mom's voice could be heard pleading emphatically for Sam to go away. He did not. After completing a full circle, he would start to beat the outside of the tarp with his stick, causing all families to wake. Most peered out their tent windows to see what the loud slashing sound was. Mom's protestations from within the tarp walls grew louder, but Sam would not stop. The whole scene had an ancient tribal feel to it. Dad and Jenny could be heard laughing uncontrollably inside their tent as they watched the spectacle through their tiny triangular window. No effort was made on anyone's part to stop Sam. The entertainment was just too good.

When Mom finally emerged, she grabbed Sam's stick and broke it in two, causing Sam to cry. She turned to Jenny and Dad's tent, which was suddenly silent and declared, "I am just about ready to go home ... I know you can hear me!"

The Sam and Lyndall show became like a miniseries for the rest of us. Parents and kids would seek out Jenny and me to hear the latest.

Jenny told Eloise about how Sam pulled out all of the pegs around the tent Mom and I shared one morning at dawn. Dad and Jenny in the next tent crawled to their triangular window to witness the silent assault while trying unsuccessfully to stifle giggles. Mom and I slept through the siege until the tent flopped down onto us with soggy nylon coating our faces and sleeping bags. Shuffling feet could be heard moving away from the tent as Mom bellowed, "Sam!"

The trip did not disappoint. Despite the unevenly matched rivalry between Mom and Sam, we all had a wonderful experience. I particularly loved the hiking. Each morning just before sunrise, a small group would leave camp to ascend a nearby peak. I was often first to summit because of my sheer enthusiasm and ten-year-old legs. Mr. Christiansen would arrive next, motivated by a need to be first even though he was second. Dad joined the hikes, too, and seemed reawakened by the surroundings, the exercise and the bonds with new acquaintances and his family. He drank what boxed wine was offered and seemed to have tiny bottles of harder alcohol squirreled away in his backpack. He also resumed his habit of eating Vick's Vaporub, which offered a high percentage of alcohol. Despite his covert consumptions, he was drinking far less than at home.

There was no hike planned for our final day since most of the group opted to rest on the shores of a nearby alpine lake. I asked Dad to join me for a final hike up Gale Peak, which we had climbed the day before. He agreed. We loaded day packs with water, lunch, sunscreen and first aid and followed the familiar route up the mountain. The weather was perfect, offering endless views of snow-covered peaks pushed to great heights by glaciers long ago. Turquoise lakes could be seen all around with darting marmots and chipmunks following our progress. We lunched just below the summit and then turned packs into pillows and watched birds and clouds drift overhead.

At some point the clouds thickened and darkened while the temperature plummeted, causing us to pack up and head back to camp with some degree of urgency. Not long into our descent, the rain started to fall steadily, then heavily. It couldn't break our mood and may have even heightened the excitement of an already perfect morning. But soon rain turned to hail, and we scrambled into a small cave-like crevice in the rocks, pulling packs and toes away from the onslaught of large ice balls. The storm only lasted for minutes, but the sound was deafening. We covered our ears as we watched stones the size of ping pong balls bounce into our tiny cave. Dad and I huddled until the rain returned. I don't think either of us had let on to the other just how frightened we were. We started to laugh. As we looked out of the cave, the sun was already making its return.

"Let's just stay here for a moment in case the hail returns," Dad suggested.

"Yeah, sounds good, Dad. I didn't get to finish my lunch, and there seems to be a chipmunk here in our cave who likes that idea."

"And I could use a drink." He plucked a tiny bottle of Jim Beam from his day pack and downed it.

I didn't care, and I didn't protest, because it was so good in that moment between me and my father. It was everything I wanted, and I believe it was everything he wanted in a relationship between father and son. His world was better on that day on that mountainside. He needed to drink when he was depressed or frustrated about bills or clients, but equally, he wanted to drink when he was happy. No matter the mood or the emotion, the response was the need to drink. Somehow it was always there when we were together. It defined my dad down to the smell. As the familiar scent of bourbon filled our small shelter up high on Gale Peak, it seemed all right. Nothing could break our mood.

17

CINDY DORSEY
AND THE BURRS

Lower School ended after fifth grade when we moved from the Cisqua campus to the Rippowam campus to start middle school. By spring, enough birthdays had passed that we were all eleven or twelve. With our "senior" status came a newfound confidence, causing kids to test boundaries and spread our wings. This new attitude manifested itself most in the interaction between the sexes. The majority of fifth graders had boyfriends and girlfriends, though this was more of an assignment than an activity. Confident, yes, but ready to do anything more than hold a hand or plant a timid kiss on a cheek? Not yet.

I liked Cindy Dorsey. She had huge, deep brown eyes and long, chestnut-colored hair, which she would curl each day before school. We weren't officially dating because I was still working up the courage to ask Cindy out. This was by no means an easy task, since Cindy traveled in a pack of girlfriends with her best friend, Sariah Pearl, controlling access to all members of the group. Their posse precluded any opportunity for my private moment with Cindy, but my quest to have an actual girlfriend and the possibility of landing my first kiss on some girl's cheek before graduation was becoming more imperative with each passing day.

One Wednesday towards the end of May, summer staged a brilliant coup on a cold spring. Temperatures hovered in the mid-seventies, while blossoms showered down on us as we entered school before the nine o'clock bell. You could feel the energy in the corridors with random pops of laughter and chatter everywhere. Mr. Fennel let the boys shed their blazers, and Mrs. Stolowitz took her biology class outside to identify bird calls.

On this balmy day, Lizzy Morgan and Storrs Lang, representatives of the Student Council for a Better School, (known as SCABS) headed into Principal Jones's office right after homeroom to suggest an extended recess due to heavenly weather. Decades into her tenure as Principal of Cisqua, Waldo Jones knew which battles to choose and which to avoid. This one was not worth it. The fact that Storrs's mom, Addie, was head of the parent's council and quite vocal in her enthusiasm about the future of the school probably did not affect Principal Jones's decision, but the fact that finals were still two weeks away may have. Besides, Waldo Jones knew every student in her school would head home that evening to offer a glowing report about the school to parents, who wrote hefty checks for both tuition and the spring auction. Yes, one extended recess was a fine idea.

The bell sounded like a herald at eleven-fifteen, and kids and hormones raced down the hallways, tumbling onto the grassy playing fields. Our thirty-minute recess had begun.

The teachers settled by the old oak near the playground with mugs of tea and tales of summer plans. Sweaters and shoes were scattered everywhere. My group liked to meet on the far edge of the field just behind the gym by the tall grasses. Technically, we were still on the playing field, but we were also several hundred yards from the teachers and well out of sight lines. It was usually just the boys, posturing about fourth-quarter goals or broken rules. Lately, we would take tally of our common quest to find or keep a girlfriend.

A few minutes after we were all assembled, Cindy and Sariah wandered around the corner of the gym. Our group went silent. The girls chatted, seemingly oblivious to our presence, though it's hard to imagine they didn't know we were there.

"Hey, cutie!" Beau called. Beau was actually dating Sariah. Cute she was, with that rare combination of red hair and unfreckled skin.

"Oh, hey, Crawford, I didn't know you guys were here. What's going on? I heard you said 'fuck' in gym yesterday."

There was nervous laughter from all. Jasper was the first to respond, standing and placing a hand on his heart, "I was in said gym yesterday during the alleged crime, and I can vouch for the fact that, when the dodge ball hit my good friend Beau Crawford in the crotch area, he did not say 'fuck'; he said 'mother-fucking-shit.'" We were doubled over with laughter now. "You guys should have seen Coach Myer's face. He was completely paralyzed, not knowing whether to help or reprimand our fallen soldier here."

More laughter. The girls were in our circle now. Cindy said hello to me under her breath and stood next to me.

Sariah wanted more. "That true, Crawford?"

"What's with 'Crawford'? Can't you call me Beau now that you're my girlfriend?"

Bing gave a hoot and then in his high-pitched falsetto sang, "Girlfriend …"

Sariah was near enough to Bing to smack him on the shoulder. There was widespread approval from all except the wounded Bing.

"Heard you cried after you went down, too. Is that true, Crawford?" Sariah continued.

"Fuck you, Sariah, I didn't cry. Why do you have to say that?"

"Just not sure I want to be dating a crybaby, that's all, but if you didn't cry, and you were hurt, I think you might need a kiss from your girlfriend to make it better." Sariah was twirling her red locks while she spoke.

Beau smiled. "It didn't really hurt. Well, maybe it did a little. Kiss might help now that I think about it. Why don't you follow me?" His arm went around Sariah and the two retreated a few steps further behind the gym to a chorus of catcalls.

Jasper, Ian, Bing, Cindy and I were left in an awkward silence on the edge of the field.

"Goddamned burrs!" Ian shouted. He had backed up next to the tall grasses and come in contact with a burr, which lodged in his hair.

Jasper spoke up, "Let me help you with that. Turn around, and I'll get it out for you."

He winked at Cindy as Ian faced away. Ian should have known better than to trust Jasper, but Ian was unfailingly gull-ible, and we all preyed on him because of it. He didn't see Jasper grab a small handful of burrs, which Jasper preceded to mash into Ian's mane. The laughter was ripe and even Ian, after a few choice curse words, joined in the fun. Cindy looked at me with a broad smile spreading across her face. This was going to be good. I grabbed a burr and tossed it at her long brown tresses. It landed just at the end of a twisted strand and took hold. Cindy screamed and ripped it out detaching a few hairs with the offending burr. She was not angry but rather electrified as she lunged forward to shove me hurtling backwards into the brush. This was heaven.

Jasper followed suit by launching a few more burrs at Cindy's hair with Bing and Ian joining in. It wasn't long before her squeals of laughter became rapid heavy breathing. The guys would not stop despite Cindy's protests. Bing held her upper arms from behind while Jasper continued to launch burrs at her head. Cindy's thrashing head looked like a nest. At this point she was on her back and starting to scream. She looked at me with panic in her eyes and I responded with a deep guttural yell, "Stop!"

I grabbed Jasper's arm to pull him back, but before I could, Sariah was there, hitting Jasper hard across the face. He fell to the ground with the unexpected force of her blow. Sariah yanked Cindy out of the grass and covered her head as they ran around the edge of the gym. Jasper and Bing bolted in the opposite direction.

Ian and I were left standing with Beau. All three of us were in a panic, unsure of what to do next.

We were soon collected by Mr. Fennel and taken to Principal Jones's office to be spoken to one by one. The gravity of the crime was real, and the remorse as strong as the confusion about what had actually happened in that fleeting moment. All of us ended up serving a Saturday detention. Sariah was the only witness needed to indict us all, except for Beau, though she did break up with him.

I looked for Cindy on Thursday. I wanted to apologize for what had taken place, but she wasn't in school. On Friday, I asked Kate, who was a member of Cindy and Sariah's circle, if she knew anything. She didn't respond except to say, "Of course I know." Then she walked away.

Cindy was back in school the following Tuesday, looking like a ghost. Her hair was cut in a short bob with a headband pushing it backwards. Her pack of friends never left her side, and I never got the chance to speak with her. She attended graduation but skipped all of the senior parties, even Kate's. She didn't come back to Rippowam for sixth grade. Kate told me she had decided to transfer to Greenwich Country Day because it was closer to her home.

I did talk to Sariah after graduation to see how Cindy was doing. She finally let down her guard and spoke about Cindy.

"She loved her long hair; that was the saddest part. She's humiliated about her hair cut, and she hates Jasper Lang. Bing, too, but she's not coming back here next year because of Jass. She's hurt, Peter, and the people who did this to her don't even know they hurt her. I'm not talking about you, or even what happened last week. It's bigger than that. Cindy can't fix what's wrong with this place. She's looking out for herself and moving on."

Me and my best friend *(from the collection of the author)*

18

CARTER JAMES

Carter James came from somewhere in Connecticut but not the nearby towns like Westport, New Canaan or Greenwich. He showed up one day in sixth grade part way through the school year, which in retrospect was unusual if not suspect. No one arrived mid-year, and in fact, no one arrived in the sixth grade. Rippowam ended after ninth grade, when everyone headed off to boarding schools like Choate or Andover. Most of the kids in my class had enrolled in pre-kindergarten and had known each other for as long as they could remember. They even spent summers together on the Island, which was known to the rest of the world as Nantucket. During my nine years at Ripp, I often felt like an outsider, but assumed it was because I started in kindergarten instead of pre-k and spent my summer vacations in Canada.

That day in late October, Carter and his mother walked somewhat sheepishly into our classroom. Mrs. James spoke for a few minutes with Mrs. Watkins. Carter was shuttled into some group activity and didn't look back at his mother, obviously mortified she had made it this far.

He had dollops of crimson in the middle of his white cheeks and wore a tweed coat, which made him look very English, which he wasn't. Tweed was allowed, according to the school handbook, but everyone opted for blue and madras blazers instead. Jackets and ties were required for boys third grade and up. Shades of preppy ran deep in Bedford. Bing would sometimes wear his royal blue pants with red lobsters embroidered on them. Ties sported whales or schooners. On the playground, we would peel back the layers inside the ties to check the quality. Four gold stripes won. Some boys wore madras bow ties in the spring. The teachers looked no less ridiculous. Carter was dressed nicely enough but stood out for not looking like a citrus-colored quilt.

He was quiet at first and didn't mix with the others. Granted it was a tight group. No one really gave him the cold shoulder; it's just that he wasn't on the soccer team, his family wasn't a member of the Bedford Golf and Tennis Club and nobody knew him from the Island. I heard Brady asking him if he went to Martha's Vineyard for the summers. Brady's uncle had a place on the Vineyard and thought they might have some friends in common. Nobody really got close to Carter.

So, Mrs. Watkins made Carter my partner for the sociology project. I was a little disappointed since I usually worked with Beau or Eric, but Carter seemed nice enough, and honestly I wanted a way to reach out to him before he cut himself off from the entire group.

We headed for the library to research the socioeconomic effect of raising the minimum wage in Westchester County on lower-income neighborhoods. Odd if you think about it, since every pool cleaner, groundskeeper, nanny, and maid in our town was paid below minimum wage with no benefits, that is, unless you count the use of the tiny guest house on the Island, the endless gifts of jam, fresh squash, or a rare Lily Pulitzer castoff.

After pulling together a small collection of social commentaries and scribbling a few notes, I asked, "So do you miss your other town, the one you left in Massachusetts?"

"It was in Connecticut and no, not really." Carter was erasing the word "douche" from the library table.

After a pause, I continued, "Do you like it here?"

"Yeah, I guess." Carter, now drilling the pages of Ralph Nader's *Action for a Change* with his fingertips, seemed ready for a new topic.

"I think you'll like it when you get to know people. Who do you hang out with?"

"No one yet."

I realized I had backed myself into a corner with that one. "Maybe you could come over to my house sometime after school?"

"Sure. I'd like that."

So, the following Tuesday, we had a half day for teacher conferences, and Carter took the bus home with me.

Mrs. Wilson made us an awesome lunch of grilled cheese with bacon, apple slices and freshly baked chocolate chip cookies plus a thermos full of chocolate milk. She packed everything into two lunch boxes and sent us to the hayloft above our barn because she had to mop the floors. We spread out our feast on the hay bales and forgot about minimum wage, Massachusetts, and the afternoon hours. The apple slices were sacrificed as bait to lure our three ponies into the barn. Apples kept hitting the unsuspecting equines in the head or back only to be followed by peals of childish laughter. We became friends.

He was over at my house often. I visited his house too. He lived a good distance from Bedford in Briarcliff Manor. The bus would take us as far as Ossining where Lia Rowland lived. Lia, Carter and I were the only three kids on the bus for the last ten minutes of the ride, but Lia wouldn't acknowledge us. I thought it was just a girl thing, but when she got off the bus, she'd say goodbye to me. I guess it was just a Carter thing. Mrs. James was waiting in her BMW just across from Lia's driveway. From there she drove us the rest of the way to their home.

His house was smallish, cluttered with stuff and close to neighbors on both sides. We hung out on their new trampoline behind the house with his little sister, Terry. We would bounce as high as we could in a covert act of espionage on the neighbor's property. One by one, we took turns reporting a finding and offering a detailed analysis. "One German Shepherd," bounce, "very dangerous, big teeth!" The German Shepherd was actually sleeping. Terry's turn: "One garden chair," bounce, "might be electric." Excessive laughter. I reported, "One lacrosse stick, must have lacrosse stick." Eventually, we were down to one rock and one tree with no good commentary, and the thrill was gone, so we headed back inside for hot chocolate and television.

Mom picked me up at five forty-five to take me home. I hadn't noticed Carter had left the living room before the end of *Gilligan's Island*. His mother called to him as I climbed into our Volvo. Just before we drove off, Carter ran up to the car to say goodbye. He was carrying the lacrosse stick.

"Peter, thanks for coming over. Don't forget your lacrosse stick."

I was speechless for a moment, looking back and forth between Carter and the moms, hoping someone would help me out here.

Finally, "It's not mine, it belongs to ..."

Carter interrupted, "It's mine, and I want you to have it as a gift."

His mother started to say something, but my mother beat her to it.

"How kind of you, Carter. Peter what do you say?" Before I could answer she continued, "Carter is such a wonderful friend, he should join us on Saturday for Peter's soccer game. They're playing Greenwich Country Day. He'll know lots of kids there. It'll be fun. I can pick him up around ten if that works for you. I'll call you. Thanks so much for having him over."

I muttered a weak thank you and goodbye as we pulled out of the driveway. Carter's mother and Terry were smiling and waving as we left. Carter headed back inside the house.

The lacrosse stick was as perfect as I had originally suspected with worn netting pulled into a deep pocket in the cradle and extra tape on the grip. It was far superior to mine. I wanted to use it but never did. It made me uncomfortable and created a moral dilemma, which I answered with inaction. It sat in my basement for years until I offered it up for a Goodwill clean-out. I didn't see any honor in Carter's act, just dishonor.

I was sick on Saturday and couldn't play soccer. Truth is, I wasn't sick but just didn't know what to say to Carter. Mom called Mrs. James to let her know there would be no soccer game. All I heard was, "Yes, another time." There was no other time, and I started to avoid Carter in school. I felt guilty about not confronting the situation, but when Bing said how relieved everybody was that I was no longer hanging out with Carter, I thought I'd probably made the right decision.

A few weeks later on a cold Monday, Eric and I headed outside for recess. We spotted a cluster of kids in quiet conversation on the far side of the playground. There was an intensity about the discussion that could be detected even from where we were. When we reached the group, I asked what was up.

Bing was at the center of the circle and seemed to be the source of information.

"Carter stole cash."

"What do you mean he stole money, from whom?"

"He stole from teachers. He went from classroom to classroom during Friday morning assembly and went in every teacher's purse and took their frickin' money."

"Why did he do it?" Eric asked.

"He probably needed a new tweed coat or something, I don't know why he did it," said Bing, who was clearly enjoying holding court. "The point is, it was wrong. He took Fennel's credit card out of his wallet!"

"That is so low," Kate chimed in.

"So, what's going to happen to him?" I asked the all-knowing.

Bing again had the answers, "What do you mean what's going to happen? He's gone, expelled, that's it, no more Carter James."

The whispering continued, and everyone unanimously condemned the perpetrator. Ironic since Bing had been caught cheating on his final last semester, and Kate and Lia were found smoking behind the gym. The varsity lacrosse team had stolen the statue of Chief Kisco from the town square last spring, and they were still hailed as heroes in our school. Carter was apparently up for a different set of rules. No trial, no jury, just expulsion.

I never saw Carter again. For weeks, I thought I should call him to see if he was okay. I also wondered if there might be an explanation. The more I thought about the lacrosse stick, the more I recognized a good intention, though misguided. But I didn't call, and I never did see him again.

19

BEAU'S PARTY

I think the boys in our sixth grade were truly heterosexual, but they were also truly horny. Porn was almost nonexistent. Every now and then, someone would uncover his father's stash of *Playboy* magazines. These would get passed around and ripped up a bit before the nervous finder would carefully return the prize to the guest room closet, where they had been discovered underneath the golf clubs.

Timmy and I would hike beyond the back of our property, where he had found and hidden an old copy of a nudist magazine called *As You Are*. We periodically thumbed through the pages, wishing they had an effect on us, but the images were all of unattractive and uninhibited people gardening, riding bikes or nailing wood planks onto the roof of their new shed.

The all-boy birthday parties in the summer between sixth and seventh grade were a different story. It had been five years since Rigby showed me his erection, and I hadn't planned on seeing another one so soon.

Though we were only twelve or thirteen, the host was responsible for supplying beer or wine. All of our homes had well-stocked bars, and our parents were invested in the contents by early evening. It wasn't much for a clever kid to snatch a bottle or two. No one was counting or noticing. Most of us had a guesthouse, cottage or apartment above the garage, so slumber parties were beyond the ears and eyes of the main house, and crimes went undetected.

Beau was the oldest in our group. He came from a typical high-pressure family; dad worked on Wall Street, mom taught kindergarten and published books of her poetry, and his older brother Dan had been valedictorian and went on to be a champion sculler. We all thought Beau had most likely repeated third grade when he moved from Massachusetts to Bedford.

On a Saturday at the end of June, before everyone headed off to the Island for the Fourth, we gathered in the Crawfords' lake house to celebrate Beau's thirteenth birthday. The lake house consisted of one central room with a vaulted ceiling and stone fireplace and a few puffy striped armchairs and ottomans. There were two small changing rooms on either side.

The distant conversations of our parents could be heard from the veranda of the main house. The Crawfords had invited them to stay for cocktails after dropping us off. As darkness fell and the early summer heat broke, the cars drove off down the long driveway one by one. Soon Mr. Crawford appeared at the lake house with three large pizza boxes. "You guys can stay up until this fire dies out, and then it's time to turn in. We're in the house if you need us, but I doubt you will. Beau, your mom stocked this fridge with sodas. Good night, boys, see you in the morning." He wrestled a bit with the latch on the door and stumbled up the hill. No one was likely to check on us again.

Beau disappeared to the men's changing room and returned with a weighted duffel bag. He pulled out four bottles of wine for the ten of us. "Dan gave me three, and I took the Cabernet from the bar just before you guys arrived," he offered with a sly smile.

A chorus of, "Oh, shit!" and "Damn!" could be heard from our group. We had never had this much alcohol before. We emptied our soda cans and poured the wine into them in the event of Mr. Crawford's return. Filling the cans took a while, but we were meticulous, knowing a spill on new sisal was not an option. Beau brought out straws.

"What's with the straws, Crawford?" Bing jested as he blew the straw wrapper back at Beau.

"It gives you a better buzz, you dumb shit."

None of us liked the taste, but we were determined not to let on. Halfway through my first can of wine, my head was spinning, and I could tell the others were feeling the effects too. Timmy looked white and Yuki had turned pink. He was sweating. I actually thought he might throw up. "Hey, lightweight, I think your mother's calling," taunted Bing. "Yuki, you no drinky wine, maybe some green tea for you," Bing said in a high-pitched Japanese accent. The teasing continued until Yuki picked up his sleeping bag and dragged it off to the women's changing room. Someone threw a slice of pizza at him, which he didn't seem to notice. It landed with a splat on his Spiderman sleeping bag. Through the laughter, we heard a weak, "Fuck off, assholes!" We were nine until Timmy started snoring.

"Let's get out of here and sit on the dock." Beau urged.

We stumbled into the full moonlight, sleeping bags in tow, helping each other along. Someone thought to bring the remaining two bottles.

Our smaller group, now down to eight, felt revitalized by the night air. As we passed a bottle around the circle, Eric suggested a game of truth or dare. The truths didn't reveal much. We learned that Jasper had broken up with Kate, Beau walked in on his brother having sex with his girlfriend and Lia Rowland wore a training bra.

"Screw the truth," shouted Skip, "let's play dare or die." None of us knew what "or die" really meant, but fear of the unknown made us accept the challenge.

The first bottle, now emptied, was spun in the middle of our circle. The spinner chose the dare for the boy the bottle selected. Beau spun first, and the bottle pointed towards Eric. After some thought: "Cannonball off the end of the dock!"

This was actually kind of scary at night. Even with the near-full moon, our imaginations offered plenty of suggestions for what might be in the water below. After some prompting and another long swig of wine, Eric shed his shirt and flew like a rocket off of the dock into the water. It was a few seconds of nothing but bubbles, and then a head popped out of the water and we heard, "Fucking freezing, you fucking assholes." He chucked his wet pajama bottoms at Beau. Someone stumbled up the dock to get Eric a towel. He was a hero for a moment, as all of us feared what the next dare might be.

Eric, now wrapped in a towel, spun and watched as the bottled eased around to Bing. Bing was a wild man and likely to do anything. He was legendary in school since the day he asked Miss Herrion, our third-grade science teacher, "What is the exact diameter of Uranus?" Poor Miss Herrion didn't get the joke and only made it worse by responding, "Now, Bing, it's not so wide, only 4,200 miles."

The group was now charged with excitement. Suggestions were coming in fast. "Make him go and get another bottle of wine!" And then, "No, I got a better one, make him go in the house and get us another bottle wearing just his underwear." Eric liked this, and the dare was presented. Much to our surprise, Bing stripped down to his boxers and trotted off across the lawn to the house.

An eternity passed as we watched the house from a distance. At one point, a light went on in the library where the bar was located. A few minutes later, Bing came racing back across the lawn with a bottle.

"What the fuck happened? You were gone for like fifteen minutes," Beau asked.

"You're not going to believe this shit. I got inside the house no problem, and I found this one bottle of rose that was in the back of the wine fridge. I was just about to grab it, and I heard your fucking dad coming downstairs asking who was there. I bolted and closed myself in the bathroom off of the library just before he walked in. I was in my fucking boxers!"

Lots of, "Oh, shit!" and "No way!"

"So, I end up talking to your dad through the bathroom door, and he's like, 'How's it going down there, Bing, I thought I heard a splash or something.'"

"Luckily, and don't take this the wrong way, Beau; he's really slurring the words at this point. My dad's the same way. So, I tell him he must have heard a fish or something. I'm actually laughing as I say this because it is so ridiculous. Then I tell him everyone turned in early, because they want to take the boat out in the morning, and we're all hoping he'll join us. I knew I had him on this one, and I could tell he was pouring something and heading for the door. Then he pauses, and I think, oh, shit, why is he pausing? And he says, 'Bing, why are you in the house?' I told him I had to use the bathroom. So, he's kind of on to me with this one, and he gets all detective on me and reports, 'There's a bathroom in the lake house, you know, and plenty of trees around, too, and hell, you can even piss in the lake.'"

"After some quick thinking, I responded, 'Thanks Mr. C, but I had to take a dump, you know what I mean, and I really didn't want to bother the others with the sound or the smell.'"

We cannot control our laughter at this point. "You guys, I am dying at this point and counting on the fact your dad will not remember any of this in the morning."

"You called him Mr. C?" Ian was clearly missing the point of the story here.

"Can you believe it?" Bing went on, "It just came out. Anyway, I heard him chuckle real low, and then he says, 'Bing, you're a good guy, just like your dad. I'll see you in the morning, and we'll definitely take that boat out. Some good trout in the pond this time of year. Now get some sleep.'"

"Then I waited five more minutes just to be sure that he was gone and went back for the rosé."

We had a new hero.

Beau was pissed about something and retreated to the lake house, not to return.

The next thirty minutes were a blur. Eric and Jasper threw Bing into the lake: the hero's reward. Bing retaliated by ripping the towel from around Eric's waist after considerable struggle.

When the towel came off, we could see Eric was hard, and Bing started trying to grab his penis while shouting, "Faggot!" Soon, we were all jumping on and off the dock naked. Sun-tanned bodies with white bottoms stumbling, wrestling and laughing. By the ladder onto the dock, Bing and Eric were rubbing against each other. In the water, I could see Jasper grabbing Skip. At some point, the alcohol, bewilderment and remorse made us stop. Someone threw up off the end of the dock, and one by one, we started to amble back to the lake house with the exception of Bing and Eric, who flopped into Mr. Crawford's boat. I could still hear them as I retreated but thought best to leave them be.

Despite the spinning head caused by an overload to my pre-teen alcohol receptors, I was also keenly aware of the excitement I was experiencing in mind and body. The sting of the word "faggot" rang in my head too. A pleasure and a pain folded into clouded thoughts. The drunken fog soon pushed me into a deep slumber.

Dan was the first person we saw in the morning through the haze of our first hangover. Mr. Crawford sent him down to survey the scene before Mrs. Crawford was up. Dan was pissed off and really giving Beau shit. The place was a total mess with pizza on sisal and spilled coke or wine on one of the armchairs. Beau was pissed, too, because his mom was also a decorator, and she had just redone the lake house. Dan got rid of the bottles, and the rest of us picked up the pizza boxes and straw wrappers. Dan made Beau go down to the dock to scrub vomit off of the wood. Apparently, some hit the boat too.

We heard Beau yelling from the dock. "Get the fuck out of my dad's boat! What the fuck are you doing in there? Are you naked, you fucking faggots?!"

Then Bing's voice, "Crawford, relax, we're just getting the boat ready for your dad to take us out , and we were putting on our Jams in case we want to swim. He said we'd catch some trout today, that's all." Somehow Beau bought this story and helped with the boat. Most of us left after breakfast, but Bing, Jasper and Beau spent the afternoon fishing with Mr. Crawford, like nothing ever happened.

It was during seventh grade that we started to make some headway with girls, kissing for real, and touching this and that. It was all very tentative and exciting. Somehow it all felt like new territory for the seventh-grade boys, even though it wasn't. The night of Beau's party, and a handful of other nights that summer with the same ending, were never acknowledged or spoken of again. Boys' code of honor, like it never happened.

20

BARCLAY'S BALLROOM CLASSES

Lenora and Vadim Markov lived about twenty miles from Bedford in the working-class town of Peekskill. They drove to the Bedford Golf and Tennis Club on Wednesday nights each fall to teach ballroom dancing classes to select seventh graders whose parents paid handsomely in hopes of refining their unrefined teenagers. Why they were called Barclay's Ballroom classes, I don't know. Perhaps the lingering Cold War prevented the Markovs from choosing to use their surname. The classes were not exclusive for kids from Ripp, but I never saw anyone from any other school there.

The Club boasted a large central pavilion with saffron walls, a black-and-white marble floor and French doors that opened onto a perfectly groomed croquet lawn. Rows of gilded sconces and an elaborate Austrian crystal chandelier suggested a miniature

Viennese palace. The space was magical, prompting even slouchy seventh graders to temporarily consider better posture.

Everyone seemed to polish up for Wednesday nights. The guys with saggy pants wore belts and combed unkempt locks. The girls arrived with carefully coiffed hair and painted faces, having just applied makeup for the first time. Their self-conscious smiles suggested each had just caught a glimpse in the mirror of the woman she would become. Hormones were everywhere.

Lenora and Vadim were impeccable, looking as if they had just emerged from the hair salon. Vadim's Russian-accented voice greeted us. "Velcome, beautiful ladies and handsome gentleman, if you will please take your seats, we can begin tonight's lesson of zee box step."

This unleashed a mad scramble as boys ran to the nearest chair to pull it out for a girl. Girls would rush towards the cute guys. Inevitably, there was shoving and Vadim would interject with his booming yet measured voice. "Ladies, please. Remember to accept zee offer from zee gentleman closest to you and to accept graciously." He then grabbed a nearby chair and swirled it in a great arc through the air bringing it silently to the floor a few feet from Madame Markova. One suspected he practiced this move repeatedly in his Peekskill apartment while looking in the mirror. A balletic gesture of the hand indicated his invitation for Madame to sit. She watched coyly, seeming genuinely surprised by the invitation, and then placed her hand in his as he guided her to the chair. She sat gently on the edge waiting for him to shuffle it forward an inch for her full weight.

White chairs surrounded the room like a lace trim. They were placed in little quartets with one couple facing another. Ladies were always seated to the right of the gentlemen. After each dance, the gents offered a chair and a new partner accepted while the lesson continued.

Learning the box step was painful, wrapping one hand around your partner's waist and still trying to stand as far away as possible was uncomfortable to say the least. Toes were crunched, and eye contact was taboo. By lesson three, we were actually not bad at the Lindy and soon-to-be masters of the foxtrot with a promise of learning the rumba and the hustle. How the hustle got in there, I don't know, but this was the high seventies.

The Markovs were really a sketch when they demonstrated. Vadim pulled Lenora in close while she gazed trustingly into his eyes. Lenora could execute any dance without a single hair moving. It was weird. Her left forearm would rest casually on Vadim's shoulder blade, but her fingers would not touch him, instead holding the shape of a five-petaled flower against the black of his charcoal-colored suit. After an unnecessarily flawless demonstration, they would separate to invite one boy and one girl to dance with them, and the lesson would take a lurch towards the awkward.

Lenora chose me for the Lindy. With her three-inch heels, we were nose to nose. Her perfume was excessive and intoxicating all at once. What a relief it was to return to Kate, who smelled of Ivory soap, after a few painful minutes of dodging Lenora's steely-toed pumps.

By lesson four, the guys were starting to stray a bit. There was talk at recess that afternoon of bringing slingshots to that evening's rumba lesson. Slingshots weren't the traditional kind with a Y-shaped stick and a stone. Instead, they consisted of a thick rubber band and a wad of paper. We'd soak the paper in spit to give it an added splat when it made contact with the target. The thumb and the index finger replaced the stick. Since paper wads and rubber bands fit into blazer pockets without detection, plenty of ammunition made it into the club that night.

Most of us were armed and ready. The Markovs might have sensed something was up because the guys were a little quieter than usual that night. Some of the girls knew the plan too. They were wide-eyed and waiting for the first strike.

After the welcome, the Markovs demonstrated their flawless version of the foxtrot and invited all of us to join them on the dance floor. The collective review allowed for some undetected whispering.

"Jasper's going down, you better duck, Sariah. Zing, splat!" Timmy said.

"Just watch your back, Ericksen!" Jasper countered.

Bing was nearby. "Screw Ericksen, I'm going for the man."

"What man?" asked Eric.

"Russian Ken Doll himself." Some kids busted out laughing.

"Who's that?" asked Eric.

"Markov, you dumb shit!"

We all figured Bing would make the first move, and he did, firing a few random shots, one of which made contact with Jasper's thigh. Jasper flipped the bird before retaliating. His shot accidentally hit Timmy instead of Bing. All three were pretty quiet during battle, knowing too much noise could blow their cover. One wayward shot hit Sariah Pearl in the ear, and there was a shriek. Vadim was there by her side as the foxtrot came to a halt. Timmy jumped in and apologized, explaining that he was trying to find the rhythm and must have lost control and hit Sariah in the ear. She did not look happy with Timmy's account, but it earned a huge laugh form the crowd. Vadim was not amused either. "Mister Erickzon, you must be careful wis zee ryzum, Everysing is subtle. Everysing is calm."

We laid low for a while, allowing the Markovs to regain control of the room. They introduced the rumba with aplomb and broke it down step by step. Lenora then approached Jasper while Vadim chose Kate. Jasper actually showed a certain confidence with the rumba. He was tall, and with his mop of blond curls slicked back, he looked like an appropriate partner for Madame. As they found their stride, Vadim ushered Kate to the sidelines to admire his wife and her new partner. Jasper, who was feeling the spotlight and savoring it just a bit, pulled Madame a little closer while looking squarely into her eyes. There may have been a blush here. Someone shouted, "Yeah, Lang!" Vadim shot a look at the heckler.

Out of nowhere. a wad of paper flew across the room and smacked into Lenora Markova's chin, throwing her head back in a wrenching spasm. She let out a haunting moan. Almost simultaneously, a room full of seventh graders shouted, "Oh, shit!" Bing hit the floor laughing in hysterics. Vadim was suddenly charging towards Jeff Greenaway, who was racing towards the fire exit, rubber band in hand, outpacing his pursuer. All of us were watching in shock, not because of the pursuit, but because we couldn't believe Jeff was responsible for the shot heard round the world. How cool was Jeff? Who knew? He wasn't even in on our plan. He must have overheard us at recess and brought his own stash of ammo. Jeff made it to the door in seconds and pushed the bar, unleashing a blaring fire alarm that would not stop. The room was in total chaos.

Club security appeared and huddled us onto the croquet

lawn while we waited for the alarm to be silenced and the building to be cleared for re-entry. The Markovs were nowhere to be found.

Fortunately, or maybe unfortunately, the fire department was very efficient, and we were allowed to re-enter the building twenty minutes before our parents arrived to collect us. Vadim was suddenly there, running his hands through his hair, but there was no sign of Lenora. Jeff Greenaway was missing too. Vadim offered us an earnest, but ineffective lecture about being a gentleman or a lady "wis zocial gracez."

Kate replaced Lenora for the second rumba demo, and the lesson limped along until eight-thirty, when we were released to our parents. Lenora and Vadim always stood at the entry doors to the pavilion and waved to the parents like a pair of tired royals during pick-up, and though I wanted to launch into the story about Jeff Greenaway's fantastic assault and the arrival of the fire department with my mom, I looked around first to see if Lenora had returned to her spot beside Vadim. Part of me wondered if I might see replacement Kate offering the royal wave, but there was Lenora at her post, waving bravely, not noticing a few hairs which were clearly out of place.

21

LIGHTNING STRIKES TWICE

I didn't expect to see the name of someone I knew in the obituaries, especially not of someone so young as Scott Abrams. The text read: Scott Warren Abrams died September 21st at his home in Briarcliff Manor. According to his father, the cause was electric shock from a bolt of lightning.

The *Patent Trader* went on to describe Scott, a young father, a volunteer firefighter, an associate broker with Bixler Real Estate, who had been nailing siding on his roof when a severe and sudden thunderstorm swept Northern Westchester County. Though Scott fell from the ladder some 22 feet, it was apparently the lightning that killed him.

At the time, I was living in New York City with my wife and our son and had returned to Bedford for the day to help my mom close her pool.

I shared the news with her. "Mom, Scott Adams was killed by lightning."

"Oh, dear. Who was Scott Adams?"

"Scott was at Ripp with me for years. You remember, the redhead, good friends with Bobby Howard."

"Wasn't Bobby Howard the Black kid? You went to his house, once, didn't you?"

"Mom, this is so weird. When we were in Mr. Fennel's fourth-grade homeroom, and we were talking about world population."

"I love it! I wish they would talk more about world population in schools. All of this traffic in downtown Bedford is horrendous. You know overpopulation was your grandparents' greatest cause through Planned Parenthood and the World Population Council. Remember when Grandfather was asked to transport all of those pelvic models to India. Imagine your grandfather explaining why he was carrying three dozen pelvic models to the Indian customs officer. Priceless!"

"Mom, he was telling us about life expectancies."

"Who was?" She was reading *The New Yorker* and making dinner during our conversation, so the focus was divided to say the least.

"Mr. Fennel. He told us that if national averages of the day held true over the next century, the boys in our class would live to seventy-three and that girls would live to seventy-six. He also told us that according to statistics, two of us would be dead by the time we were forty. I thought it was such a weird morbid fact to tell a group of fourth graders. We all just started looking around the room at each other, wondering who the grim reaper would choose first. Scott was in that classroom. Now he's the second one to die and we're only in our thirties. Fennel was right."

"Who else died?"

"Mom, tell me you don't remember Jasper Lang. You worked at Fox Lane then."

"Oh, Jasper Lang, what a sad story. There was no getting through to that mother, and the father was incorrigible. What was her name? Even her name was silly. Addie! I kept wanting to call her Batty."

My mother was a social worker, having graduated from Swarthmore College and the Simmons School of Social Work. She also earned a second master's degree from the Columbia University Teachers College. After running the Social Service Department at Northern Westchester Hospital for a decade, she became the social worker at Fox Lane, Bedford's massive public high school. Her multiple attempts to communicate with Jasper and his family were a bust.

Jasper left Ripp abruptly after eighth grade, even though Ripp went through ninth. He ended up transferring to Hotchkiss, which was not far from Bedford in rural Connecticut. His dad attended Hotchkiss and was on their board of trustees. Mr. Lang was a Yalie too, and apparently, he, Timmy's dad, and Principal Porter were all roommates at Yale.

I never liked Jasper. In Mr. Fennel's fourth-grade class, we created a mock society that lasted the entire year with banks, bogus currency, stores and even a stock market. The competition became pretty intense between abnormally entrepreneurial ten-year-olds. Each kid had a store where he or she sold all kinds of stuff like erasers, pens, batteries and snacks. The families were in on it too, with the moms making Jello cups and Rice Krispie treats and the dads emptying their closets of old neckties and golf tees, all to be sold for a profit. Jeff Greenaway's dad worked at IBM in Armonk and got an unlimited supply of free batteries, so Jeff was making a killing selling them at a quarter apiece.

Of course, there were white-collar crimes, too, and we had to put a judicial system in place. Mr. Fennel selected five judges to determine the fates of their peers. I was one of the five and quickly regretted the appointment.

One sun-drenched day in April, everyone was outside for recess. Yuki and I were stuck inside helping Mr. Tower with a massive wall map of pre-World War I Europe, when we ran out of staples. Mr. Tower's room was next to Mr. Fennel's, so I ran next door to borrow his stapler. I rounded the corner to see Jasper's unmistakable mop of blond curls as he climbed out of the window. The pockets of his blazer were weighted with something, and one hand was full of AA batteries. He tumbled out the window and bolted without seeing me.

I didn't say anything and didn't need to. When Jeff came back from recess, not only was his meticulously tended store-front trashed, but most of his batteries were gone. Jeff was quick to finger Jasper, who had it out for Jeff since the day he showed up at Ripp. Jeff was a total brain with a 4.0 GPA. He was also pint-sized, with thick eyeglasses and greasy hair, which made him ripe for teasing. The previous spring, after lacrosse practice, Jasper and Bing hung Jeff by his underwear on a hook in the boys' locker room. Jeff cried and kicked the wall while a group of boys and a few brave girls stood around laughing. The noise was enough to attract Coach Myers, who hoisted Jeff off the hook and dispersed the crowd.

Jasper and Bing escaped with only one Saturday deten-tion and no mark on their records. Mr. Lang was tight with

Principal Porter and gave him the old boys-will-be-boys speech. "Remember the stuff we did at Yale, Preston? These boys are practically angels by comparison."

The incident was bad enough, but Jasper would not let things go, and he was constantly finding ways to retaliate. For the rest of the year, poor Jeff would discover underwear hanging from his locker, in his pocket, at the bottom of his school bag and even in his lunchbox. Apparently, years later, a perplexed Mrs. Greenaway opened a FedEx package, and a pair of tighty whiteys was there to greet her.

Luckily our fourth-grade society didn't have to endure trials. Instead, students submitted written explanations of why they had committed a crime and why they regretted having done so, or why they were innocent. Judges were presented with the testimonies, given some time to deliberate, and then asked to deliver their verdict or sentence during a private audience with Mr. Fennel. Jasper's defense read, "I didn't do it. I was at recess. Ask Bing or any of the one hundred other kids at recess."

I sat in my room that night dreading my morning meeting with Mr. Fennel. I knew I had to report what I had seen, regardless of the consequences.

I jumped when I heard the phone ring. "Hello, Laurence," Mom said, "No, he gets home around nine, can I have him call you then? Yes, I'll tell him. Definitely, we are all looking forward to it. See you Saturday, and I'll be sure to have Brad call the minute he gets home … my best to Addie. Bye."

I heard Dad's Jeep pull into the driveway and ran downstairs to meet him at the door. Breathlessly, I told him the whole story about Jasper and Jeff and my role as a judge. We were interrupted by Mom's voice calling, "Oh, Brad, I didn't know you were home, you have to call Laurence Lang, he says it's important. It's something about Ripp." Dad was a trustee of the school, and this type of call happened all too often. He heard me out, sensing the urgency of my message and then headed for the phone.

"Don't worry Pete, you have to do what's right, and I trust you will. You always have."

I sat in Dad's study for the call. Mr. Lang's voice was clearly audible through the receiver.

"Hey, Bradlee, thanks for calling me back. Listen, I just had a great conversation with Dan Wilkins, Skip's dad, and I wanted to talk to you as well. Has Pete told you about this whole thing?" Dad confirmed that I had. "You see Brad, this is all just a big misunderstanding, Jasper was with Bing playing four square or something. This Greenaway kid has it out for Jass, but it wasn't him. Jass thought he saw a kid come from behind the building, but he wasn't sure who it was. Jasper's a great kid, I mean he's made mistakes, but he has such promise, like Pete, and now he's getting blamed for some other kid's actions. I just think Peter has a chance to do the right thing here, and I know Jass and all of us will be truly grateful to Pete for setting the record straight."

My dad was a lawyer and an excellent one at that, so I was interested in his response.

"Laurence, I appreciate your call, as I'm sure you know, Peter's an honorable kid. He'll do the right thing, and you can assure Jasper of that." Dad winked at me while he said this. There was some more talk from Mr. Lang, and I heard my dad say, "Access to an unlimited supply of free batteries does beat the market." Mr. Lang's chummy laugh could be heard through the phone. "Goodnight, Laurence. Will we see you this weekend? Good. Until then."

At eight-fifteen the next morning, before the first bell rang, I reported to Mr. Fennel's classroom. Skip Wilkins was walking out when I arrived. He avoided eye contact.

The room was empty except for Mr. Fennel, who gestured to a chair in the front of the room. He asked me how I was, and I told him I was nervous. "Don't need to be; this is just a conversation." I told Mr. Fennel exactly what I'd seen. He asked a lot of questions, like if I'd actually seen the batteries, and was I certain that it was Jasper. Weren't there other kids at Ripp with blond hair? He lectured me about the dangers of drawing conclusions, even when they seem obvious, and about my responsibility to my peers and our fourth-grade society. It was confusing for me because I had seen the guy with the double As in hand, leaving the scene of the crime through a window. I wasn't expecting to be challenged on this.

That afternoon, Mr. Fennell called me back into his classroom to inform me four out of five judges swore Jasper had never left the playground. I was the only one with a differing version of events. Majority ruled. Jasper was innocent.

A few years later, Jasper was caught cheating on his final math exam at the end of eighth grade. He was dating Kate Renwick at the time and persuaded her to tape a mirror to the bottom of her calculator, which she held on an angle just above her answers. Jasper, seated close behind, could decipher Kate's answers and mark his paper undetected. If Kate hadn't dropped the calculator as she left the study hall, with shards of mirror flying everywhere, their plan might have worked. Neither admitted any wrongdoing, but when both scored an eighty-eight percent with the same four problems incorrect, the school was forced to take action. By then, Principal Porter had moved on to the Spence School on the Upper East Side of Manhattan, and Jasper was expelled.

Jasper was one of the first to start smoking pot at Ripp, and the new principal had little patience for him or his dad as incidents kept occurring. Apparently, he graduated to cocaine at Hotchkiss. After Hotchkiss, the rumor had it he was being kept alive on lithium at the Silver Hill Retreat during spring semester of tenth grade. Dad was the first to know he was back in Bedford after seeing him at an Alcoholics Anonymous meeting. With few options left for schooling, he enrolled in Fox Lane.

The money crowd was small at Fox Lane, but they found each other by their BMWs and still played above the law. It wasn't hard to get drugs on campus grounds, with almost 1,200 students between the high school and the middle school. Jenny had graduated from Fox Lane the prior year and managed to sail through, ensconced in her AP classes and small clubs.

Jasper never got back on track. Alcohol and drugs were his easy escape. I'd see him at parties around town, and he was always completely wasted. When the news broke that his BMW was crushed by an eighteen-wheeler on Interstate 684, I wasn't surprised. Jasper, a kid from Horace Greeley, and another from Fox Lane were killed instantly. There was a girl in the car, too. She lived, but there was little hope that she would walk again because of a severe pelvic fracture and a shattered femur. She had been on the varsity field hockey team. The truck driver was fine but shaken. The BMW was clocking close to 100, going south in the northbound lanes with Jasper behind the wheel. His blood alcohol level was almost three times the legal limit. He was sixteen.

Fox Lane made a huge deal out of it and placed the crumpled blue pile of metal that used to be Jasper's Beamer on the school green until a group of parents insisted the reminder of friends lost was just too painful for the children to see every day.

I ran into Bing a few weeks later during spring break at Fox and Sutherland Books. He was pawing through the rack of Cliff's Notes. I hadn't seen him in almost two years. We started talking about Jasper. The two had been close since kindergarten.

"Yeah, what a waste. Jass could have had everything. His dad wanted him to work for his company; they had money, what a waste. I miss him."

"I didn't really keep in touch with him after he left Ripp," I offered. I didn't want to tell Bing that I had never really liked him. "What happened at Hotchkiss—was it drugs?"

"No, he was definitely doing drugs, but Jass was smart about that stuff and never got caught with anything. He was actually nabbed for stealing. One afternoon, during some school prayer or something, Jass went from classroom to classroom, taking money from the teachers' wallets and purses, which made no sense since his dad would have given him all the money he wanted. The only reason he got caught was because one of the teachers was having an affair with one of the students and was in the Goddamned closet going for it when Jass walked in to lift some cash. Jass thought he had them because he threatened to report the affair if they talked. Turned out the teacher was one of those, I-have-to-do-the-right-thing people and told his wife about the affair, then called the girl's parents and then the principal, vomiting truth everywhere."

"So, what happened then?"

"Dude, it was fucking Hamlet. The teacher gets fired, or

'put on indefinite administrative leave,' the girl freaks out and has a total breakdown, and Jass gets expelled, goes to public school and dies. Shakespearean, man. Moral of the story: go with the lie."

"Sounds like what happened to Carter James, only worse."

Bing looked up, surprised by the name, and then laughed. "That wasn't Carter, that was Jass."

"What do you mean?"

"Jass took that money, but he needed a scapegoat, and Carter was perfect. He told Porter that he left the assembly to take a piss or something, and when he was walking back to the gym, he passed Carter heading towards the classrooms. Porter believed him, and Carter was toast. Jasper was slick like that; he never got caught. I guess he never thought lightning would strike twice. What a waste."

photo by Evelyn Carmichael

22

TRAIN STATION

I made the 7:27 by seconds. As I ran through the closing gate, the stationmaster hollered, "You better run, kid!"

"Always do!" I said flashing a grin. Five nights a week, I'd ride the Metro North trains home to Bedford after my ballet classes. I got to know all of the conductors and stationmasters. There just weren't that many twelve-year-old commuters, and I suppose they kept an eye out for me.

"You're right, kid, you always do. Have a nice night. Hey, where's your dad?" He was letting one more passenger through.

By then I was almost on board. "Went home early today!" I shouted.

"And left you working late, how you like that?" I could hear him laughing as the train pulled away.

The creaking of metal was deafening as the train meandered through the underground labyrinth of steel tracks. I wandered through the train cars, careful to mind the shifting plates as I worked my way to the front. Dad was picking me up in Bedford Hills, and I knew I wanted to be in the seventh car to be right next to the stairs at the Bedford Hills Station.

The cars were dark, which was often the case on the 7:27. It was an older model train, but it also went express to White Plains, which got me home fifteen minutes before the 7:33, making it worth the run on a school night. By 125th Street, when the train reached its maximum speed, the electricity usually kicked in full force, and the lights came on. Commuters would offer a weak cheer as they raised their *New York Post*s and *Wall Street Journals* and started to read the day's news.

Car #7 was not only dark, but also empty. It was Rosh Hashanah, and at least a third of the commuters needed to be home by sunset. I settled into an empty bank of four seats under one of the emergency lights so I could get a start on my algebra homework. There were about a dozen others spread throughout the dark car.

After I propped up my book, the train car door opened, and I looked over, expecting to see Dave coming through to collect tickets. Dave was one of two conductors on the 7:27 who collected tickets. It wasn't Dave who pushed open the heavy door. An enormous blond-haired man with a full beard filled the door frame. He stood there for a few seconds looking at me. We made eye contact, which I regretted immediately. He shuffled to the nearest seat as the train lurched from side to side and sat facing me, his penetrating eyes never losing their focus. I tried to keep my attention on my textbook, but I also wanted to know if he was still looking at me. Twice I looked up to check only to be met by his sallow eyes. The door opened again. It was the conductor this time. "Tickets, please!"

I didn't recognize the conductor. He approached the blond guy asking for his ticket, which he didn't have. With a smoker's growl, he asked for a ticket to White Plains.

"One way?"

"Gimme a round trip."

"You goin' back tonight? Round trip's gotta be same day."

"I said round trip, White Plains."

The conductor collected cash, punched holes in the receipt and returned it to the man. He then placed the "paid" marker on the seat back.

I was relieved because White Plains was the stop after 125th, which meant he would be getting off the train in about thirty minutes and well before Bedford Hills.

The conductor came to me, and I showed him my monthly pass.

"Where's Dave tonight?" I asked. I wanted the blond guy to know that I was a regular on the train.

"Rosh Hashanah."

"Oh, yeah, that's right. Hey, are we getting lights soon?"

"No, not tonight, power's weak. Might get them in #2, but it's the smoker. Sorry about that." He walked on, "Tickets, please!" Before I turned back to my book, I cast another glance at the blond guy. He was still watching me though he'd slumped lower in his seat.

Once the conductor left the car, the man stood up, gathered his coat, and moved one row closer to me. I didn't look up again.

A few minutes later, the conductor came through to head back to his seat in car five. He stopped at the blond guy's seat and told him that if he changed seats again, he would have to take his seat tag with him. Then he turned to me and asked, "You, okay, kid? We got full lights on in #2 if you want to come on back."

"No, I'm good. Need to be at the front for Bedford Hills. Besides, I don't smoke." The conductor laughed, and I thought I heard a low chuckle from the man.

"Okay, kid," said the conductor as he left the car.

I don't know why I didn't move because I was honestly scared to the point I thought I might be trembling. I thought if I got up to move, he would follow. I didn't want to show my fear, so I locked my eyes on the algebraic equations and counted the minutes until we reached White Plains. He smelled my fear. Though I didn't look at him again, I could feel his eyes on me. I heard him moving in his seat, and I could hear his breathing. The dirty blond ring of hair and full beard glowed in the weak light of passing streetlamps.

Near Hartsdale, the train whistle screeched, and I jumped. I heard him laugh again. Another train rushed by us within inches. Only a few more minutes until we reached White Plains.

When we pulled into the station, one or two people got on, and I waited for my silent observer to get off, but he didn't move. As we left the station, I could feel my heart start to pound with fear. Maybe he meant North White Plains, which was the next stop and the same price. He didn't move as the doors opened at North White. A combination of fear and dread consumed me.

I felt sick to my stomach and started to sweat. I thought about heading for car #2, but I would have had to walk past him. I was afraid to walk between the cars where no one could hear you.

I picked up my books, loaded them into my bag and headed to the other end of the car as we pulled into Pleasantville. I timed it perfectly, so I reached the doors just as they opened and then ducked into the seat on the far side of the doors, out of sight of the blond man. Three more stops until Bedford Hills.

I hoped my dad was at the station on time. He wasn't known for his punctuality, especially at night. He'd left the city early for a planning board meeting and inevitably would have stopped at Nino's on the way to the train station to have a drink before collecting me. I started to devise a plan in the event Dad wasn't there. I would just keep walking past the waiting cars and taxis and cross back over the tracks as if I were heading towards the commuter parking lot. My plan didn't go beyond this first move.

When we finally pulled into the Bedford Hills station, there were only a few people left in my car. I looked out the window to see if I could spot Dad's car. Nothing. I didn't look back to where I'd been seated, fearing the stalker was still there watching me. Once on the platform, I took a quick look to the right before heading up the stairs and saw the blond guy heading towards me. My heart was racing. I ran up the stairs two steps at a time like I usually did but tried to keep a calm pace, determined not to show the panic that pulsed through my body.

As I ran down the steps on the other side of track #1, followed by a half dozen commuters, I saw wives in Audis and Land Rovers but no Dad. Usually, I knew a few of my parents' friends, but none was there. The station cleared out quickly at that hour of the night. Cars pulled away from the commuter lot while taxis collected stragglers. I walked past the meeting point and headed up the far steps to cross over to the commuter parking lot as I had planned. He followed. I tried to walk at the same speed but knew I was getting faster. So was he. I could hear him light a cigarette, and soon I could smell it. Once at the top of the stairs, I started to run. I decided to head back down the far side, cross over the tracks again and get into one of the cabs if there were any left. As I ran along the dark side of the tracks, he ran after me. I could see the light of the train disappearing. After an hour spent stalking his prey, the game was now over; time was up.

I broke into a sprint bounding up the stairs, stumbling as I went. As I returned to the meeting area, I heard Dad's voice yell, "Peter!"

"Dad! Let's go, where were you, Dad? You're late!"

"I was at my meeting. Come on, let's get you home. Are you all right?"

"Just go, Dad, please, I want to get home." Once inside the car, I could see the blond guy coming down the stairs. He was breathing hard and looking left and right. He saw me through the car window and watched as we drove away, taking a long heavy drag on his cigarette.

Once on McClain Street, I said, "Dad, someone was following me, and I got scared."

Dad immediately replied, "Peter, was it that tall guy with the beard?"

"Yeah, he sat next to me on the train and watched me the whole trip."

"Goddamned son of a bitch! I saw that guy walking past the meeting area, and he gave me the creeps. If that guy or anybody ever laid a hand on you, Peter, I would fucking kill 'em."

I had never seen my dad so angry. He always said the word "shit," but that was the first time I'd ever heard him say "fuck." The severity of his response legitimized all of my fears, and emotion washed over me as I started to sob. Soon Dad was crying, too.

"Pete, you're not commuting alone anymore. I don't need to be at these meetings, and I won't have you ride the train alone ever again."

"I don't want to tell Mom about this, is that all right, Dad?"

"Don't worry, we won't tell Mom, and it won't happen again, I promise."

photo by Evelyn Carmichael

23

BLACKBALLED

My parents weren't exactly a force in Bedford society, but they were on people's radars. Dad was a Harvard-educated lawyer who served on the all-powerful planning and zoning boards in addition to his responsibilities as county legislator. He was a member of the board of trustees for both the Hammond Museum and the Rippowam-Cisqua School. My mom was the director of social services at Northern Westchester Hospital where many Bedford matrons did their volunteer work. Everyone in town knew of her connection to the Cadbury Chocolate family and probably assumed by the look of our house and our heritage that we had money. We didn't; at least we never seemed to have enough, but a charitable trust created by my great-grandfather ensured we were able to make generous contributions to worthy local causes.

We seemed to be on the social fringe, inspiring interest, curiosity, and caution. Besides the Woods's annual ice cream and rhododendron party, we didn't receive many invitations. I lived closer to the nucleus of Bedford's social world than the rest of my family because of Rippowam. There was a sort of social triptych in Bedford, which included Rippowam-Cisqua, St. Matthew's Church, and the Bedford Golf and Tennis Club, known simply as "the Club." Ripp was my world, and I spent a fair amount of time at St. Matthew's and the Club.

I don't know if it was true or not, but my mom told us the Club did not admit Blacks or Jews and for that reason, we were not joining.

"But we aren't Black or Jewish, so we could join, couldn't we?" I offered.

"Pete, it's discrimination, and that's why we want no part of it. Do you know during World War II, all of the Jews in Denmark were ordered to wear a yellow star?" This seemed a bit extreme in comparison to the unproven discrimination of the Bedford Golf and Tennis Club. Mom's story was apparently just getting started, "The King of Denmark was outraged at this offense against his people and, though he was one hundred percent Christian, he wore a yellow star on his coat to support and help conceal the identities of the Danish Jews until the war was over. Other Danes followed the King's example, and when the Nazis came to collect the Jews, there stood the King and every citizen of Denmark, waiting to greet them with yellow stars sewn onto their lapels. The Nazis couldn't tell who was a Jew and who wasn't. It was like that wonderful story by Dr. Seuss, what was that called?"

"The Star Bellied Sneetches," I mumbled.

"Yes! 'With stars upon thars.' When that pompous group of families is ready to admit all citizens of this town—men, women,

Blacks, Jews, Muslims or Swahili—then we might think about filling out an application, but until then, we are just fine. We stand with the King of Denmark and stand up for the rights of Blacks and Jews!"

"Are there really any Swahili in Bedford, Mom?" I asked.

"Yes."

"Who?"

"I think one of your bus drivers is Swahili, but now you're just being difficult like your father." She was shaking her head. "You are the son of a lawyer if ever there was one."

Membership at the Club remained an issue for our family. One afternoon, after a particularly fierce tennis game with Timmy, his mother, Luly, complimented our skills and reminded us both to sign up for the round-robin. Timmy headed straight for the sign-up sheet on the clubhouse door while I fixed the strings on my racket. Mrs. Carson called, "Peter, you have to sign up for yourself. Timmy can't do it for you, remember? Club rules."

"Thanks, Mrs. Carson, but we aren't members, and only members are allowed to play in the tournament."

Without looking up from her issue of *House and Garden* she responded, "Oh, heavens, I forgot you were not a member. My apologies. Why is it your family chooses not to belong?" Louisa Carson still boasted a southern accent; she was from the Carolinas.

I tried to explain we had our own pool. "But your friends are here, and besides, I see you here all the time. You could play in the round-robin if you were a member, and by the looks of that game you just played, you might just win, right Timmy?" Timmy wasn't listening as he tried to crush a fleeing ant with his tennis ball.

My parents would get questions too but seemed to brush them off more easily. Honestly, my mom had no interest in sitting by a pool or playing tennis with Luly Carson. She preferred to focus on social change rather than social status.

My dad's clear defense of a woman's right to choose in his political campaigns had made him some enemies in Bedford, but they were unseen enemies behind closed doors who worked in the shadows. It was an era of change, and when Jane Canfield, wife of Cass Canfield, the president of Harper and Row Publishing, made a very public showing of her support for R. Bradlee Boal in the '78 primary, his candidacy took a turn towards victory. My dad and mom were respected and admired, but not by all.

Tripper Harley was a close friend. His daughter Hope was in my class at Ripp and had professed her undying love for me in kindergarten. Wallace Harley was a good friend of my mom's. The Harleys owned a whole pack of Bassett hounds, eighteen in all, and would lead spirited hunts across Sunnyfield Farm on autumn weekends. Tripp would lead the charge on horseback, sporting his plaid blazer and a hunting horn. Wallace would reassure with knowing wink, "Don't worry, Lyndall, neither Tripp nor the hounds ever catch anything, but the excitement and exercise are unparalleled. I think the rabbit and the fox are having the last laugh!"

Tripp was also head of the nominating committee at the Club and was tasked with bringing in new members each year as the old guard expired or relocated to Palm Beach. One evening, Tripp called my dad to ask if we'd consider applying.

After the pleasantries, Dad cleared his throat. "Lyndall and I have some concerns that the Club may have some official or unofficial discrimination policies against minorities. Is this the case?"

I couldn't hear Tripp's lengthy response, but Dad said, "We suspected that wasn't the case, but we wanted to know for sure. Of course, if they choose Rockrimmon over the Club, that's another matter. Remember when those real estate agents were steering certain buyers away from Bedford? What a mess. It ended up in county court. Can you imagine refusing to show qualified buyers homes in this town—based on what? Against everything we believe in, isn't it?"

After a measured response that I couldn't hear, Dad said, "Tripp, thank you for the call. We're flattered by the invitation. Let me talk it over with Lyndall and the kids and get right back to you."

We talked about Tripp's offer at dinner that night. Getting a call from the nominating committee was a virtual guarantee of membership, and I was elated.

"Dad, I can walk there after school, and I'll get so good at tennis. All my friends are there, and they have the best hot dogs!"

Jenny was not interested. No one from Fox Lane went to the Club, and a few of the mean girls she had dealt with in third grade before transferring schools were a constant presence. "I'm not going."

Dad offered a tally, "That's one for, one against. Lyndall, looks like you have the swing vote." Jenny rolled her eyes as she stabbed peas on her plate.

"I am so pleased they have changed that wretched admissions policy. We should probably support them just for changing their ways. I suppose we could join. Can we afford it? If I could ever find time for lunch, I would meet Wallace there."

Dad chimed in, "And I haven't played enough golf lately, this might be my chance. Do you think we'll get a discount for our disgruntled daughter if she never shows up?" I laughed.

"Brad!" Jenny left the table crying and Mom followed, turning back to glare at Dad.

Dad gave me a wink, "I was just trying to lighten the mood. Listen, I'll call Tripp. This will be fun."

Every day after our application was submitted, I asked my parents if we were members yet. Mom told me we had to wait until the membership council met and voted; soon after that meeting, we would hear back from Mr. Harley.

It was close to two weeks later when Tripp showed up at our door. I heard the knock and ran to answer it, hoping he might give me the good news first. Instead, he asked for a moment alone with my parents. Tripp was all about formality, and I suspected speaking to the parents first met Club protocol.

The three of them retreated to the living room. Dad offered Tripp a drink, which he refused, but fixed one for himself. Jenny and I had learned over the years that sitting at the top of the front stairs offered a perfect perch for eavesdropping in the living room. I nestled in to hear what I could.

"You see, Brad and Lyndall, the Club has a system called Blackball."

"Oh, my," my mother interjected, "wasn't that how decisions about landownership happened in the South during the Jim Crow era?"

"Lyndall, I don't know about that, but this has been the way Club leadership has voted for decades, and the members are satisfied with the process. No one has to stick his neck out to influence a decision. Objections are anonymous and, in turn, approval is unanimous. When we vote on anything, members of the governor's committee are given a black ball and a white ball. Each voting member puts one ball in his right hand and one in his left. I should say his or hers, I keep forgetting Luly's a member of the committee now. Anyway, both balls are dropped simultaneously in two covered containers. The right hand holds the vote, and the left the other ball. You must understand once we nominate a prospective member, we almost always have a unanimous acceptance, but in your case, one black ball was in with eight white balls. When we have one or more black balls, we repeat the instructions for voting and repeat the process. We had the same results the second time around. Lyndall and Brad, I'm so sorry to put you through this, but the committee has rejected your application to join the Club."

There was an extended silence, which I knew Mom would fill. Instead, she rose and walked to the door to close it.

I tiptoed down the stairs to stand motionless next to the door to hear what ensued.

"I'm not supposed to do this, but I spoke with some of the other members of the committee, and we would like to reintroduce you as a nominee with letters of recommendation. We rushed the first one through thinking you were a shoo-in, but we just need more opportunity to educate this committee about where you stand on certain issues. I think a letter from Cass Canfield or Natalie Hays Hammond would make a real difference, and Brad, I think something about your excellent work on behalf of all residents of Bedford regardless of income or religious preference would also help make your case."

"This is about abortion rights, isn't it, Tripp?" Mom said. "I don't believe it. This will haunt us to our graves in this town,

Brad. You cannot even swing a golf club with these people. Unbelievable!"

"Now, Lyndall, the Club and this town are changing and, in my opinion, for the better," Tripp said. "But there are still a few members of the old guard who need a little time. Pulling back on some of the issues some of the time may be the best course in the long run."

"Tripp, honestly, this is no reflection on you, but Lyndall and I are not only rejected by the committee, we are also unsure of whether or not we want to be a part of the Club. We were really doing this for Peter. I think we leave this where it is. I trust this will not affect our friendship with you or Wallace. Now, if you'll forgive us, I think we want some time alone. Can I show you out?"

At the door Tripp made another pitch to my dad for re-nomination, but Dad wouldn't hear of it. I could hear a loss of patience in his tone. As Tripp headed down the stone steps, Dad closed the door tightly. I watched from my bed as the lights of Tripp's Mercedes pulled out of our driveway and headed off into the black night.

24

A CHILL IN THE AIR

On my train rides home with my dad, if I finished my home-work, I was rewarded with sections of *The New York Times*. It was a conscious nod to my impending adulthood, and I savored the privilege. On a spring night in 1979, I looked at the front page in disbelief. On the top of the page, I saw the headline, "Four Murdered in Two Estates in Bedford Hills." As the train careened through tunnels with a deafening whistle, I read the detailed account in horror. At two homes on Succabone Road and Bisbee Lane, four individuals had been shot execution-style in the back of the head after being bound and pummeled. One victim was twenty-one years old. Another was his nanny.

"Dad, Succabone is where the clocktower is, right? Isn't that where we walk to meet the Harleys for fox hunting?"

"That's correct, Pete. It's a little more than a mile from our house. Why do you ask? You look like you've seen a ghost."

I turned the paper around to show him the headline.

He took a moment to scan the article, placed his drink on the floor, and turned his attention to me, immediately understanding what was going through my mind. "Pete, we're safe in our house. We have Rex and Henry. They are good watchdogs, and I'm there to make sure you and all of us are safe … Jesus, this is shocking." He picked the cup full of bourbon up off the floor and took a swig. "The police are on this and right now—fifty of them. Bedford is probably one of the safest places to be. We don't need to tell your mother or sister about this, right? Jesus Christ, I know Croydon Sperry. He was the father of the boy. You okay?"

I nodded, but I wasn't.

When we walked in the back door, Jenny had already gone to bed. Mom looked worried. We knew she had heard the news.

"Yes, the police came by earlier. They're conducting a door-to-door search of all homes within a two-mile radius of the Sperry and Frankel estates." She could see I was rattled. She put her hands on my shoulders, "I'm scared too."

"I thought of Mrs. Hattie," I offered.

"I know, Pete, I thought of her too. She's safe in her apartment in Mount Vernon with plenty of locks on her door and Butch across the hall. She's probably watching the Mets game. I can give her a call tomorrow. She may not know about this, and I won't tell her. If Mrs. Hattie were here though, she would remind you it's time for you to go to bed. Homework all done?"

In the morning, I had forgotten about the murders as we pushed through the usual somewhat frantic morning routine trying to get to Rippowam on time. It wasn't until first recess that I was confronted with the news again. As I exited the library onto the courtyard, I could see a group of teachers huddled in quiet conversation. Their intensity gave them away. On the far side of the lawn, my friends were in a similar grouping. As I approached, I could hear Bing leading the conversation. The group leaned in.

"She was like a hundred years old. She raised the mother and the kids, and here's the sad part; a few years ago, she retired with the full pension and all the glory. She headed home to Ireland, and guess what. She got lonely and came back. Welcomed with open arms and a .32 caliber to the back of the head." Bing pointed his fingers at Beau's neck, but Sariah pushed his arm down.

"Jesus, Bing, this is scary. Stop making light of this. We're not safe anymore." Kate trembled as she spoke.

Jasper weighed in as he kicked the ground, "My dad knows Sperry and talked to him last night. Sperry and his wife were in Manhattan at a benefit for Cassy's school. They had no idea. Chris tried to fight 'em. It's totally tragic. Sperry thinks it's Rastafarians 'cus his older son's Beamer was stolen and then found near a Rasta hangout in Brooklyn."

An angry voice pierced the conversation. "Why do white people always think it was a Black person who committed the crime?" Lia Rowland was one of two Black kids in our grade.

Bing looked Lia in the eye, "Maybe because it's always Black people who commit the crimes, Lia." All eyes went back to Lia.

Lia started yelling, "That is racist, Bing Spofford. Shut the fuck up." Jasper prepared to defend his friend but didn't get a word out. "You too, Jasper. It is not always Black people. There is so much crime, fraud, sex abuse and discrimination that happens every day in this country, and right here in this town too, and it's done by white people. They just get off because the system is rigged for white folks and against Black people. Do you have any idea what happens to me when I walk into Erin Pritchard's to shop for a dress?"

Jasper responded, "Yeah, no Lia, I don't. Could you chill the fuck out?"

Still yelling, "They follow me and they whisper to each other, and then they suggest I try the mall in Mount Kisco. You don't know what it's like, Jasper Lang, and I suspect you never will in your mansion and your country club and on your fucking yacht." Lia was shaking by now. We were all a little stunned.

Jasper continued but we wished he wouldn't. "So, Sperry might be wrong about the Rastas, but the Frankels were Jews, and we all know Blacks hate Jews, right? So that makes it even more likely Black guys did this. Are you going to tell me Blacks don't hate Jews, Lia?"

Lia paused in disbelief. "No, because I'm not even going to talk to you anymore, Jasper Lang, but I am telling Parkman you are prejudiced and acting like a total prick." With a decisive turn, Lia left the circle. We watched silently as her long legs strode with purpose across the field towards the huddle of teachers.

When she was well out of earshot, Bing spoke. "What a bitch. So, Parkman's going to say all the right things about not standing for racist comments and the need for real consequences and all that fucking shit, and then when Lia and her parents leave his office, he's going to remember that the library is now called the Laurence Lang Library, and nothing's gonna change. Besides, it probably was the Rastas." He looked around for a laugh but there was none.

Tina spoke next, "I wish you could hear yourself, Bing. And you too, Jasper. Show a little fucking compassion. It's not easy for Lia or her family. I don't want to talk about this anymore." She was starting to cry. Hammy moved towards her to put his arm around her. The bell rang, summoning us back to class.

That night the heated dialogue on the playground repeated again and again in my sleeplessness. Lia's raw hurt, the utter callousness from Jasper and Bing, and the pathetic inaction from the rest of us haunted me for hours. A systemic failure laid bare in a corner of the schoolyard.

At home, there was no further discussion about the murders or whether or not anyone was caught. My parents seemed to ignore the threat and returned to normal with a steely resolve. I asked my mom if we had started locking our doors at night. Turns out we had no lock on the kitchen door or on the back door, so our house was open to anyone at any time. I did not sleep well. When Rex barked at night, I remained awake and wary. The safety of childhood and of home were interrupted, and I was changed. Bedford was changed.

I scoured *The New York Times* for several days. Six articles appeared over the course of the next few weeks. Details of the lives of Dr. Charles Frankel, Helen Beatrice Lehman Frankel, Christopher Sperry and Nellie McCormick filled the front page and the obituaries.

On July 20th, another article appeared on the front page of the *Times*. It detailed a hearing where Junius Gray and Jimmie Lee Allen, two incarcerated Black men, were accused of committing the brutal murders of four individuals in the town of Bedford Hills. Jimmie Lee Allen asked the judge why he didn't have a lawyer present. Weeks later, they were found guilty by an all-white jury and the case was closed.

The District Attorney spoke at a news conference after the hearing. "We are satisfied ... they broke into two homes, committed robberies and killed the victims. It's as simple as that."

Nanny, Grampy and five cousins at Little Alum *(image courtesy of the author)*

25

GRAMPY

Grampy always seemed so old. Even in the pictures from his forties, he looked old. Granted, he had already lost his hair by then and wore impossibly thick gold-rimmed eyeglasses. He dressed in a dull gray three-piece suit every day, even after retirement from his job as the chief financial officer of the American Optical Company. He puttered, too, like a man twice his age. I guess he got an early start in life, thanks to the example of his eldest brother, Arthur, who found his way out of the poverty-stricken rural parts of West Virginia and into the halls of Harvard. Arthur paid his younger brother Eben's tuition to Harvard, and Eben paid for Howard's and on down the line through all six brothers. Poor Aunt Augusta was last in line and the only girl. Harvard didn't admit women back then. Radcliffe or Wellesley were the only options for Gussie, and the brothers didn't see much point in an education for their sister, so she chose Wellesley and footed the bill herself.

Grampy entered Harvard at 16 and graduated at 19 to attend the Massachusetts Institute of Technology, with Arthur and Eben once again helping to pay his way. He met Thane Lee, married and had two sons, Howard and Richard. Neither son liked his given first name, preferring their middle names; Bruce and Bradlee. Grampy, known to most of the world as Howard Waller Boal, was forty-four years old when Bradlee was born.

Howard and Thane chose the small Massachusetts town of Brimfield as their primary residence and the ideal place to start a family. The house was solidly middle class with two stories, four bedrooms, a proper dining room, a study full of all the right books for a Harvard grad, a welcoming hearth, plenty of sensible furniture and oriental carpets, all tucked onto a small lot on Elm Street, which was within walking distance from the American Optical Headquarters and the Elks Lodge. There were five houses in a row that looked remarkably similar. The Boal residence was smack in the middle.

Only twenty minutes to the west, on the shore of Little Alum Lake, was the Boal's summer house, known as the Camp. Despite not having heat, the Camp came pretty close to perfection. We visited every summer. Jenny and I loved it; Mom did not, deeming the house "filthy." Mom slept in the tiny guest room off of the kitchen next to the house's only bathroom. In the morning she would tell us all about the sounds Grampy made on his midnight run to the bathroom. "It was like a pipe burst!"

Little Alum Lake was big enough for sailing, and the family had two boats, a small sunfish and a smaller sailfish. Howard also had a rowboat known as Grampy's ark. When Dad was a kid, young boys had to meet two challenges as part of their passage to manhood. The first, to be completed on a boy's tenth birthday, consisted of swimming across the lake. A three-mile swim circling the lake was required for the twelve-year-olds. The exhausted swimmer was trailed by a pack of cheering boys bobbing along in Grampy's ark. Dad and Bruce both succeeded.

Aside from happy summers, I'm guessing there wasn't much love or affection in the Boal house. Dad left for Exeter at thirteen.

A few years later, Thane died, which was difficult for Howard and Bruce and devastating for young Bradlee. Howard withheld the news thinking it would spare his young sons the pain of cancer's quick claim on their mother. But Christmas break was grim, with both boys in shock and a mother so weakened she was unable to love, care or communicate. Bradlee's excessive drinking started then and didn't stop. After Grampy buried Thane, he met Margaret and remarried. Margaret was a librarian and looked the part, sporting thick glasses with catlike tips and a silver safety chain. She wore plain beige dresses. Her thick gray hair was cropped mid-forehead, which would have been a difficult length for any woman and really did nothing for Margaret.

We called her Nanny. She was nice enough to her step-grandchildren but always seemed to recede, as if believing that without the blood connection, she really couldn't claim the true bond of a grandmother to her grandchildren. She had the oddest habit of saying "hmm" constantly. The more nervous she was, the more it would happen, making lulls in the conversation—of which there were many during our visits—a virtual cacophony of "hmms." At first, I would try to react to them by repeating what I thought she had missed, but Nanny would curtly let me know that she had heard what had been said.

One summer evening after a long day of picking apples

at Cheeney's orchard and touring the eternally dusty Old Sturbridge Village, we sat under the towering pines while Grampy began the ritual of grilling his famous fried chicken. The adults were moving through various cocktails at a rapid clip, and the kids were busy munching on apple slices.

The grilling of the chicken was especially tense during drought years. Despite Grampy's eyeglasses thickening each year, his vision continued to worsen and, unable to properly measure anything, Grampy erred on the side of excess. The charcoal was doused with enough lighter fluid to cause an inferno. Grampy hurled a long-tipped match at the charcoal as protestations rose from all around. The first two or three matches missed the target and hit the dry carpet of needles around the base of the barbeque. Dad jumped up to stomp out the random flames, spilling bourbon as he went.

"Brad, sit down!" Now my mother was up doing the same.

"Hmm .... hmm."

"She told Dad to sit down." I'm in on the action too. Apple slices could wait.

"Yes, I heard her ... hmm." Nanny was trying to look at the lake.

Mom, back in her chair, just covered her face with both hands.

Voosh! Up the flames would shoot, stretching perilously towards the drooping red needles of the pines. Above the crackle could be heard, "hmm, hmm ... hmm."

Twenty minutes later, severely over-spiced chicken was served. By then, Dad was sloshed, Mom was livid, and Jenny had started gagging. We left the next day, despite plans to stay the week.

After Nanny died, we stopped making the trek to see Grampy, preferring to have him come to Bedford. He seemed to be eternally aging and dying and yet living on through it all. Six of his seven siblings lived past the age of ninety, and Grampy was no exception, pushing on until ninety-five. He had already celebrated two twenty-fifth wedding anniversaries, and we were starting to wonder if there might be a third in his future.

On one of his final visits to Bedford, Mom decided Grampy needed a walk. A walk was the answer for everything in our family and might just be the cure for a dull visit from the father-in-law. Out they went down Guard Hill Road towards the golf course. Dear Grampy was quite stooped by then and really could only focus those huge lenses towards the ground. Looking ahead involved reclining the small of his back to raise his chin. Unfortunately, this tipped the scale, and Grampy would totter backwards in fright. Chairs were really the best course for Grampy, but Lyndall was strong-willed, and he needed a walk. At first, they shuffled side by side, Mom running out of comments about the neighborhood since the pace was now tortuously slow. Then Mom's arm went around Grampy's shoulders as he started to look down the road. Soon Mom was behind him, leveraging the upper back to prevent a crash. The pace dwindled, Grampy was scared and breathing hard, and my mother was at a loss.

"Grampy, this was not a good idea. I'm so sorry."

"No, it's my fault. I can make it. How far do we have to go?" He shuffled a few more steps but the motor was clearly dying.

"We don't have to go anywhere Grampy. Let's just go home."

"I don't think I can go any further. Can we just sit down here?"

"Oh, Grampy, we can't sit on the side of the road, you'll just have to walk home with me. Come on, we've made it this far, we can make it home." They were only as far as Mr. Hockley's house, which was a few hundred yards from the western edge of our property.

"If I can't sit, then I'll just have to stand, but I am not walking another step."

Grampy's voice trembled.

Then he craned his neck, moved his chin up and looked my mother right in the eye to let her know that she may have been a strong-willed, independent woman of the 1970s, but he was not moving another inch. He glared, she understood, and then back he went like a redwood in a three-piece suit, crashing down in the leaves onto his bottom.

"Oh, Grampy! This is a terrible mistake, and it's all my fault." She pulled him back onto his feet. "Stand here and wrap your arms around this tree and keep looking at your shoes. I'll run home and get the car."

Grampy, quite rattled by then, obeyed orders and gripped the maple, which was older and more stable than he, as he focused on his shoelaces. Like a Tai Chi master, he held this pose for close to ten minutes as cars trundled by and a nearby dog barked. Soon he was flopped into the Volvo and returned to the living room chair with an extra shot of gin.

My dad died in 1986, a year before Grampy. Bruce and I debated whether or not to tell Grampy since he was deep in the vacuum hole of dementia and unlikely to comprehend even the news of the death of his child. Bruce felt he owed it to his dad to inform him, and we set off to the Elmhurst Home for the Elderly to break the sad news.

As we passed scores of mumbling and disoriented denizens in musty corridors, I realized this was going to be a tough visit. We came to Grampy's shared quarters. The smell of aging flesh and soft foods wafted through the stale air. Bruce had called ahead to request that Mr. Philbert, Grampy's bunkie this month, be relocated for our visit. I entered first. Grampy looked up with the wide eyes of a child. The three-piece suit was long gone, replaced by a stained white tee that revealed Grampy's birdlike frame. He greeted me with startling enthusiasm, "I know you! I do." This surprised me because we weren't especially close.

"Hi, Grampy, it's Peter, I'm so glad to see you." Sort of a white lie. I kissed his cheek, which was discolored and chapped.

"Yes, I remember, you and I, not long ago, we rode in the cavalry together." I didn't answer, but I think my head started shaking from side to side. He re-confirmed, "We did! The Great War. I remember." Now, I had studied World War I in history class, and there was no mention of the cavalry. Who knew?

I didn't stay long. This was not the Grampy I remembered, and he was miffed by my inability to remember my horse's name. Bruce stayed in the room to tell him about Brad.

Ten minutes later, Bruce emerged blinking back tears unsuccessfully.

"Did he understand?" I asked.

"Yes and no. He thought my son had died, and he was very sorry for me. He didn't remember having a second son."

26

SILVER HILL

Nanny died. There was nothing particularly tragic about her death. Her life had been long and pleasant, or at least without incident. She was working as a librarian in Worcester, when she met Grampy who was not only quite literate but also quite lonely since the untimely passing of his first wife, Thane, from pancreatic cancer a few months before he wandered into the Worcester Library. Margaret and Howard moved quickly from books to vows and enjoyed a good twenty-nine years of marriage. I couldn't attend her funeral because of my eighth-grade midterms, but the rest of the family traveled to central Massachusetts to pay their respects while I stayed home with Henry and Joe.

Rooms were booked at the Publick House Historic Inn and Lodge in Old Sturbridge Village for most of the family, but Dad and Bruce decided to stay in the house on Elm Street with Grampy. Dad spent the night in his boyhood bed at the top of the worn wooden stairs with Bruce across the hall. Haunted by the death of his mother decades prior, Dad paced, drank, obsessively smoothed his thinning hair, bit his short nails, and woke Bruce three times, finally sleeping on the floor, huddled like a fetus outside the room his mother had slept in thirty years before.

Bruce worried about the stress his brother was adding to their father's already fragile state, so Dad moved to the Publick House the following night, sharing Mom's room. Unable to sleep again, he headed for Ebenezer's Tavern adjacent to the hotel lobby. He was the last to leave the lounge, with a guilty bartender helping him out the door and watching him as he stumbled along the corridor and up a few menacing steps to find his room. He woke before dawn in a panic about a fire in the hotel. There was no fire, but he made Mom get up, banged on all the doors, and forced both his family and complete strangers to evacuate into the cold night. Mom was livid, Jenny was mortified, and Bruce decided Dad needed professional help.

A week later, Dad said goodbye to Jenny and me in the kitchen. We promised to visit him. After two stilted hugs, he hoisted a duffle bag onto his shoulder, rubbed Henry under the chin and walked out the door to Mom, who was waiting in the Volvo. She drove him to Silver Hill, a highly respected treatment center for alcoholics in nearby New Canaan, Connecticut for a seven-week inpatient stay.

That evening we gathered in Jenny's room, Mom slumped in the old rocker in robe and slippers. Jenny and I sat on the bed. Mom seemed exhausted, but we wanted to know how everything went, what Dad's room was like and when we could see him. As she sipped her gin and orange juice, Mom told us about the day.

During the check-in process, Dad had been reluctant but

cooperative, realizing there was really no other path forward. He pushed through forms and his welcome interview. Mom waited in the reception area, having taken the entire day off from work. Once forms and interviews were completed, they followed a young man named Hector to Dad's plush third-floor room in the grand white mansion that looked very similar to our grand white mansion. Mom described Hector as "all business with a clipboard and big biceps." He was a member of the Silver Hill care team and would see Dad through his entire stay and his re-assimilation period.

"Wait, is Hector coming home with Dad?" Jenny asked.

"No, love, if Dad makes it though this part of his recovery successfully, he can return home, and Hector will call or visit periodically to make sure he's getting back on track with his life. He was very helpful to your dad, but he was strict, too. They have to be. That's what your father needs. I don't think I was strict enough."

She went on to describe the day. Hector asked Dad to empty his duffle and lay all of his possessions on the bed. He sifted through Dad's clothes, checking pockets and reaching into shoes and socks to see if there was any hidden stash. All of this made Mom uncomfortable, so she looked out the window until she saw someone she knew from Swarthmore, which made her even more uncomfortable. Hector then gave permission for Dad to place all of his clothes in drawers. Mom helped.

"You know your father could never fold."

Next came the toiletries. Toothbrush, Crest, comb, athlete's foot spray, Old Spice, shaving cream, aftershave, toenail clippers, razor and Vick's Vaporub were laid out on the bed.

Mom recounted the conversation between Dad and Hector.

"'Sorry, Mr. Boal … ' Hector couldn't remember your father's name, so he glanced at his clipboard then said, '… Richard,' I know this makes your father angry, and I feared for what was next. Then Hector said, 'We'll need to remove the aftershave and the Vick's. Both contain alcohol which is not permitted on the premises for the benefit of our patients and to align with your treatment plan.' I looked at your father, knowing this conversation was going from bad to worse.

"After a pause, Dad cleared his throat and spoke. 'First of all, Hector, it's Brad. Calling me by my name aligns much better with my treatment plan.' Even in times like these, your father's sense of humor is absolutely barbed.

"Dad had been patient during a very long morning check-in process and was probably starting to yearn for his lunchtime martini. He was clearly annoyed when he responded, saying, 'You can take the aftershave, but I need the Vick's for my allergies.' Of course, we all know Dad doesn't have allergies.

"Now, Hector made it very clear he had dealt with clever alcoholics before, saying, 'My apologies, Brad. The form says your name is Richard, but it also notes that you prefer Bradlee, but I will call you Brad. Our pharmaceutical department will find you a replacement for the Vick's that can help with your allergies …'

"Just then, Brad lunged for the Vick's, and with equal speed, Hector grabbed your father's clenched fist and held on tight. While their hands trembled, Hector calmly explained if a patient is unable to follow the house rules, he or she needs to leave the facility. He reminded your father he would be in clear violation of the consent form he had just signed during the welcome interview. A few feeble and embarrassing moments followed with Dad tussling with Hector. They seemed equally matched in determination but not in strength. I'm afraid I dissolved into tears. Hector left with the Vick's, and I left without a goodbye. Honestly, it was horrible." Mom was visibly upset, and Jenny and I left the bed to surround her with embraces.

Patients at Silver Hill cannot receive visitors for the first twenty-one days of their treatment period. On the twenty-second day, Mom visited. She returned every Wednesday and every weekend. She was filled with optimism for Dad, for their marriage and for our family. Jenny and I looked forward to our visit, but as the designated weekend approached, Mom thought it might not be a good idea. The following weekend, she also advised against it. Dad was not doing well, consumed with anger and resentment towards everyone, and especially his family, whom he blamed for putting him through this painful period. Mom warned us we would find a very different dad when he returned home.

After a month without Dad, we started to notice how easy life was at home and how devoid of stress, confrontation and worry we all were. There was laughter at the dinner table, and we didn't wonder whether or not we should have friends over. We joined Mom in the living room by the fire each night. Jenny pulled out our weighty volume of works by William Shakespeare and divided up parts for *Two Gentlemen of Verona*. We read for hours. Soon, we didn't think about Dad, and we didn't ask to visit him. In the end, we never did.

We let go of Dad. I was thirteen, but I knew, as we all did, Dad was a crippling weight for us to carry, like an albatross. During his time at Silver Hill, we felt the weight lifted. When the phone rang, we didn't expect the police to be calling about a crash Dad had caused on route 172. We didn't dread the nights, wondering if Dad could make it up the stairs on his own or if another glass would be broken. We exhaled, and with the release, we knew not only that we were fine, but that life was easier without him.

We also felt guilty for finding relief. I know each of us harbored hope for Dad, whom we genuinely loved and pulled for. But we were also not surprised when white wine was surreptitiously poured in the pantry a few weeks after his return, and calls from his sponsor were ignored, and the disease marched back into his life and all of our lives, taking hope and trampling on it on the way in. He wasn't the one who was changed during his seven-week absence; we were. I stopped needing a father to fill a void or offer counsel or give love. He was gone, and I knew I could move on without him—we all could. It was survival.

After his seven-week stay at Silver Hill was successfully completed, the Volvo rolled back into the driveway with Mom at the wheel. Dad was home. He graduated to outpatient care with a hefty dose of required activities and trust. He wasn't yet allowed to return to the law firm, and travel for International Planned Parenthood Federation was off the table. He could live at home, but his days and nights were filled with mandatory check-ins with his sponsor, journal entries, exercise and attendance at Alcoholics Anonymous meetings. He seemed to forget the "anonymous" part, reporting with some surprise how many acquaintances from Bedford were in meetings. He let us know Anna Harley from Jenny's tenth-grade class was a regular.

On his first day back, I was the last to see him, arriving home just after nine o'clock from the Mount Kisco train station in a cab. Both nervous and excited to see Dad after almost two months, I found him in the living room by the fire with Berlioz playing on the record player. Henry sat nearby while the fire warmed the room. At first, he didn't see me, so I stood still in the doorway and looked at him. His glasses were on as he studied *The Wall Street Journal.* Everything appeared as it had been two months ago, but there were small differences. A mug full of tea sat on a coaster to his right. He chewed on the stick of a lollipop. He was thinner; he looked gaunt and older than I remembered.

"Pete!" He was up and heading towards me. "How I missed you, kid. You're taller!"

We hugged, with the newspaper crumpling between us. "I missed you too, Dad. I'm sorry we didn't come visit. Between Ripp and ballet, there's been so much going on. You look good. You lost weight. How are you? How was it?"

"It was rough, and it was good, I guess. I want to hear everything about school and about ballet."

"I'm sorry we didn't come see you," I said again.

"Yeah, I'm sorry too, Pete. Here, sit down with me for a minute." I sat on the floor next to Henry. "One of the things we talked about a lot at Silver Hill is being true to ourselves and leading with honesty, which can be the rough part. I'm going to be honest with you now; it hurt when you and your sister never showed up to see me. I've struggled a lot over the past two months, and you two were my strengths, but I didn't get the strength I needed from either of you."

I was looking at Henry, and I started to cry. "Mom told us to protect ourselves and focus on what we needed to do to stay on track. I'm sorry. It felt wrong, but I think we needed a break too … from you."

"From me?"

"I guess. From you drinking so much all the time."

"Pete, that hurts to hear." There was a silence filled only by crackling wood and Berlioz. "I wasn't drinking when I was there, and I was really struggling with that. Damn it, Pete, I was only twenty-five minutes away." He picked up the mug, then put it back down after a sip. His tone changed, "Listen, this is a new day for us, and your dad doesn't drink anymore. I won't ever again, I promise. Do you hear me?" I nodded. "I promise. I still have work to do, and I'm going to need help, your help, but I'm on a better path, and you and I and Jenny and your mother get to walk this new path together." I looked up at him and smiled through tears.

The phone rang. Mom's voice called from the kitchen, "Brad, it's Hector, do you want to take it?"

"Yeah, thanks, I'll get it." He turned to me. "My care team knows tonight is a big night in my recovery process, and this is a required check-in. I've got to take this." Our conversation was over.

In the end, unlike the late-in-life dementia that erased his elderly father's memory of his son and so much more, my dad was gone for almost everyone who knew him well before his last day. As the years passed, my relationship with him became estranged, his relationship with Jenny was strained, and Mom opted for divorce after decades of frustration. His law firm was still tolerant, but the major accounts had moved on. Even Bruce, who had attempted this unsuccessful intervention, had largely turned his back on his brother. He had died for many long before his heart stopped.

27

IMAGINE

Every now and then or perhaps quite often in the history of New York City, lives are defined by real estate. I know two people who didn't know each other that well, but they married and later divorced for the sole purpose of transferring a lease. A man wouldn't leave his rent-controlled apartment even though it tied him to a life he no longer wanted to live. A family of six squeezed four kids into their tiny one bedroom, with parents on the Murphy bed in the living room, because they had a garden.

My New York real estate story began with a promotion that created a timing issue with my education and resulted in a new apartment and a new life.

Not long after Dad returned from Silver Hill, he broached the subject of my schedule conflict. "Your mother tells me they're promoting you to the Advanced Men's class at SAB. She says you'll be the youngest one in the class, is that true?"

"Yes, all true. They tried to move me up last year, but I

couldn't go because of Rippowam. Advanced starts at twelve-thirty, and the earliest I could leave Ripp is two forty-five. I can't wait another year. We have to figure this out. I might need to move into the city."

"At fourteen? Surely this can wait."

"I'll be fifteen in October. Ballet careers start young. This is what I want, Dad. More than anything. And I'm good at it, I promise."

"Peter, listen, I know you're good. I've seen you dance, and that school won't stop talking about your potential, but do you know what dancers make for a living? Seriously, you have to consider this when you are making a life-altering decision. The average salary for a ballet dancer in one of the top U.S. companies is about $25,000 a year. That's if you make it. Jobs are scarce. That's less than my secretary makes and more in line with what Mrs. Wilson is making." Someone had been doing his research. "Do you know how long those careers last? And then, where are you? You don't have a degree, you don't have a college education, you can't afford a family, a home, a vacation, or a car. Do you really know what you're getting into?"

"Dad, I'm good. I'll make it. I promise I will." My impassioned plea was having an effect on him, and I suspect he already knew there was no alternative path for me.

He wasn't done. The trial lawyer was uncovering a new angle. "Besides, you're an outstanding student with a shot at a good school like Harvard. Your whole family on my side attended—Bruce, Grampy, and all of my uncles, which makes you a legacy applicant, but you don't even need the edge. Do you know what graduates from Harvard are making five years after graduation?" A brief pause.

"Let me guess, more than your average ballet dancer?"

"Yes. In fact, they are making six-figure salaries. Do you know how many ballet dancers are making six-figure salaries? One, and his name is Mikhail Baryshnikov. Okay, maybe two if you count Rudolf Nureyev. I know you're good. I know you have a shot. I know you love this, Pete, but I want you to be practical and sensible. This is a crucial moment for you." He could see he had lost.

He walked closer and looked directly at me. "Can you promise me you're good enough to earn a respectable salary and not just follow a fool's passion? If you can, I'll support you in this decision, and I'll help you, but you may be choosing the harder path in life."

"There's no other path for me, Dad, and I just may be needing an apartment in New York City."

Dad heard about a sublet at 10 West 74th Street, just off Central Park West. This was prime New York real estate, steps from the San Remo, the Beresford and the Dakota. Steps from the homes of Dustin Hoffman, Mia Farrow, Mary Tyler Moore, Lauren Bacall, Barbra Streisand and John Lennon. Knowing his son was headed into ninth grade at the Professional Children's School (PCS) fourteen blocks south, Dad grabbed the deal for $495 a month. With academic classes starting at eight-fifteen or nine each morning, and ballet classes ending at seven at night, I found myself living alone in my desirable sublet on West 74th.

I immediately recast myself as a New Yorker. I had the apartment, the plan, the purpose. I bought a Walkman and a pair of red Converse high tops and strode down Columbus each morning like I belonged. A few weeks after my residency was established, I crossed West 60th to get to PCS before the bell rang. A boy about my age appeared before me. He stopped me to ask a question while another boy grabbed my arm from behind, bent it behind my back and slammed my torso over the hood of a parked car. The first boy took my wallet, removed the cash and started running, dropping the wallet as the two bolted down the block. A cab screeched to a halt, and the driver took off on foot after the boy with the cash, tackling him to the ground and holding him until the money was surrendered. He then shoved the perpetrator, who ran off. The hero cabbie scooped up my wallet, stuffed the cash inside and tossed it to me. I caught it and stood still in disbelief.

The cabbie walked back to his car, which was blocking traffic, and turned to me and shouted, "You could fuckin' thank me, kid, you ungrateful asshole!"

"Um, thank you," I said. For some reason, I waved to him. Off he went. Now I was a New Yorker.

The apartment was on the eighth floor, surrounded by brownstones, allowing for far away views of the Hudson River and a side view of Central Park. It was also huge by city standards at 1,300 square feet with a sunken living room, a decent kitchen and dining area, plus a large bedroom, four closets, and three exposures. Dad spent the night with me every so often after a squash game or before an early litigation. He stocked the place with bourbon and *Playboy* magazines and used it to as a safe place to drink and unwind.

Once friends got a look at my place, it became a popular hangout. Friday nights were particularly raucous. Everyone else lived with parents or host families or in a rooming house. With no one but me at my place, curfews were ignored, drink was available, smoking permitted, and life without rules was fine as long as we made it to class on time the next morning. Older kids, like Reed and Dago, introduced us to pot, supplying it and telling us where we could find more. Our two local options included a seedy-looking store on Columbus with chipped yellow walls and grubby books called the Paperback Exchange, and a pair of shadowy dealers just inside Central Park named Chico and Lenny. Dago told us Chico was John Lennon's supplier and could always be found across the street from the Dakota, where John and Yoko lived with their son Sean.

Columbus Avenue was populated with the entire dance world and much of the rest of the world in the early 1980s. The atmosphere was like a cross between a Moroccan souk and the Vegas strip. You could hardly walk the streets at night, with crowds filling sidewalks and spilling onto the street as rubbery break dancers spun on cardboard with boom boxes blasting Grandmaster Flash. Accomplished Juilliard students offered up Rachmaninoff and Saint-Saens, earning extra dollars for their talents. The smell of espresso wafted past chatty diners and street vendors outside of Cafe La Fortuna. Tina Ying held court inside her trendy new restaurant, while fashion-conscious shoppers flocked to Parachute, To Boot, Ylang Ylang and Only Hearts. The energy was surreal and almost giddy. Everyone knew everyone else. The risk of being spotted ducking into the Paperback Exchange was not an option, so Anne, Kareen and I would head for the less-traveled corner of 72nd and Central Park West. I was elected to venture into the park while my new best friends remained on the sidewalk, keeping watch.

Dago told me once I was inside the park, head to the left under the trellis, whistle once and wait for Chico or Lenny to respond with a whistle of their own. Leaving the lighted path and descending the hill towards the lower path, I took a deep breath, steadying my nerves, and whistled. All of my instincts predicted certain death. Three seconds later came a distant whistle. A few more courting whistles, and I was face to face with Lenny's gold-capped teeth.

"Nickel or dime?" he uttered through an extensive beard while reaching into the pocket of his long coat. He wasn't alone, but I couldn't quite see the other figure.

Still certain of death, I responded, "Uh, nickel bag please ... thank you." I'm sure my voice cracked. I was failing at hiding my country club origins and my recent bout with puberty.

"It's good stuff. You'll be back. Now you know where to find me."

I passed him a five. "Thanks again." I turned to leave.

"Hey, kid, how old are you?"

My heart was already racing as I turned around. "Fourteen."

"Huh, you look twelve. Careful getting out of here, it's not safe at night. I'll watch your back." This from the drug dealer.

I tucked the bag in my pocket and scrambled up the hill in disbelief that Lenny was my cover. Anne and Kareen stood across from the Dakota, puffing nervously on long Virginia Slims. We did go back but not often. The Paperback Exchange didn't seem like such a bad idea after all.

On a Monday in early December, Dad stayed over. The nights with him were always pleasant. We had all the windows open to battle the excessive heat produced by our radiators. The thriving pulse of New York could be heard all around us. I was holed up in a chair, reading about the Austro-Hungarian Empire in anticipation of my midterm. Dad watched Walter Cronkite on CBS. It wasn't conversation I yearned for with

Dad, just proximity.

"It's almost eleven, Pete. You should go to bed." His words had their late-night drunken drawl.

"Almost done, Dad. Just need to finish this section."

Just then, several loud blasts punctuated the night air. The noise came from outside the kitchen window, which faced an alley that led to 73rd Street.

"Sounded like gunshots." Dad was headed to the kitchen to see what had happened. There was some shouting.

"It's probably just a car backfiring. This is New York, Dad."

"Yeah, it's New York alright, and that was no car."

Soon it became clear that the cracks of noise had not been from a car. Sirens could be heard coming from several different directions.

"Hope they didn't bust Lenny," I muttered. Dad looked at me for clarity, but I shook my head.

Returning to the television with his refreshed drink, Dad switched channels to watch the Patriots/Dolphins game. The familiar voice of Howard Cosell filled the living room. People on the street below were making noise. Some were calling, and some were crying. I walked to the windows facing 74th and looked down onto the sidewalk. People were out on their stoops all up and down the block. I saw our doorman, Kurt, who served as the unofficial mayor of our block, talking with some of the other residents.

"What is going on down there, Dad? Should we go look?"

"Wait. Listen." Dad was turning up the volume on Howard Cosell and Frank Gifford.

Gifford said in a somber tone, "Howard, you have to say what we know in the booth."

Cosell followed, "Yes, we have to say it. An unspeakable tragedy confirmed by ABC News in New York. John Lennon, outside of his apartment building in New York City, the most famous, perhaps, of all the Beatles, shot twice in the back, rushed to Roosevelt Hospital, dead on arrival …"

"Holy shit, Pete, those were the gunshots." We looked at each other in disbelief. The air felt cold and heavy. "The courtyard of the Dakota is maybe 200 yards from the kitchen window."

From the street below, there was crying, consoling, and faint singing. A procession of candles floated past our building, merging with more candles as New Yorkers headed by the hundreds for the Dakota. The vigil lasted for hours, then days. After heading downstairs to talk with Kurt and some of the passing mourners, I finally climbed into bed. The window was still open, and distant voices could be heard singing the words to "Imagine."

Me, Michael and Stanley Williams during rehearsal, photo Paul Kolnik

2 8

THE QUAKER MEETING

Between Mrs. Hattie, Mrs. Wilson, my mother, sister, grand-mother and much of Bedford, strong women surrounded me growing up. They were the decision-makers and the influencers. Men were more distant. I've heard others cite splendid male role models in fathers, brothers, preachers, teachers, husbands, coaches and unlikely examples and heroes. Some are equally defined by the absence of men, or by women. The men were there for me, but the connections weren't.

Grandfather was fine company and a decent-enough role model, especially as a public servant, though he had two bad habits. One was constantly and publicly praising his granddaughters, Jenny and Jessica, as his clear favorites in the grandchild department. Their strengths were evident, but the constant professing of favoritism seemed unnecessary and even hurtful. Nick and I were glum and resigned to second-class status, knowing there was no changing Grandfather's mind.

He was also a formidable cheat at Scrabble. I wasn't close to Bruce or Grampy or either of my male cousins on that side of the family, and the fantastic bond my dad had with my cousin Jeff and with Joe Guay seemed to stand in the way of what he and I might have had. Dad certainly had his shining moments, ripe with love and valuable wisdom, but from my perspective, alcohol came first, and from his perspective, he couldn't find his way out of the hold of his disease.

A few male teachers stood out. Our fourth-grade math teacher, Mr. Bruninghaus, was wonderfully old school, in wool tweed jacket and sharply knotted tie. His classroom had bare walls with all twenty wooden desks and chairs in perfect alignment facing the blackboard. The 1970s philosophies of learning did not dare to enter his classroom. He was a shouter, but we learned our fractions and common denominators and felt his sincere admiration. Monsieur Morissette at the Professional Children's School was an inspired French teacher. He was as flamboyant as Mr. Bruninghaus was austere. "Pamplemousse is my personal favorite word in the entire *langue Français*. J'adore pamplemousse!" Dr. Longo stayed with me during a very wayward senior semester, recognizing a nascent thinker and writer. My senior thesis was on the Quaker Meeting, a subject I knew a little about. Research and curiosity coupled with my family history, plus unwavering encouragement from Dr. Longo, pushed me to write something of value and insight, at least to me.

The ballet teachers at the School of American Ballet were devoted and empowering. I had very few in my seven-and-a-half years of study; Elise Reiman and Helene Dudin shepherded me through my first year, handing me off to Richard Rapp, Andrei Kramarevsky (Krammy), and Jean-Pierre Bonnefoux in years two and three. Each of the three men in very different ways gave me great confidence and knowledge. I savored these relationships, taking in all I could from the ninety-minute lessons I shared with my classmates and teachers. The world seemed to fall away during ballet classes as we all focused on physicality, technique and music. Each of them lives in me to some extent today, as a teacher, as an artist and as a person. I had no relationship with any of them outside of class, which seemed ideal. I felt their favoritism and encouragement, but there was something so pure in the relationship as it only existed through classical ballet.

I first took Stanley Williams' class at age twelve. Stanley was somewhat of a legend as a teacher. He turned the study of ballet into zen meditation but focus and calm were only the beginning. He accelerated preparations for jumps and allowed for accents and variations that spoke to the dynamics of dance and music. He studied Balanchine's choreography as closely as he had studied August Bournonville's in his native Denmark, distilling the principles of great choreography and technique and bringing it to fresh light through his approach.

Professionals from all over the globe would flock to his classes, most of which were taught at SAB. He also gave company class on Tuesdays for NYCB, at American Ballet Theatre each fall, and in Denmark each summer for his alma mater, The Royal Danish Ballet.

I didn't know any of this at twelve. Entering the immense white studio for Stanley's class was not unlike attending Quaker Meeting in Katonah. White walls, wooden barres, elevated natural light, everyone had their chosen place on the perimeter of the room and the collective commitment was understood. Stanley moved into the room soundlessly, dressed in slacks and a button-down shirt and carrying his pipe. He spoke, but almost inaudibly. He conveyed ideas through hand and arm movements and carefully chosen musical notes.

The poor pianists would fall by the wayside in droves as Stanley would guide them to submission with the weakest framework of musical structure. The Russians would rebel with flowery doses of Tchaikovsky, Prokofiev and Rachmaninoff. Stanley would quietly thank them, and off they'd go, never to return.

What so few understood was his desire for dancers' limbs to define music and not keys or pedals on the piano. Notoriously, pianists were guided to play only the counts of one and four, leaving the dancers to round out phrases and create articulation. The roundness, expression and intensity of music needed to live in the dancers' bodies and not just in the ear. Overpowering music could only be followed, while two softly played cords allowed for melody, meter and bravura to be overlaid and explored. Brilliant movement complemented, enhanced and even conducted great music. He wanted to build from the essence, investing meaning and shape into every step. In the end, the music lived within our bodies and our movements.

My first year with Stanley was an epiphany. Other teachers, as wonderful and effective as they were, had asked for more physicality, higher legs, more pirouettes, better beats. Aside from complicated combinations, they hadn't allowed for the students' intelligence, musical phasing, or decision-making in the process. Stanley taught for my mind as much as he taught for my body. I would have quit if I hadn't walked into his world.

He taught once a week when I was twelve. When I turned thirteen, he taught four times each week, and at fifteen, I took his class six times a week with an occasional added Bournonville variations class on Wednesdays, plus rehearsals for his staging of a Bournonville piece for SAB's annual graduation performance, known simply as Workshop. After graduation, I continued to take classes two or three times a week until he died in the fall of 1997. During that time, he often called on me to show the class what he meant or to put his corrections into words for the class, which he never felt capable of doing himself. Like the spare chords on the piano, we would only hear phrases like, "Go front," "Big toe," and when we succeeded, "And you're there." His final year, he helped to train me as a teacher, which, in fact, he had actually done since my very first class with him so many years ago. He was a great constant in my life and an almost daily presence for twenty years.

When my father died, I returned home from tour in California in order to attend the funeral. I stopped by Stanley's class to stay in shape and to return to what was routine and reassuring. Stanley asked why I was there when the Company was on tour. On learning the reason, he looked devastated, not simply because he knew my father, which he did, but because he felt such a close bond with me. All those years of profound connection with hardly a single conversation.

Stanley would tour with us on occasion, especially for the trips to Denmark. Loved by all, Stanley fell right into City Ballet's tour culture, drinking far too much in hotel lobbies and rooms and at company parties. Returning to my room at night, I'd pass him at the hotel bar, surrounded by a jovial group, who would be laughing with and at him as he would topple through the Rose Adagio from *The Sleeping Beauty*, wobbling before various suitors. I resented his companions for letting him drink too much. I never joined in the fun, seeing too many similarities to my father and the potential erosion of the ideal relationship I shared with my teacher. The studio was our place, almost every day, with a mutual respect that bordered on love.

I don't know how Balanchine felt about the cult of Stanley. Stanley was certainly devoted to advancing the principles of Balanchine's technique in his school, but his extensive following was really unlike anything I have ever seen in ballet. His twelve-thirty advanced men's class had about twenty-five students enrolled, but three times that many would attend. Legends like Rudolf Nureyev, Fernando Bujones, and Mikhail Baryshnikov would take a place at the barre alongside most of the men from NYCB and ABT, including Helgi Tomasson, Ib Andersen, Peter Martins, Joseph Duell, Adam Luders, Jacques d'Amboise, Robert Weiss, Peter Fonseca and Patrick Bissell. Technically, women weren't supposed to take the class, but Galina Panova came with her husband. Merrill Ashley, Colleen Neary, Heather Watts, Kyra Nichols, Maria Calegari and Darci Kistler were regulars. Rudy would always take the place next to me, offering coaching between combinations. It was honestly a bit of a zoo, with Stanley puffing away on his pipe, Lynn Stanford chain-smoking while playing piano, and some of the pros lighting up mid-class. Lynn's music was not only compatible with Stanley's teaching philosophies, but a joy to hear. He played Mary Wells's hit, "My Guy" every time his boyfriend Todd would dance across the floor. Viewers lined up along the wall to look through the haze of smoke to see the most concentrated collection of balleterati anywhere.

Stanley would constantly remind the professionals to let the students have their space and their turn, but there was no space. We all had to turn on an angle at the barre just to extend our leg in tendu front.

Balanchine came to watch one day when we capped out at about eighty. You could see his dismay. The following week, a list was posted with eight students' names on it: Michael Byars, Jeff Edwards, Gen Horiuchi, David Liu, Pablo Savoye, Sean Savoye, James Sewell and me. We were to attend a new class called "special men's" at ten-thirty each weekday morning, just prior to the advanced men's class. No company dancers or guests were allowed to attend.

Balanchine never taught special men's class but did observe several times during the inaugural year. Of the five weekly classes, three were taught by Krammy and two by Stanley. Balanchine wanted Krammy's influence to shape our education in tandem with Stanley's and not to have one teacher define us. Where Stanley was cerebral, Krammy was pure showman, performing in the front of the room with testosterone-infused character flair. He was still throwing impressive double tours en l'air in his sixties.

Balanchine entered soon after class had begun, wearing a sharp blue blazer, colored cravat, and small, polished shoes. His thinning white hair was plastered back with pomade. He looked down over his long-arched nose while his eyes blinked as if confronted with new light. The first class he attended was taught by Krammy. The bond between the Russian teacher and the Georgian ballet master was beautiful to witness. Even though they conversed only in Russian, we could feel the camaraderie, hear the laughter, and see the nodding and the gestures of agreement. Balanchine kept suggesting combinations to Krammy, demonstrating them while seated in his chair. He also requested time to speak with us at the end of class.

He explained that his personal work and coaching with

future male principals started when dancers were twenty-two or twenty-three years of age, "So late, can't make a difference then." Often, he explained, he knew who his principals would be when they were just students, like us. Our egos were swelling as he continued. He asked why the detailed work and individual attention couldn't start at sixteen or seventeen. We all nodded, ready to sign our principal contracts. This, he explained, was the purpose of special men's class. He cautioned it wasn't just talent or promise, but serious work on our parts. He wanted that work to start now. He then launched into a lecture about dress code, which had fallen by the wayside. He pointed to the holes in Jeff's tights, to Pablo's raggedy sleeveless shirt and then Sean's dirty socks. He said we looked like hot dog vendors on the street. Dress code would be strict for special men's. He told us not to take sweatpants, warm-ups or towels and throw them on the floor, but rather to fold them neatly and place them on our bag.

Each of us remembers different lessons imparted on that day. But it may not have been his words that mattered; it was the standard he aimed to impart. We had a shot at being principal dancers and maybe even principals for his company, but we needed to start to live by higher standards in order to achieve the honor. It was the folding, dressing, respect, reverence and so many other qualities and attributes. We felt the honor of his selection, his presence and the privilege of the opportunity. It was a turning point, and none of us wanted to disappoint him.

The ballet class has always been like a higher ground for me, and I believe it is for all dancers. Words seem to fail when describing it. The shared meditation and the chance to take our human form and rise to its epitome through movement and music is a pinnacle of existence. I'm an atheist, but the ballet studio, like a temple or a ziggurat or Quaker meeting house, is where I come closest to recognizing something bigger than me. It is still the place I go to almost every day.

29

BALANCHINE

Apparently, my alarm clock didn't know it was Saturday. For a seventeen-year-old, seven forty-five a.m. on a weekend was almost rude, but of course I wasn't your average teenager, and this was no ordinary Saturday. I finally pushed out of bed, surrendering to the second alarm fifteen minutes later, showered, ate some breakfast, packed my bag and headed down in the elevator. It was already eight forty-five. Class was at nine and our final rehearsal on stage was at eleven. My last few bucks would need to pay for the cab.

I got a taxi right away and told the driver to take me to 165 West 65th. My ride was only about twelve blocks, but I was already running late and wanted to make up time. Sometimes traffic rewards walkers, but on this day, we trundled down Columbus in a couple of minutes. New York had this all-news-all-the-time radio station called 1010 WINS. Cabbies chose this or NPR. 1010 WINS was the station of choice in my cab that day and was offering us a pleasant spring forecast for the New York metro area.

I did a quick check of my bag while exchanging unnecessary dialogue about the weather with the driver. 1010 WINS had moved on to the next story.

"Early this morning, choreographer George Balanchine died at the age of seventy-nine from a rare neurological disorder. Mr. Balanchine, known to New Yorkers as the Ballet Master in Chief of the New York City Ballet was considered to be one of the most influential artists of the 20th century, his name often compared to the great artists of our time: Igor Stravinsky, Pablo Picasso and ..."

"Oh, my God!" I uttered louder than I should have.

"Something wrong?" the driver asked in his melodic Haitian accent.

"No. I sort of knew that man."

I first saw George Balanchine eight years prior at the School of American Ballet's *Nutcracker* audition. An older student offered me a huge piece of gum minutes before the audition. Not knowing anyone and being a head smaller than most, I was happy to have the offer. It seemed like a friendly one. I stuffed the gum in my mouth and chomped away. I actually never chewed gum and thought it might not be allowed in the school. I regretted accepting the gift but by then found myself in the middle of Studio #2 in a crowd of several hundred children with no means of disposing of the gum.

A hush fell as Mr. Balanchine entered the studio. David Richardson, the children's ballet master, scurried to his side. There was hardly a whisper from anyone except my supposed friend. He leaned close to my ear to say, "Mr. Balanchine hates boys who chew gum." Gulp. Down it went, that huge piece of Hubba Bubba. To say I had a lump in my throat the day I first met George Balanchine was no exaggeration.

Now, eight years later, I had another lump in my throat. I got out of the cab and made my way through the Juilliard School to the northeast corner of the third floor, where four studios and a handful of offices and dressing rooms constituted the School of American Ballet, founded by Balanchine and Lincoln Kirstein in 1934. I wanted to cry. I walked the long corridor towards the double glass doors of the school as I had almost every day since I was nine years old. I knew I needed to keep it together because I was the student everyone would look to for a reaction. Our graduation performance, known as Workshop, was that night. Kids were nervous anyway.

Just outside the doors, two kids laughed while playing jacks. Inside the doors, students were preparing for their warm-up classes just like on any other day. I saw my friend Cathy and asked her if she had heard the news. She said she had and was sorry she'd never met him. She asked if I was okay. Mr. B. had spent most of the year in the hospital, a distant figure for the current students. The previous year, he had attended final rehearsals for our Workshop performance, but we hadn't seen him this spring.

Everyone seemed to know this was coming. We heard reports of a bad week, of his priest, Father Adrian, being called to the hospital, of weekly casting being read, and of Mr. B. stopping the reader to ask who one of his ballerinas was. He hadn't recognized her name. He wasn't eating. It wouldn't be long. If we knew it was coming, why was the pain so sharp and the fact so shocking?

I was between two worlds on that day, a top student at the school and also an apprentice with the New York City Ballet, hired last January supposedly by Balanchine himself. I remember the day when I was standing against the back barre of Studio #3 before class, and Peter Martins, recently appointed as ballet master and unofficially acknowledged as successor to Balanchine, arrived at the door with Stanley Williams. Stanley was our primary teacher and had served as Peter's, too, when he was a boy at the Royal Danish Ballet School. The Danes were clearly talking about me. The following week, I was told by Natasha Gleboff, executive director of the School, I was an apprentice. I assumed, with Balanchine in the hospital, Peter was making decisions about hiring. Rosemary Dunleavy, the company's ballet mistress, needed two more men for *Union Jack*, and I got my first job.

I was offered another job when I was sixteen. The offer came from Mikhail Baryshnikov, then artistic director of the American Ballet Theatre. After the 1982 Workshop performance, ABT extended corps de ballet contract offers to Rita Norona and to me. I learned about the offer in an odd way.

Before SAB had dormitories, my friends and I all had our own apartments, packed with roommates and very few rules. We grew up quickly, and seeing drugs or alcohol passed around at a Friday night party was common. SAB ran a tight ship, and some kids always seemed to be "in the office." Everyone was buzzing about Dago Nieves, who had been called in the past week and suspended after a teacher found him smoking pot in stairway D. A lot went on in stairway D, and Dago's infraction was by no means the worst offense.

So, there I was, having just smoked pot the past Friday,

when Mary Cornell, Lincoln Kirstein's secretary, found me in the hallway to let me know Mrs. Gleboff would like to see me in her office. I recalled the guilt I had felt about chewing a piece of gum at nine. That guilt was now multiplied exponentially. I wondered if my imminent suspension would apply to my academic school as well. What about the honor roll? Did my parents need to know?

At the appointed time, I was told to step into Mrs. Gleboff's office. Years later as a faculty member at the School, I became great friends with Mrs. Gleboff. She was wise, intuitive and very funny, but not then. She was the stern Russian warden. In truth, she was neither Russian nor warden, just Czech and powerful. I walked into her office for the first time and found Stanley sitting next to her. Stanley was a favorite teacher and sort of a father figure to many of us. Did he need to be here for this? Mrs. Gleboff told me to sit down and also told me I looked nervous. She and Stanley exchanged glances and chuckled. Cruel messengers of punishment.

"We wanted to inform you that Mr. Baryshnikov has extended an offer for you to join the American Ballet Theatre, but Mr. Balanchine has turned it down." Huh? No suspension.

"What should I do?" I asked, still a little shaky, but also hugely relieved.

"Absolutely nothing. We just thought you should know. Congratulations. You can go now." And there it was.

Rehearsal for the evening performance went smoothly. Though faculty members were clearly rattled by the news, they put on a strong front for their students. I didn't see Alexandra Danilova, Balanchine's second (common-law) wife. Antonina Tumkovsky took me by the shoulders, fixing her piercing blue eyes on me as she wished me luck in her thick Russian accent, "Dance well; it is the only thing to do." Tears were everywhere. Peter shuttled Suzanne Farrell past us, wrapped in his embrace. Natasha Gleboff stood in the wings of the Juilliard Theater, a tiny woman and a great pillar of strength for anyone who might need it.

By one, I had to leave in order to report to the neighboring New York State Theater for the company's matinee performance. The scene at the State Theater was completely different than the one I just left. Balanchine had not been a presence at the school for many months. So many students knew only the name and the reputation, but not the face or the man. Where Balanchine may have devoted himself to the school in 1934, it had long since passed into the capable hands of others whom he trusted. The company was his true home, brimming with collaborators, muses, lovers and friends. It was his house, his temple and his stage. A pall hung over this house, and I felt it as I approached.

Arriving at the stage door, I was met by a half-dozen camera crews and reporters who bobbed around the stone stairway that descended to the stage entrance. It was almost half-hour, and gaunt dancers wearing sunglasses pushed through the buzzards to find their way to safety. One reporter stopped me to ask if I was a dancer with the company. She then asked for a comment about Balanchine's death. I had none and pushed past.

Inside the dark theater, there were not words, just heaving sobs, muttered consolations, and an eerie silence. We were summoned to the stage for a company meeting. Peter and Lincoln were there with Rosemary, Betty Cage, Eddie Bigelow, John Taras and Jerry Robbins. The sobs didn't stop, and tighter embraces didn't help. Peter spoke, telling us performances would go on as scheduled since it's what Mr. B would have wanted. As I left the meeting, Patricia McBride gave me a powerful embrace, and Robert Maiorano patted me on the back. I was the second youngest member of the company.

We really had no time, so I left the stage to put on makeup. I was in the second piece on the program, which was Jerry's *Mother Goose,* the same ballet I had danced in as a child. The company performed admirably on that somber matinee. At one point, Lisa Hess, who played the Princess Aurora in one vignette, pricked her finger and showed each member of the ensemble. I looked at her offered finger and then at her face and saw tears streaming across her cheeks. Many on the stage were crying too. The wound was so fresh.

There was no talk in the dressing room after the performance. I showered, found food and made my way back to the Juilliard Theater for Workshop. I was to perform the lead in a premiere by Helgi Tomasson called *Ballet D'Isoline* and Balanchine's *Western Symphony* that night. It was almost a relief to return to the environs of the school.

At that time, New York City Ballet's agreement with the American Guild of Musical Artists, the dancers' union, dictated that an apprentice who performed in three ballets with the company in one season must immediately be elevated to the corps de ballet. *Mother Goose* was my third ballet, but I hadn't noticed or kept count. Backstage in the wings prior to the Workshop performance, the beacon that was Natasha Gleboff found me and said, "Amidst all of this, you know you and Sean are now in the company. You can sign your contract on Tuesday." An ending and a beginning.

I loved dancing *D'Isoline* that night. It was a wonderful work and the outgrowth of months in the studio with Helgi. Whereas so many young male dancers looked to Peter Martins, or Mikhail Baryshinkov as their idol, for me it was Helgi—so understated and pure, but always fresh and honest. The work was made on Zippora Karz and me, with my future wife, Kelly Cass, and James Sewell as the alternate cast. There was a third cast, too: Cathy Ryan and Sean Savoye, but we assumed they wouldn't perform. A few weeks before the premiere, Helgi made a switch and pulled Zippora, replacing her with Cathy. Artistically, Cathy was probably the right choice, every bit a regal princess, and Zippora was a filly, like a young Farrell, but the switch still hurt.

Performing *Western* in SAB Workshop was difficult. After months of preparation under the meticulous eye of Suki Schorer, we were ready for anything except the death of the choreographer on the day of the show. That night, I danced the Jacques d'Amboise role in the fourth movement. I felt dishonest entering the stage with a cheesy grin. Zippora was my leggy partner, and she too felt strange. We turned in a solid performance, but it was not how we wanted to honor the choreographer we felt so close to. I once read dance critic Arlene Croce's words about that day: "We all just went to the temple (New York State Theater), there was nowhere else to go." I was two blocks north of the temple, a lost yet grinning cowboy.

Zippora and I had developed a Balanchine bond. During the course of the year, she and I spent many months sitting together while second or third casts worked on ballets. We talked about the world of ballet, and we talked about Balanchine: his taste, his technique, his philosophies and, of course, the works he would one day create on us. We lived and trained to work for him and dreamed, literally dreamed, of dancing for the New York City Ballet. We breathed Balanchine.

For years, I kept a note taped to the inside of my locker at SAB. The note, written on a pink memo pad, was from the SAB receptionist. She had written, "Zippora will meet you at Roosevelt at 12:15." The date was December 10th. Balanchine had re-entered Roosevelt Hospital in early December of 1982, and the rumors swirled that he wasn't doing well. Zippora convinced me we had to go see him in the hospital. I never would have done it on my own, but Zippora empowered me, and I agreed.

The 10th was a cold December day, but I stood outside on Columbus next to the old hospital operating theater watching for Zippora. I was early and nervous, but seeing my friend stride down the street with her infectious confidence changed that. We asked the woman at the main reception desk where George Balanchine's room was, thinking she would tell us lowly students were not allowed to see the wizard that day. Instead, she said, "Fourth floor to the left." Long corridors took us all too quickly to his room where, like the pair of nervous seventeen-year-olds that we were, we sank back against the white wall a few yards from the door to his room. There were voices inside, and we didn't need anyone to tell us we were lowly students at that point. We knew.

I don't know how many minutes passed. There were several times when we considered bolting, but Zippora had resolve. We'd come this far. What if this was our only chance to speak with him? Eventually ballerina Karin von Aroldingen emerged from the room and spotted us. "Oh, are you two here to see Mr. Balanchine?" Nervous nods. "He will be so pleased, can I take you in and introduce you?" More nodding. When we entered, dancer Frank Ohman was requesting a favor from Mr. B., and we waited at the door until Mr. B. agreed to Frank's request. I think he might have agreed out of curiosity to learn who his next visitors were.

Karin brought us into the room and spoke in her thick German accent. "Mr. Balanchine, these are two students from your school who've come to see you." He sat up in his bed with the bright eyes of a child. He looked right at me and said, "Well, I know you, but I haven't met your friend." Mr B. had coached me in rehearsals for the role of *Nutcracker* prince a few years before. Frank bowed and left, and Karin stayed for a few minutes, pulling up chairs and assuring Mr. B. she would return shortly. She was a constant presence at his side in his final years, as strong as a cane, as caring as a nurse and as close as a lover.

We three spoke so freely. For that moment, we shared so much. He wanted to know about our teachers and our studies. We wanted to know about Western Symphony and all the other treasures he had given us. Two seventeen-year-old Americans and a seventy-eight-year-old Georgian, and yet we were three dancers with so much in common. People have asked me what I remember about that meeting, and there are two things etched in my memory, neither profound. First, there was a Christie Brinkley Sports Illustrated calendar on his wall. Second, I didn't know he had lost part of his finger in a gardening accident, and he repeatedly made emphasis by shaking his shortened digit at us.

Before long, the phone rang and the caller asked Mr. B. who was with him. I knew he wouldn't remember our names. He responded, "I'm with one very beautiful woman and one very ugly man." Thanks, Mr. B. Soon, Karin returned and expressed some surprise that we were still there. I looked at my watch. We had been with him for an hour. He thanked us repeatedly for coming and made us promise we would return. He told us to bring others and that he was so very proud of us.

Weeks later, I received my apprenticeship, and I worried people would think I received it as a result of having visited Mr. B. in the hospital. Zippora and I chose never to tell our peers about our visit.

December 10th and April 30th were days I would never forget. I signed my contract on May 3rd, and the following day at eleven a.m., I attended Balanchine's funeral at the Synod of Bishops Russian Orthodox Church on 93rd and Park.

The day seemed sweltering, with the small and exquisite church brimming with dancers, teachers, devotees, friends and patrons. The oppressive pall was still present for the extensive family, who loved their patriarch more than anyone or anything else. Many shuffled past the open coffin trembling, crying, clutching one another, but I refrained, preferring to remember my audience with the boyish man in the hospital with the teasing tone, who enjoyed his twelve-month relationship with Christie Brinkley.

Everyone was weighted with sadness, but one stood out to me. She was Nina Fedorova, an exquisite dancer in the corps de ballet. Double doors topped by transom windows stretched along the street-side wall with narrow spaces separating them. Nina stood in one of the gaps like the figures carved into the marble support columns seen on the buildings of St. Petersburg. Her location shielded her from harsh sunlight, but I could still see a face that hadn't stopped crying. Mascara surrendered to the tears while her endless tendril legs, extended by heeled shoes, seemed to buckle under grief, architecture so weakened it threatened to collapse at any minute. She was shaking and staring blankly forward towards the coffin. Disbelief. A story that was hers alone.

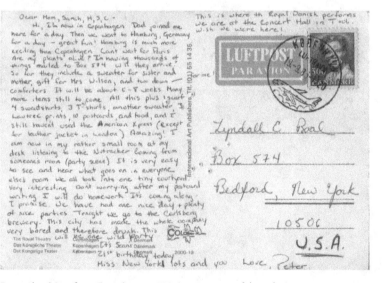

Postcard to Mom from Copenhagen, 1983 *(image courtesy of the author)*

30

SUNNY VON BULOW'S SHEETS

My first year with New York City Ballet flew by. A fledgling member of the corps de ballet learns dozens of roles in the first full season. The work is physically and mentally exhausting but also completely fulfilling. A typical day starts with a ninety-minute morning class, followed by six and sometimes seven hours of rehearsals plus an evening performance. This happened six days a week with double shows on Saturdays and Sundays. NYCB dropped the Sunday evening show in the late 1980s, citing low attendance, but troop fatigue was also part of the decision. Spent and exhilarated by the end of our eighth performance on Sunday evening, one would think we would collapse in bed and crawl to a massage on Monday. But knowing a day off was coming at dawn, we would head to a nightclub.

There was a sort of celebrity status that came with the job—

instant recognition around town, entree into this club and that restaurant, magazine shoots and a general feeling of invincibility. The combination of a good paycheck, fewer rules, little to no parenting and a lot of alcohol quickly went from exciting to unsustainable.

My tenure with the Company began when I was in eleventh grade. Though twelfth grade would only require one semester consisting of three classes, it was a challenging fall for academics. When senior year began, I was in Europe on tour with the company. The three-city tour lasted six weeks, with two in London, two in Copenhagen and two in Paris. English Lit would have to wait.

The overnight flight to London was a debacle, with dancers drowning themselves in cocktails before, during and after the flight. The plane was filled with laughter, limbs, cigarette smoke and hundreds of little glass liquor bottles. A principal dancer vomited all down the front of his white suit, a new corps member was making out with an inebriated senior ballerina, whose husband was joining the tour later in the week. The smell of alcohol and the ensuing epidemic of hangovers made for a sorry sight deplaning at Heathrow early the next morning.

Despite impressive performances in each city, the company was in mourning after the death of Mr. B., and behavior was off the rails. At seventeen, I was both elated and alarmed by the new world I was entering.

I stayed with my Aunt Caroline in London but saw little of her and my cousins with all of the pomp surrounding New York City Ballet's return to England. At Covent Garden, Princess Margaret came backstage to greet the principal dancers from *Divertimento #15*. Lord and Lady Sainsbury (friends of my grandparents) hosted the entire troupe at their country estate for an afternoon party that stretched well into the night. Alicia Markova hosted a group of twenty, including me, for tea at the Savoy Hotel. Seated at the head of a long table, with perfectly coiffed hair surrounding her head like a silver helmet, she summoned staff and sipped her tea like the Queen. Dame Ninette de Valois watched our company class, asking ballet master John Taras for an introduction to the newest hire.

John introduced me in the same way throughout the tour, "This is Peter Boal, he is our future."

Small but slightly elevated by sensible heels and smartly dressed in mauve florals, Dame Ninette approached me with a glint in her eye. "I wish you could stay in London and join the Royal; we could use you."

"Thank you, but I can't stay, I just joined the New York City Ballet, and besides, I'm still in high school."

"High school or not, we are unable to hire anyone unless one parent was born a British citizen, so we'll have to let you go."

"My mother was born in London, but I would still need to go home."

"Oh, well, that changes things doesn't it. In the eyes of the Commonwealth and the Royal Ballet, you're a Brit. Please do remember the Royal if you ever want to return to Covent Garden. You could be our future, too." With a wink, she was off.

I saw Dame Ninette again at a lecture demonstration presented by principal dancer Joseph Duell on Balanchine technique. Joe used me to demonstrate to an assembled group of London critics and writers. You could feel the fascination in the hall as Joe articulated methodology mixed with insight and inspiration. The event was not only informative for me and all in the room but also signaled an important step forward in the post-Balanchine era. Joe was seen as a bright light in the future of New York City Ballet. When he jumped from his fifth-story window two years later, we were stunned and left wondering what we had missed and when and why the bright light extinguished.

Receptions in Denmark and Paris proved equally as celebratory. A full orchestra awaited our plane on the tarmac in Copenhagen to salute our new Danish-born ballet master in chief, Peter Martins. Poor Sean Lavery, one of our workhorse principals, whose back had gone out in London, was made to wait supine on the plane until the festivities were complete; a dancer on a stretcher makes for an awkward homecoming. A raucous party, with far too much aquavit, was held at the Carlsberg Brewery. In Paris, Ambassador Pamela Harriman hosted the entire company at the U.S. Embassy. Each invitation and evening seemed to top the last, but the best invitation by far was for an elaborate dinner at the baroque chateau Vaux-le-Vicomte outside of Paris, where Rudolf Nureyev joined the fun. Needless to say, I didn't miss English Lit at all.

My father came to see me in London. He and I had grown more distant since I left home two years prior, but I was pleased to have the time with him. Apparently, the divorce with my mother was final. They had been waiting for Jenny and me to leave home. After I moved into the city and Jenny headed for college, the time seemed right. There was nothing left between them, and the disconnect was hurting those around them and each other.

Though both remarried, Dad was in a downward spiral, and one by one, his defenders stepped away. Friends and family lost patience as well and would no longer step in or compromise reputations to help. Mom was glad to be done.

The New York City Ballet became my world, and I was thrilled to breathe fresh air, regardless of how dysfunctional my new family was.

The company seemed sexually charged, with older dancers looking to newer hires for relationships. I was well aware of interested parties but always felt respected. Everyone in the company had watched me grow up. It didn't take long on tour before I found a girlfriend, or rather she found me. Despite the passions of a new relationship with an older and far more experienced partner, I was struggling with my sexuality, recognizing my attraction to men and unsure of how acceptable that attraction was to my family, my hometown, and my new world.

A veteran corps dancer named John was always nearby. I spent little time with him at first, but he found a way to connect about art, alcoholic parents and our peculiar small-town upbringings. John was from Tarboro, North Carolina, where his father had been the editor of the *Tarboro Times*. He was refreshingly witty, well-read, caring and classically handsome, with straight brown hair that flopped across his forehead covering his pale green eyes.

For my nineteenth birthday, John asked if he could take me to dinner. I wasn't naive and knew accepting the invitation would be seen as encouragement. We met at Ruelle's, a swank spot on Columbus Avenue. After animated conversation, a bottle of pinot noir and a delicious meal, we retreated to John's apartment on West 75th and talked. A leg touched a leg, and I panicked, claimed friends were waiting for me, and left.

Nothing happened that night, but a torrent of feelings of

desire and love was unleashed, and a few weeks later, I had a dresser drawer, a toothbrush and a boyfriend on West 75th.

Friends were fine with the news of my coming out. I heard mostly, "Yeah, we knew," or "Whatever."

Mom cried for four consecutive days. I kept calling to check on her, and all I got was, "He-he-lo ... no, I'm fine, se-se-seriously, I am ... I-I ... can't talk ... I-I'm fine, really." And she hung up. Later she would explain she had always supported homosexuals but just didn't think she would have one for a son. She countered, "But I thought you wanted children?" I told her I wasn't especially keen on the situation either, but it was a truth I could no longer avoid.

I didn't tell Dad because he was in a new marriage to a kind Catholic woman named Elizabeth, and they were dealing with issues with her daughter, his drinking, and a reality that was crumbling around them and being propped up at the same time.

On my nineteenth birthday, I launched into five months of bliss. I spent my days in the studio working on new creations with Twyla Tharp, Jerome Robbins and Peter Martins. I was learning and performing many of the roles I had watched as a child and hoped one day to dance. In the evening, after the performance, I would head home with John.

John was at a very different point in his career. After a decade in the corps, he was dancing many of the same parts without new opportunities. He appreciated his job, but the reward was staying in line with other dancers, helping Rosemary Dunleavy, our head ballet mistress, recall which wing the corps entered from, and taking class with Maggie Black. His passions lay outside of the company. In many ways, though our time together was brief, John offered a much-needed positive influence at a time when I could have been pulled down many different and more destructive paths.

Inspired by his close friend, artist Jane Wilson Gruen, John took great pleasure in learning to cook, paint and write. He frequented museums and galleries with a combination of kid-like curiosity and acquired knowledge. Jane's daughter, Julia, was one of his dearest friends, and a partner in many crimes, and John Gruen, the writer, photographer and aesthete, completed the adopted family along with a carefully curated group of authors, artists and dancers. It was a family I needed and lacked.

The nightlife changed but in no way slowed down. The Gruens held regular soirees at their West 83rd Street floor-through. The guest list was impressive and well-chronicled by John in his many tell-all books. Weekend nights were still spent in clubs like Area, Pyramid and Studio 54. John and his circle were often at the newest hot spots in Manhattan or the Hamptons, rubbing elbows with the fun and the famous. I sat through long conversations with Jack Nicholson at Nell's while he pined over a young NYCB corps member named Liz. We would see Julia's boss, Keith Haring, in his studio and at the Palladium with Grace Jones. Calvin Klein was at the Swamp in Southampton with his entourage. We would jump when Paige Powell called to let us know Andy Warhol wanted to meet for dinner at the Algonquin.

In February, dancers were counting the overtime minutes while Jerome Robbins put finishing touches on his new work, *In Memory of* ..., a new creation for Suzanne Farrell. John and I were angels.

John had started to experience severe tooth pain, which triggered disorienting headaches. He had to pull himself from the cast. No dentist could determine the source of the pain, so more tests and more doctors followed. I, like John, was convinced it was his teeth, and when we were told it was actually cancer, I was in disbelief.

Weeks earlier, John and I were watching television late at night when an obscure cable channel reported the increasingly widespread appearance of a new gay cancer. Though we didn't realize it at the time, John's diagnosis of Burkitt's lymphoma was an AIDS-related cancer.

In 1985, we knew little or nothing about AIDS. It wasn't until I visited John at Columbia Presbyterian Hospital and saw a red warning posted on the outside of his door stating "protective clothing must be worn in this room at all times," did I realize John might have the new gay cancer. A friendly nurse named Fred told me it was just a precaution, and I wouldn't need to wear a mask when visiting. Fred didn't wear protective clothing either.

John's condition worsened quickly as we moved to chemotherapy treatments and radiation. A catheter was placed under the skin on his forehead to help administer chemo, and two magenta X-es were inked onto his temples to pinpoint the exact radiation sites. His beautiful brown hair disintegrated to wisps, which he kept far longer than anyone thought he should. His face and head grew hairless and round. He lost weight, and he lost the will to live.

I changed my routine from frequenting night clubs and chic restaurants to boarding the A train at the end of each rehearsal day to head for 168th Street to eat hospital food with John. His appetite was lacking, and bland food wasn't helping, so I would eat what was on his tray while he sampled the takeout I brought from Zabar's or Ying's. He insisted on a beer, which had to be smuggled in. He wanted to hug and hoped to kiss, but I was struggling.

The company work didn't slow down for me. I was depleted on many levels, and everyone either avoided me or approached with tears in their eyes, needing to unload about what they thought I was going through.

After Christmas, John and I found a quiet night at home. Our prized Abyssinian cat, Ted, purred on John's lap. As the fire blazed and the last of the wine was poured, I broached a topic I had avoided. I needed a break. I couldn't do it anymore. I was cracking. Even at home, I was rehanging IV bags, scheduling treatments and apportioning drugs. After performing *Tschaikovsky Pas de Deux*, I was jumping in a cab to rush home to spoonfeed an exhausted cancer patient whose spirit was gone, and who didn't even remotely resemble the man I had fallen in love with months before.

The decision to break up might have been justifiable, but it was also selfish, and John told me in no uncertain terms that I could not break up with him. Through tears, he explained he would die. He granted permission to do whatever I wanted outside of the relationship but implored me to stay by his side, hold his hand and help him fight until he was through his illness. I had set love aside to heed self. A low moment. I heard and understood.

I started an affair with his friend, but I never left John's side. Cedric had been in relentless pursuit since I joined the company. Even while John was sick, Cedric was there, approaching, offering, offending at every turn. I should have walked the other way, but he was extremely attractive and provided an escape.

The clandestine nature of the affair made it more thrilling, and the outlet allowed me to love John and care for him as he required and deserved. Still, John took a downturn during the spring. His oncologist asked for a private consultation with me, knowing I was closer to John than any family member or friend. He explained treatment could only do so much, but without a patient's will to live, the challenges of recovery were greater, and the chances of improvement were slimmed.

Several stepped forward to help John in this dark time, like Julia and John's friend Bruce Padgett, who had attended North Carolina School of the Arts with John and then joined NYCB the same year. Heather Watts came to the hospital regularly. Somehow the Red Stripe beer she brought him was always more appreciated and more delicious than anyone else's offering. She had a gift for making John laugh. They spent entire visits planning guest lists and menus for their next summer on Hydra, a frequent destination for John and his friends in Greece. Lincoln Kirstein was a surprise visitor. He came to the hospital on three occasions, always checking with me on what time would be most suitable for a visit. He stayed for exactly an hour each time, discussing art, dance and literature for the first thirty minutes and then reading a pre-selected passage or chapter during the remaining time. John thought of Edith Wharton and Jane Austen as divinities, and Lincoln obliged with *House of Mirth* and *Emma*.

I asked my mother to visit John. After those first four days when I'd told her about my new beau, she came around and realized first, that she loved me unconditionally and no other person would stand in the way of our bond, and also that John was completely likable and fine company. We spent a fair amount of time together in her home, in our home, on trips and at the ballet, and now she wanted to help me in this darkest time.

I don't know exactly what happened on that spring day when Mom went to Columbia Presbyterian Hospital. Long ago she had done a residency there before moving to Mount Sinai. Re-entering felt familiar. I do know John suggested they visit the hospital garden to sit in the shade among the early blooms. Both said it was pleasant but odd to have one-on-one time without me. I wanted Mom to see John because she was an effective and compassionate social worker, not just the mother of his partner. She suggested John identify all of the reasons he had for beating cancer and reclaiming his old life. My name came up a lot, and apparently, so did Sunny Von Bulow's.

John, despite all his passion centering around the recipes of Julia Child and the paintings of Caravaggio, was not above buying an issue of *The Enquirer* to read the latest on Claus von Bulow, his comatose wife Sunny, and her Newport mansion. New Yorkers had been riveted by the story of the heiress and the sensational trial of her husband Claus, who was accused of putting her in an irreversible coma through an insulin overdose, which, in turn, put her in a suite in Columbia Presbyterian Hospital. After John's first visit to the hospital, he asked his favorite nurse Fred, if Sunny von Bulow was really upstairs; it didn't take Fred long to divulge the truth about Sunny's whereabouts.

"Oh, Fred," John said, "you must promise me that once, perhaps on my last date on this earth, if I'm here, you will give me Sunny's sheets."

I was actually in the room when this was said, reading a copy of *Persuasion*, which Lincoln had dropped off.

"John, you know I can't even divulge who's here in the

hospital." Fred's principles on hospital ethics were already compromised.

"Oh, Freddie, you already told me Sunny's upstairs, so stop pretending you are a good nurse. Jane's the good nurse." John's other favorite nurse was Jane, whom I rarely saw since she was working the morning shifts.

I chimed in, "Sorry Fred, he told me you outed Sunny, so quit pretending." We saw a lot of Fred, and I suspect John was one of the best parts of his job.

"What's the thread count?" John was back at it.

Fred countered, "Do you really think they tell us nurses the thread count of Sunny von Bulow's sheets? You need to eat something and stop dreaming about linens you will never, ever see."

"Fred, I just need you to do this one thing for me, and then I'll eat this green Jell-O."

"I'm leaving now, bye Peter, bye John. Jane's on in the morning. Visiting hours are over, but you stay as long as you like." As the door closed, Fred called out, "Frette sateen, 500 thread count … I didn't say that."

And so it was that John confided in my mom. "I'm also hoping to sleep in Sunny von Bulow's sheets—just once," John offered.

"John, what does that mean? Freshly cleaned sheets, I hope."

"Yes, of course. Sunny lives just above me, and apparently, according to the tabloids, the most exquisite sheets are brought to the hospital each week. My nurse promised to pinch a set for me."

After my mom's spring visit, John seemed to improve considerably. I don't know if the upswing was a coincidence or if Mom deserved some of the credit. There were others who helped John fight back. NYCB's physical therapist, Marika Molnar, paid visits to our apartment regularly. As she spoke with John about company news, she put pressure on his toes and made him point his feet. She massaged and manipulated, helping to wake the dormant dancer inside. Maggie Black visited on Tuesdays. She helped John stand at the kitchen counter, his feet in first position, and gave a short, modified ballet barre with corrections. As these two women coaxed John back to the familiarity of classical ballet, I wondered if they knew he would never return to dance. I suspect they did, just as Heather understood there would be no trip to Hydra that summer or the next. But with each tendu and each repetition, life returned to a man who was fighting back from the brink of death.

By August, John was restless. He had gained weight, started to see some regrowth of hair and found the will to live. He attended ballet performances, and as I prepared for the company's return to Washington, D.C., John was planning his own visit. With principal dancer Gen Horiuchi due to appear in the Broadway production of *Song and Dance*, Ib Andersen was the only Oberon for *A Midsummer Night's Dream*. I was chosen to debut in this role at The Kennedy Center, sharing a week's worth of performances with Ib. John was excited to see my debut but probably more excited to attend Heather's birthday party. The Gruens hired a car, and Julia would travel with him on Saturday. John was giddy with anticipation.

The night before his travels, I called from D.C. to say goodnight. "Are you sure you're up for this? It's a lot. You know you don't have to come down here."

"I wouldn't miss this for anything, my dear. I'm just tired and need to sleep. I have a bit of a headache.'

"Have you taken anything for the headache? Did you let your

doctor know? Is it anything like the ones you had …"

"Peter, stop, I'm fine, it's a headache. I'm excited, and I'm tired. Stop worrying, I'll see you tomorrow night. I suspect Oberon needs his rest, too."

"All right then. Goodnight, I love you."

"I love you more. Goodnight, my treasure."

As soon as we hung up the phone, I called Julia and asked her to give John a call. I then called my friend Anne, who lived a few blocks away. Anne had a key to our place, and I asked her to stop by in the morning before she went to work to check on John and help him prepare for the trip.

When Anne arrived in the morning, John was dead. Ted was by his head, nuzzling and pressing his paw against his face. Anne, in horror, felt no pulse, called 911 and tried to call me. Unable to reach me, she called New York City Ballet and spoke with company manager, Patricia Turk, who found me in my hotel room.

I opened the door and saw Pat's white face. Sitting beside me on the hotel bed, Pat told me what I already knew. The room was so cold, the light was harsh, the news crippling. Pat hugged me as I cried inconsolably. She had booked a flight on the next shuttle to New York, gave me some cash and told me a car would be downstairs in ten minutes. She asked if she should stay, but I told her I was okay.

When she left, I sat in silence for a moment on the bed and then let out a deep, guttural moan that filled the heavy air, followed by heaving sobs. I thought we had defeated cancer and defied death, and just when optimism felt earned and appropriate, John was ripped from life so abruptly. Part of me was torn in the process.

Hours later, I was in New York. I walked slowly up the three flights of stairs and entered our apartment. Anne sat in the corner holding Ted. She was shaking. John's body was on the bed with a sheet over his head. The scene was more gruesome than I had imagined. The ambulance arrived quickly, but when the patient is pronounced dead, the ambulance leaves and the morgue wagon is called. The morgue wagon moves at a much slower pace, which is why John lay underneath a sheet on the bed. I couldn't look under the sheet just like I couldn't drop a handful of earth on his coffin in Tarboro the following week.

I spent the day in our apartment in a complete stupor before flying back to D.C. Anne stayed to help, and various friends tried to do what they could. There were credit cards to cancel, sheets to wash, family to contact. It was overwhelming. I needed to find something to hold on to. I wanted to dance. On Wednesday night, I stepped on stage as Oberon, woefully under-rehearsed. Maria Calegari gave me a pewter Russian orthodox cross on a chain, which Mr. B. had given to Joe Duell years before. She said it had helped her cope with Joe's death. I tucked it inside my tunic. Ib Andersen stood stage right telling me what to do before each entrance, and ballet mistress Sally Leland did the same on stage left. It wasn't a great debut, but I needed dance more than ever. Just as Maggie and Marika had helped John to heal through dance, I needed to heal in the same way.

The day after John died, I called my dad.

"Hi, Dad."

There was a long pause. "Hey, kid, I heard about your roommate from your mother. I'm so sorry."

I was already crying, "Dad, he wasn't just a roommate, he was so much more, I loved him."

"I know, Pete, your mom told me." He paused, and I could

hear his measured breathing. "I'm so sorry."

"I'm so sorry I couldn't tell you about us, but I need you to know now. I need you to know what I'm going through." The sobbing was making it difficult to get words out. "I'm really hurting, Dad. I'm really hurting."

"I know, Pete, I know. It's going to be all right. I'm going to help you. I am. I love you, son."

The days after John's death were a cloud of disillusionment. I thought I had reached the bottom, but I hadn't. My landlord knocked on the apartment door the next day and informed me I would need to be out by the end of the week. I could tell it pained him to tell me this news. He offered a guest room in his duplex below us, but I needed to go. After forty-eight hours of sifting through a lifetime of collected objects that included paintings, photos, *Gourmet* magazines, spices, books, clothing, Greek pottery and hundreds of albums from the Inkspots to Patsy Cline to David Bowie, I was both despondent and at the end of my ability to function. Though friends were in and out, I felt completely alone, holding a shell of an existence, wondering how to go on. Dancing was a ladder I could climb, and I added a serious focus on education, starting with drawing and painting classes and soon adding a full core curriculum by enrolling in Fordham University. I also focused on my dad, who was holding on to a different shell. We had one year left, and it was a difficult one, but he had very few people he could talk to, and I felt equally alone. He had a drinking apartment on the east side, where I stayed for a while. We grew closer. We had no secrets and a shared demon in his drinking. I couldn't save him, but we healed together and moved forward until his time was up almost exactly a year after John's death. It was time.

31

A ROUGH NIGHT

New York City Ballet took up residence for three weeks each July in Saratoga Springs. At first, the town seemed to be a fairly typical if not attractive college town about twenty miles north of Albany. It had a bowling alley, Pizza Hut, Dunkin' Donuts, Friendly's and scattered taverns, motels, shops, parks and restaurants. Saratoga has a few distinctions that set it apart from other towns. Sulphur springs could be found everywhere, with spigots coming from rocks right next to the post office. Grand European-style mineral baths could be found on the southern edge of the town. These extensive and antiquated spas had served to attract health seekers and wealthy travelers for hundreds of years. A large community of Hasidic Jews resided nearby in order to take the waters. Since 1863, Saratoga was home to a legendary thoroughbred racetrack, attracting bettors, glitterati and a freewheeling moneyed crowd in the month of August. Mary Lou and Cornelius Vanderbilt "Sonny" Whitney had a palatial home there called Cady Hill. Mary Lou presided over the social scene during the twenty-eight-day racing season. Along with about twenty golf courses, dozens of quality antique stores and a handful of Victorian mansions, there is also a writer's retreat called Yaddo that at various points in time housed Leonard Bernstein, Truman Capote, Sylvia Plath and David Sedaris.

This was my summer destination for twenty-four years, the first two as a summer course student at the New York State Summer School for the Arts and the next twenty-two as a company member.

As professional dancers, we became adults before our time and yet in Saratoga, we felt like adults for the first time. We all looked forward to this break from routine, but Saratoga was also a place where rules and laws were broken, and the police force was busy when we were in town. For many of us, this was the only three weeks in the year when we drove cars, lived in houses, took out the trash on Tuesdays and set out the lawn furniture on weekends. Many of our summer rentals had swimming pools, and the chance to barbecue with friends was a novel and welcome experience.

My first Saratoga summer as a company member, I rented a moped. I hadn't found the time to get a driver's license, and it turned out a moped could be rented without one. It couldn't go faster than fifty miles an hour, but on local roads, it was fine for my needs. I wore a helmet and rode responsibly. Carrying the helmet down the corridor at Saratoga Performing Arts Center (SPAC) always prompted questions.

"You really ride a motorcycle?" asked Afshin.

"Actually, no, it's just a moped."

"Are you safe? They seem so unsafe." Afshin's girlfriend Liz now joined the unwanted conversation.

"Very safe."

"You be careful," Liz warned.

"Don't worry, I am."

I wasn't the only one with a moped. Doug had one too, but somehow, I was the most talked about moped rider in the company.

In my second week, I was cornered by Rosemary Dunleavy and Heather Watts.

Rosemary began, "Peter, we are very concerned about you riding a moped. Is it really safe? Do you wear a helmet?"

I didn't want to be rude, but I was holding the helmet under my arm. I just looked at it.

"You have to return it," said Heather before I could respond.

"But Sean and Doug have one, too; do they have to return theirs?" I countered.

"You have to return it because you're too young and too talented to be running the risk of hurting yourself. Besides, there's no one else to dance the third movement of Bizet," Heather declared.

Bit of an insult to Sean and Doug, but she was correct about the third movement of *Symphony in C*. I could see I wasn't going to win this, and besides, I was outnumbered two to one.

Rosemary added, "Peter insists you return it as well."

Make that three to one. Nail in the coffin. I returned the moped and rented a bicycle. The following summer, I obtained a license and borrowed my sister's Saab.

Mom and Dad were now divorced. Both asked to come visit me in Saratoga, knowing I had some plum roles to perform and a bit more down time than I had in New York City. Mom came with Pepper Crofoot and stayed at the Adelphi Hotel. I suggested Dad come the following weekend on the train. Even though he was seeing Elizabeth at the time, he came alone. He was to arrive in the evening in time to see me perform.

SPAC is a covered outdoor venue that seats five thousand with lawn seating for many more. From the stage during matinees, we could see the picnics and small children dancing on the grass. The theater was home to the Philadelphia Orchestra and a popular spot for summer concert tours. Returning to work on Tuesdays, we were delighted to find the names of weekend occupants on our dressing room doors, like James Taylor, Cindy Lauper or Tina Turner. This led to speculations about which toilet Cindy sat on and which mirror Tina used to tease her famous wigs.

Dad would see me in Jerome Robbins' *Interplay*. I asked him to meet me at the stage door following the second ballet. The stage was adjacent to the loading dock on the side of the theater at the base of a long driveway. My best friend, Alexia, hadn't met my dad and waited with me during the second intermission. Dad didn't show. Intermission ended, and the music of *Brahms-Schoenberg Quartet* could be heard coming from the orchestra pit as the last ballet began. I told Alexia to head home while I continued to wait. She and I shared a split-level ranch with Stacy Caddell and Julia Hays.

Ten minutes later, during the quieter second movement of *Brahms-Schoenberg Quartet*, as I sat on the edge of the loading dock, I spotted a figure in the dark, staggering downhill along the driveway towards the stage door. His walk was irregular, off-balance and serpentine. An usher hovered nervously a short distance behind him.

"Peter? Peter ... you there?"

Dad drank too much every day. Somehow, he functioned behind the wheel of a car, as a trial lawyer, at a dinner party and as a father, but there were days when Dad's drinking was beyond his usual amount (five bourbons to my count). As he stumbled down the hill, slurring words loudly against the sweet melodic sounds of the New York City Ballet Orchestra, I was filled with dread, anger and embarrassment.

I quickly ran up the drive to intercept him. "Dad, what happened? Why are you so late?" He was humming to the music. "You need to be quiet."

"I saw you dance ... you were in ... cred ...ible. You're a really good dancer, Pete. I needed a drink after I saw you dance ... to celebrate ... and I, I had a glass of white wine." Dad thought for a moment, then continued, "I had one glass, just one." He seemed pleased with this "... and then, I had another ... but it wasn't wine ..." The usher still hovered and moved a bit closer.

"Dad, let's go. I need to get you home."

"I can't walk back up that hill." He was shaking his head. He leaned closer and changed to a whisper, "And I don't think the usher likes me." The smell of scotch was an affront.

I was frustrated and humiliated. Company members peered out of the stage door to see what all of the talking was. The usher offered a flashlight.

"Yes, you can, Dad, and you will. Let's go." I took him by the arm and pulled him back up the hill, relieved Alexia had left.

We drove for about thirty minutes even though the house was only five minutes away. I wanted an opportunity for Dad to sober up. He slept during the drive, snoring loudly. Now nearing eleven, I needed to get him into our guest room, past a house full of friends, including Stacy's visiting boyfriend George McPhee, a hockey player on the New York Rangers.

When we pulled into the driveway, I woke Dad up. I gave him water and a mint. He seemed better. He strode confidently into the house unassisted, eager to meet my friends. I was far less eager.

We walked into full lights and full company. The television was hastily turned off, and everyone stood. I introduced my dad and explained he was exhausted and ready for bed. Hands shook, heads nodded, and I took my dad by the arm.

"Wait, I don't want to go to bed." His words were still a bit slurry. Julie started to laugh. "I want to meet your friends, Pete."

Julie was the first to speak, "And we want to meet you, Mr. Boal. Can I get you some pizza?" This was not the plan.

"Thank you, Judy, I'll take some pizza, why not? And a drink if you have one. Not water please, I'd like a real drink." Dad spotted George, "Pete, who's this? You look like George McPhee."

George laughed, "Pleased to meet you, Mr. Boal. You must like hockey?"

For about fifteen minutes, things seemed to go relatively smoothly, though Dad seemed completely inebriated to me. He finished the slice of pepperoni and a wine cooler. He conceded to George that the Rangers were a decent team, but the Bruins were far better. After a little protesting, George took it in stride.

When George and Stacy headed to bed, Dad asked me where the liquor cabinet was. I told him we had no liquor in the house and that he did not need another drink.

Dad was always a passive drunk, more melancholy than angry or violent, but tonight was different. He was adamant that he have hard alcohol, and a heated argument between father and son ensued. Alexia and Julie went upstairs. But I knew everyone was listening.

Dad was opening cabinets and slamming them shut. He was wearing himself down. He leaned against the kitchen counter, unable to stand on his own any more. "Peter, you don't understand, I need a drink, dammit, and I don't mean another watered-down wine. I need some bourbon ... now."

"We don't have anything in this house, it's almost midnight and you need to go to bed."

Dad grabbed the Saab keys with unexpected alacrity and headed for the door, hitting the stair rail hard as he tried to head down the half flight of stairs. "I'm going. I paid for that car. I saw a liquor store in town, and it's open 'til one, I checked." The clarity alcoholics can have when it comes to obtaining alcohol is astounding and infuriating.

"Dad! You cannot drive a car. You're too drunk. How many accidents do you have to have? You are embarrassing me again, like you always do. Give me the keys." He wouldn't let go of them, so I pulled the keys from his clenched hand. He let out a pathetic shout as he flopped to the floor.

"I'll go buy your fucking bourbon for you, but this cannot continue. I can't do this. You can't do this."

A few minutes later, I pulled into the lot of Saratoga Spirits and Liquor. There were more cars than I expected. Only the dregs of Saratoga were there. I moved quickly to locate the bourbon and bought a fifth of Bulleit, hoping no one from the company, the audience or the police force was watching. The drinking age was nineteen, but it had just been lifted from eighteen, and at midnight in downtown Saratoga Springs, the clerk, behind his protective plexiglass, didn't seem to look too closely at my fake ID.

I ran up the steps of our house, but Dad was nowhere to be seen. Alexia was on the couch waiting for me.

"He went to bed. I put some water on his nightstand. He seemed okay. He's still dressed in his suit."

"Thanks for waiting up. I'll get his clothes off when I go to bed. Did you notice if he was on his back or on his side?"

"He was on his side. Why does that matter?"

"It does." I took a deep sigh. The last few hours had been horrible, and the release of emotion was coming. I tried to speak but couldn't get a word out, just a heaving sound.

Alexia hugged me. She was a devoted friend. She was also a Mormon and had never seen anyone, especially not someone's father, as inebriated as my dad was that night.

"I … I'm so embarrassed. I wanted him to be okay to meet you. I wanted to spend some time with him. But this isn't him, or maybe it is. He's like this all the time, and I hate it. Sometimes I hate him. Sometimes I wish he wasn't my father."

I was sobbing uncontrollably, then, and I know Alexia must have been unnerved, but she just kept hugging me tighter.

"Remember, you're not him" she said. "And he's a good person who's troubled." This felt a bit like Mormon church doctrine, but I had no choice but to agree and find solace in her words.

"Things can't go on like this."

It might have been the roughest night I spent with my dad, but in the morning, he was in the kitchen before anyone else, cooking bacon, which woke George up first, then the others. The Bruins/Rangers debate was on again. Dad found pancake mix and made batch upon batch to the delight of all. He was articulate, humorous, insightful and admired, even by me. He never apologized for his behavior, and I'm not even sure he remembered what happened that night.

Lyndall and Dart, Dartmoor, 1946 *(image courtesy of the author)*

32

CLOUD NINE

Passions are passed from generation to generation, sometimes without any awareness of the developing legacy. And sometimes they are placed on the next generation by the previous one, unrealized or unwanted. My grandparents shared their love of ballet with my mother, and to no lesser extent, with my father. From my parents, it came to me, and I ran with it, letting it fill my life in every way. Jenny excelled on so many fronts, but none seemed equal to my unique passion for ballet. Law became her chosen profession, and she proved a cunning lawyer, eventually ascending to chief magistrate judge for the State of Massachusetts, clearly a high achiever with no need for the parents to worry. But the excitement surrounding my early success in a most unusual profession for boys eclipsed so many of Jenny's more commonplace successes. Jenny experienced the usual slights and bruises of a teenager navigating her way through private life and public high school, but her younger brother's story, and the attention it warranted, posed a different conundrum. Mom stood by her side all too often as acquaintances gushed about the ballet and me. She recognized her daughter's discomfort and sought a solution. In an all-out effort to help Jenny find her passion, she turned to ponies.

Horses ran in my family. Granny's steed was named Lady, which sounds so much better when you hear it in my grandmother's Edwardian accent. During World War II, Granny's youngest sister Freda relocated from blitz-torn London to pastoral Devon to serve in the land army. Helping to plant trees and work the land was an integral part of the U.K.'s war effort. Freda took to Devon, and to a local farmer named Clary, and never left. Clary's farm, named Baybenny, housed chickens, goats and cows, a house cat named Crème, Clary's lab, Jeb, Archer, their prized sheep dog, and half a dozen horses. Freda loved her barn horses as much as she loved her children. There were also her herds of wild horses that roamed the moors with no attachment to humanity except for the Baybenny brand on their bottoms and their shared love of Freda. As she bounced across the moors in her mud-splattered Land Rover, the herd would come to attention. They knew Freda was armed with pockets full of carrots, which caused her horses' bold necks to curl, their endless manes, forelocks and tails blowing in the winds. The wild herd became docile. Freda would hug and hold as many as she could before the herd bolted at the sight of Archer in the distance.

On my mother's tenth birthday, Freda offered her the greatest of gifts. The pony's name was Dart, after the Dart River that coursed past Baybenny. Though Dart lived with Freda in Devon, my mom visited often, building a truly special bond.

On the other side of the Atlantic, some thirty years later, I started out with Cricket, and there was no special bond whatsoever. Marilyn Schroer, our riding instructor, kept Cricket for the little ones who were just starting out. By the time Cricket was introduced to me for my first lesson, the pony had become both rotund and stubborn, having dealt with a few too many snot-nosed brats during her sixteen-year tenure in the riding ring. I slung her saddle onto her back without incident and then heaved on the girth. Cricket's head launched upwards while an angry hoof stomped against the stone floor in protest, but even I knew this was just for show. Next came my failed attempt to insert the metal bit of the bridle into Cricket's mouth. Cricket's pink tongue continued to reject my efforts. Mrs. Schroer was there to help. "Too cold for you, Cricky? Let's see if we can fix that." She warmed the bit in her hand and produced a chunk of carrot from her pocket, placing it alongside the metal mouthpiece. In they went. Soon, Cricket and I were headed up the hill to the ring. Cricket seemed happy if not a bit indifferent to our little stroll.

At the entrance to the ring, the plan suddenly changed. With eyeballs bulging, Cricket stopped, sinking her full weight into the earth and letting her nine-year-old master know who was boss. I turned to face my opponent and stared back. Two iron wills and a trembling lead rope separated us. My body was barely inside the riding ring, and Cricket's was rooted like an anchor just outside. Memories of Rippowam's field day and the crushing tug-of-war defeat for the red team returned. Boy and pony pulled and grunted while Mrs. Schroer laughed a few feet away. Cricket flung her powerful neck skyward, and I lost my footing and my hold on the rope, dropping into the mud while the victor trotted over to the long grasses just outside of the ring for a morning snack.

"Oh, dear, I'm afraid that's not a good start, Peter." Mrs. Schroer called to me in her singsong British accent. "We must first show them who's the boss in the relationship, and at this point, I'd have to say it's Cricket." Really, Mrs. Schroer, what makes you say that?

"Do you think you can manage to hold on to Nutmeg while I collect Miss Cricket?" Nutmeg had clearly been through this before and didn't even acknowledge my defeated presence.

Mrs. Schroer grabbed Cricket by the nose and then by the reins. With a few encouraging clucks and a wallop on the rump, the two trotted right back into the ring. The weekly lesson began.

I lasted about a year and learned to ride quickly. I was happy to graduate from Cricket to Heather, but my heart wasn't in the whole riding thing, and the few times that Heather stopped short of a small jump, causing me to slide up her neck and then down onto the dusty earth, were enough to persuade my mom and me riding was not my thing.

Jenny was a different story, showing far more talent in the equestrian arts. By the time she was twelve, Mrs. Schroer had entered Jenny in a local horse show. Jenny came home that night with a beaming smile, a long yellow ribbon and a new passion. As her interest increased, so did the number of lessons per week. Jenny joined a select group of jumpers Mrs. Schroer helped bring to Westchester County horse shows on weekends. The star of this group was Susie Schroer, Marilyn's daughter and Jenny's classmate, who not only helped care for the ponies, but also claimed most of the prizes.

Jenny enjoyed the whole thing, finding a new confidence in herself and discovering a small circle of friends whom she desperately needed. My parents bought her the right boots, jodhpurs, a plush riding jacket and an expensive Crosby saddle. She looked rakish on her cream-colored pony's back with her black velvet helmet tipped just so. I loved watching her concentration in the ring, as the determination of a small girl triumphed over a mammal several times her size and weight.

One day, outside of Richard Oliver's clothing and gift shop, we bumped into Wendy Tweedale who had recently been to *The Nutcracker*. My mom reconfigured her routine frequently to avoid Wendy Tweedale, but we were on a collision course with no escape.

"I do believe I see a prince right here on the sidewalk, how is his highness doing? Oh, Lyndall, how proud you all must be of Peter."

My mom was already rubbing Jenny's shoulder while Jenny squirmed to the left. "It is fun. Happy New Year, Wendy, it's good to see you. Family's well I trust?"

"Yes, yes, Chad found out he's headed for Princeton following in his brother and his father's footsteps. Another Tiger! Anyway, we all went to see *The Nutcracker* just before Christmas and were so pleasantly surprised to see Peter's name in the program. You must have been over the moon." She looked at Jenny, "I'm so sorry, I've forgotten your name, honey."

"It's Jenny."

"Jenny, you must be so proud of your brother; do you dance too?"

"No."

Mom jumped in, "Jenny is doing so well in school, and she

rides horses ..." You could see the confusion on Wendy's face. She was not ready to move on from *The Nutcracker*. "She's in all advanced placement classes at Fox Lane and getting such good grades. Aren't you high honors again this semester, Jenny? I can't keep track."

Silence.

"And she's quite the accomplished equestrian these days. Her instructor suggested we look into a circuit of horse shows in Virginia this winter with the thought that she might one day ride at Madison Square Garden."

Whoa. News to me, but apparently it was true. From that point forward, my mother ramped up Jenny's equestrian life. We switched trainers to a man named Emerson, with whom Susie Schroer rode. Emerson worked at Sunny Field Farm, an expansive stable in Bedford where prized racehorses were bred. He was known up and down the East Coast as one of the finest and most competitive trainers. He was also great for Jenny, encouraging and supportive, and we could all see the results. With Emerson came Slipstich, a better show pony than any Mrs. Schroer could offer. Slipstich came with a lease price, too, which my dad thought should include four white wall tires and air conditioning. Soon Jenny, Mom and I were jetting off to Virginia and Southhampton on weekends in order for Jenny to compete in the most prestigious horse shows, collecting fistfuls of ribbons and accumulating points in a national ranking system.

In retrospect, the horse shows were a kind of disease for our family that none of us, except maybe my dad, could see. My parents' marriage had never been great, but their fierce devotion to travel, children, jobs, politics and social causes left little time to evaluate the plagued relationship. Though my dad's law firm continued to employ him despite the frequent missteps his alcoholism caused, he was no longer pulling in or retaining the high-paying clients. Mom was done, tired of the embarrassments, wrecked cars and excuses. A weekend at a horse show in Virginia was far better than another pointless argument with an incoherent husband.

Mom threw herself into the world of horse shows, even after Jenny started to tire of them. We built a barn and fenced in land to house Jenny's ponies. (At one point she had two!) In the end, Jenny's ponies needed to be at Sunny Field. With a vacant barn, we took in three of Mrs. Schroer's flock. Heather and I were briefly reunited, and with her came Snodgrass and Georgie Gal. Jenny and Mom started a weekend routine of waking at three a.m. to trek hundreds of miles to Pennsylvania or Virginia, arriving just in time for the early Saturday morning classes. Sometimes, they would hit the road after school on Friday to reach some sad motel after midnight. Soon, I started spending the weekends with friends or with Mrs. Wilson. Dad was happy to accept business trips with colleagues who preferred pouring to protesting. The bills were coming in quickly, and we were soon sliding into a financial hole that we would never climb out of.

Then came Cloud Nine, known in the stable as Herman. Cloud Nine was a beauty through and through. Just three years old and fourteen point two hands tall, making him about a half centimeter shy of being classified as a horse, his endless legs and tapered ankles bragged of pedigree. The gleaming chestnut coat was all thoroughbred. Emerson brought him to our attention, and before my dad could object to the purchase price, my mom was in the barn nuzzling.

Jenny was now almost eighteen and moving through her senior year with a high GPA, plenty of friends and encouraging college prospects. How she managed a schedule brimming with horse shows on dozens of weekends, I don't know. I never saw her. Ballet was now my entire life. I had moved into my first apartment in New York City. Our family was starting to fracture, and my departure from our unhealthy home was a welcome one.

In a sense, my mom left too, completely focused on Cloud Nine's ranking on the national circuit. According to Emerson, Herman had a shot at Green Pony of the year, a category reserved for the most prized three-year-old in the country. Jenny was eligible to ride ponies until she turned eighteen, making this a deadline year.

Columbus Day weekend caused an awkward reunion, with no horse shows, no business trips and my return home. The house was quiet. Jenny had retreated to her room, and I was reading in the guest room just off of the living room where my parents sat by a roaring fire. Dad was a master at making fires, and this one crackled loudly, competing with the songs of his favorite album by Carly Simon. Mom was armed with her latest Nevil Shute novel while Dad pored through old copies of the *Journal* and the *Times*, which surrounded him on the floor like a moat.

I could hear Mom's voice. "Jenny and I are off again this weekend, it's the Virginia Beach Classic. Emerson thinks Herman can win this one too, though he wants to put Susie on her for the final class if he's doing well."

After a pause Dad responded, "Why would Susie Schroer ride Jenny's horse?"

"Brad, my goodness, it's not a horse, it's a pony. I've told you a thousand times. Susie is the stronger rider, and in a close call, that can make a difference between a blue ribbon and none at all. We are so near the top of this national ranking system, and at this point, Emerson doesn't think we should take any chances."

Dad folded his newspaper and placed it on the floor. I could hear the clink of the ice cubes in his bourbon. "What's wrong with not winning? Do we have to win? How does Jennifer feel about this?"

"Don't be ridiculous, Jenny wants to win too. She knows how this would look on a college application. We are talking about the number one Green Pony in the country, Brad, honestly. You know it would mean a great deal to your daughter if one day you showed up at one of these horse shows."

I heard the creak of floorboards in the upstairs hallway and knew Jenny had heard the tension rising in my parents' voices. Sometimes she and I would gather on the top step, unseen but able to listen to the arguments my parents were having in the living room.

"I thought we were doing this for Jennifer, not the horse. I don't give a Goddamned shit about the horse. How does this make Jennifer feel when another rider gets called in for the important rides?"

Mom put her book down. "Brad you are turning this into something it is not. Jenny has ridden this horse almost every day for a year now and has ridden him in more winning classes than anyone else. She wants this, and we need to support her in this quest however we can. And speaking of supporting Jenny, Emerson's office called again about the August bill. They are not even mentioning his fees for September. I need to pay that. Can you please make sure we have enough in checking for that?"

Conversations about finances were toxic at this point in

our family. I knew wherever Jenny was perched, we were both now cringing.

A painful silence hung in the air until Dad's voice broke the tension.

He was on the verge of shouting. "Do you think this Emerson gives a Goddamned shit about our daughter? No, he cares about his fees and having a highly ranked pony. He's not the parent here, Lyndall, we are, and as a parent, I don't want Jennifer pulled off her horse so the Schroer girl can get the prize."

Mom was up. "How can you even suggest you understand this situation? Emerson is wonderful with Jenny, like a father to her, which she certainly doesn't have at home. You're never here, and when you are, you're completely intoxicated. I can't even have this conversation with you."

I could hear Jenny's muffled crying from the top of the stairs.

"Lyndall, this is about you! You're the one who wants this. You want to succeed at something because you can't make this family work, just like you can't make this marriage work." He was slurring his words. "You are the one failing our daughter as a parent, and you can't even see it."

My mother's voice was now trembling, "That is grossly unfair, Brad!"

In a rage, my mother grabbed her fleeced-lined bedroom slipper and hurled it across the living room, hitting my dad square in the face, causing his glasses to fall on the carpet and bourbon to splash onto his chest. At that moment, Jenny was at the door to living room. I stood just behind her.

"Mom, stop it!" Jenny shouted.

My mother pushed past us, ran down the hall and up the stairs. The door to her cavernous bedroom slammed. Her crying could be heard in the distance.

Jenny turned to my dad. "Look what you've done. Why do you always have to ruin everything?"

Dad was speechless and wet with alcohol but still held his half-empty glass. Jenny wasn't done.

"Why can't you stop this? Why? You're killing us, Dad." Jenny walked into the room and stood in front of my dad at the edge of the ring of newspapers. "Give me the glass."

Dad chuckled and shook his head, "I'm not gonna give you my drink. This's not your problem Jennifer, this's mine."

"Dad! It is my problem. It's all of our problem. It's ruining all of us."

Dad stood up in an attempt to hug Jenny but forgot about the piles of newspapers and stumbled. Jenny jumped back and looked at her father in disgust.

"Dad!"

She ran from the living room, down the hall and up the stairs until we heard her door slam shut, and quiet returned. Even Carly Simon had been replaced by the repeated click of the record player's needle. The fire still crackled.

I waited a few moments, not really sure to whom I should go. I opted for my dad.

As I stepped into the room, he greeted me with, "Hey, kid, hope you didn't hear all that." He wiped a tear from his eye as he put his glasses back on.

"I did hear some of it, Dad, is everything okay with you guys?"

"No, Pete, it's not okay. You want to know the truth, your mother and I are going to separate when Jenny heads for college. And we're broke." He paused to sigh and swallow. The tears were back. He took a few deep breaths and sank back into his chair. "We need to sell this old house and see where we are."

I hadn't expected this much disclosure, but I suspected all of it. It was almost calming to hear it articulated so concisely.

"Dad, I think that's the right thing to do. This is just not working for any of us."

Dad was crying again. "The funny thing is, I still love her, Pete. We just can't make it work. After twenty-three years of marriage, we just can't make it work."

I wanted to hug him, but he was now so sunken into his chair, I just walked over to put a hand on his shoulder, and he placed his trembling hand on mine.

"This whole thing with the horse has wrecked us. We can't afford this in any way, and Jenny won't even speak to your mother. I should've stepped in sooner. It's my fault too." He was on his feet again and headed for the closet by the Steinway for more bourbon.

Months later, the separation was official, and Cloud Nine was Green Pony of the year. Susie Schroer rode in the important final classes, and Jenny watched until it was time to stand with Cloud Nine to have her picture taken with the president of the horse show, holding on to a clueless Herman, who was temporarily decorated with an elaborate trio of ribbons while Jenny held the silver-plated trophy.

Despite the high costs associated with our ownership of Cloud Nine, the prized pony was suddenly worth a great deal. Purchased and insured for $9,000 the prior year, he was now worth near $80,000. He could also be leased for close to $10,000 per season for showing or breeding. We opted to lease instead of selling. A few months into the first year's lease, on the opening day of the Southampton Classic, Herman suffered from a nasty cold. He was lethargic and glassy-eyed. His new trainer ordered a shot of butane in each nostril, a known trick in the equestrian world that perks up a drowsy horse for a short while. Herman didn't perk up, and a second round of injections was administered. According to the vet who was called, there might have been a third. Soon, Herman was dancing frantically in his stall like a moth in the light. He wouldn't stop, worrying both groom and trainer. By the time the vet arrived, Herman had shattered two ankles and collapsed on the earthen floor of his stall with eyes bulging and froth bubbling from his month. His condition was deemed beyond hope. The vet administered a final injection in order to euthanize the suffering animal, and Cloud Nine was no more.

Me and Heather before a ride *(image courtesy of the author)*

33

CHRISTMAS EVE, 1981

There were moments of utter bliss during my childhood in Bedford, and they often occurred on Christmas Eve. My mother frequently proclaimed December 24th her favorite day of the year. "It's the anticipation of all things wonderful."

During the years when we boarded three of Mrs. Schroer's herd in our barn, we would take them out on a ride just after our robust breakfast of eggs, bacon and waffles. My dad and whichever set of grandparents were visiting that year would settle in the living room with a blazing fire and newspapers or knitting. Mom, Jenny and I would head for the barn for a morning ride, bundled up in scarves, parkas, hats and mittens.

Bedford was laced with myriad riding trails and dirt roads, fiercely guarded by the Bedford Riding Lanes Association and the zoning board. Diminutive yellow and black BRLA signs were posted throughout the town at the entrance to paths and along the roads warning hikers and bikers of the official purpose of the trails. Passing a horse while driving in Bedford was a daily occurrence, and drivers knew to retreat to pedestrian speeds and veer to the opposite side of the road.

It always seemed to snow the day before Christmas. Big, geometric flakes wafted downwards onto parka sleeves and my waiting tongue. On Heather's waddling back, sandwiched between Snodgrass and Georgie Gal, I would turn my face skyward and take it all in, eyes closed, mouth open. Some conversation was traded back and forth between the three of us, but often just the rustle of evergreens, the hypnotic clop of hoofs and the periodic knocking of the woodpeckers sufficed.

When my maternal grandparents would visit, we were all at our best. Granny and Grandfather were passionate about the same social causes and political leaders as my parents. Dad often crossed paths with Grandfather around the globe while volunteering for the International Planned Parenthood Federation. Hearing my dad debating and cajoling with a peer was rare and wonderful. How articulate and humorous he could be. Sometimes, on these occasions, the alcohol was an afterthought and didn't take hold until late in the evening.

My mother seemed fortified by the presence of her parents, reminded of what she had aspired to in the first place before life took over. We would often host guests and gatherings, and the afternoon meals would last for hours. Our formal dining room with two fireplaces boasted fine china and glassware, along with the silverware pulled from its mahogany chest. Napkin rings and tiny silver salt and pepper shakers dotted the starched white tablecloth with an endless array of serving spoons and holly. Distant memories of Mrs. Hattie groaning over all the silver pieces that needed polishing made us smile. Mom was not a great cook, leaving the task to Mrs. Wilson whenever possible, but roast beef and Yorkshire pudding were two regular triumphs from her kitchen.

Once everyone was served, Dad would rise with glass in hand. We were a family of polished public speakers, especially on the Cadbury side, but my dad was different, both unscripted and genuine with an inevitable dash of humor.

I remember his toast the last year we gathered for Christmas before my parents' separation. It must have been 1981. Standing at the head of the table, eclipsed by the oversized sweater given to him the previous Christmas by Grampy and Nanny, he removed his eyeglasses and raised his crystal wine glass.

"Ahem ... I just want to say ... pass the Yorkshire pudding please." He sat back down, picking up his knife and fork to peals of polite laughter.

"Brad, really!" Mom was laughing, too, and scanning the faces around the table to see the reaction of the others.

Back on his feet, Dad began again. "Let us thank Lyndall and her helpers in the kitchen for this formidable feast we are about to enjoy. We're also so pleased to have George and Barbara with us again for Christmas. It's getting harder to find left-leaning liberals in this town, and if we have to import them from Canada, then so be it." More laughter.

"Corinne, we are so pleased to have you with us today. You know you are an important part of this family, too." Corinne Blum was a waif of a woman, always impeccably dressed, who befriended my grandparents after the war when they lived in New York while Grandfather worked for the United Nations. She still lived in Manhattan and often joined us for holidays, having lost her son and husband many years prior.

"Holidays are about family, and sometimes I think I'm blessed to have Lyndall and Peter and Jennifer and all of you." Dad's voice was starting to tremble. "I love you kids and your mom, and I am so proud of you two, Jennifer with your riding and Peter with your dancing, and most of all, we are proud of the remarkable young adults you two are becoming. Watching you two blossom is the greatest gift your mother and I could ever have. I am a lucky man, and I don't even know if I deserve all of you, but I thank you for putting up with your old dad."

He set down his glass, placed both hands on the table and bowed his head, unable to continue.

Mom chimed in from the other end of the table. "Well, here's to family!" Dad sat down and wiped each eye with his handkerchief. The clinking of glasses could be heard echoing around the room. "Let's all join hands for a Quaker grace."

Eventually, we'd all follow one conversation, navigating from the merits of Norman Manley's leadership in Jamaica, and his disdain for my grandmother's coffee, to the civil unrest in Sri Lanka, which my grandparents still called Ceylon. It was another language to me, but I savored the tone of excitement, inclusiveness, and harmony. After Jenny asked to be excused, I stayed at the table, mopping up sauces with another piece of Yorkshire pudding, not ready to let the moment pass.

After naps and glasses of sherry, accompanied by the music of the Mormon Tabernacle Choir and the last-minute wrapping of presents, we'd load into our cars and head for the Village Green. Families congregated around the massive Douglas fir in the center of the green. Organ music was piped in from nearby St. Patrick's Church, and volunteers distributed carol books with colorful drawings and taper candles. Many brought thermoses filled with hot chocolate or cider, and everyone shared everything. Around a massive bonfire we gathered, leaving behind our arguments and failings for the moment to sing together. My tiny grandmother clutched her towering husband's arm while pulling the slight Corinne close to her side. Jenny nestled against my mother, and the feel of my father's arm around my shoulders was everything I could wish for.

BRADLY AT BOAT HOUSE, LITTLE ALUM LAKE, BRIMFIELD, MASS. EARLY 1940'S

Bradlee at Little Alum *(image courtesy of the author)*

EPILOGUE

GHOST

If you add up all the time I spent with my father over twenty years, it wasn't much. Yet his presence, or absence, loomed and still does.

When he died, I was on a West Coast tour with New York City Ballet. We were performing at Zellerbach Hall in Berkeley, California. Jerome Robbins's *Glass Pieces* was about to begin when I was summoned to a pay phone near the dressing rooms. Mom was on the line. She told me the news of my dad's death. Alexia was there to console me, and a small gaggle of ballet masters and stage managers hovered nearby wanting to know how long they should hold the curtain. Minutes later, I was on stage walking. Robbins had asked us to move through space with purpose and without emotion, like the commuters at rush hour in Grand Central Terminal. Coworkers crowded the wings watching me perform with tears rolling down my face and neck. Later that night, I boarded a redeye for New York.

Dad had been attending an International Planned Parenthood Federation conference in Jamaica. His friends said he drank too much at the Wyndham Rose Hall Resort bar, then stumbled to his room after last call. His doctors had warned him repeatedly about the weakened state of his liver, but he continued to test fate like a slow suicide. That night he lost. When he didn't show up for breakfast, friends worried. The body was found in his hotel bed with empty bottles from the mini bar on and around the nightstand. Elizabeth, his new wife, was adamant the body be flown home for the funeral, but the heat in the tropics was too great and decomposition too fast.

The funeral was held at a small Presbyterian church in Katonah not far from the train station. Elizabeth was a Catholic. Her piety was not in question by the Church, but her divorce was, so she and Dad had been attending the less judgmental Presbyterian house of worship. Mom was seated towards the back with Marilyn Schroer. Jenny and I were in the front with Elizabeth, Bruce, Mrs. Wilson and Joe Guay. Most of the Guay family attended.

I was surprised how many people were in attendance, given my dad's withdrawal and demise. He was still loved, just like the young father who had carried his son around the Police and Firemen's Fair eighteen years prior on that hot summer day in Bedford Hills. Partners, secretaries and law clerks came from the city. Members of the Bedford planning and zoning boards sat beside neighbors, friends and even a few rivals. I saw Tripp and Wallace Harley, Mrs. Hammond, Waldo Jones, both of my dad's roommates from Harvard and so many people I didn't even know.

I sat there not listening to speeches and wanting to scream at all of the assembled and myself. How had we let this happen?

So many assembled had stepped forward to save him and each had failed in the face of his gripping addiction. I remembered Jenny shouting through tears, imploring Dad to stop drinking, and Bruce pulling the family together for an intervention. Mom had shouldered all she could during a twenty-five-year marriage. I did what I could, but I also had to step away acknowledging a losing battle, and the need to save myself in the process. One by one, we pulled away leaving Dad so alone and teetering on the edge. Elizabeth adored him, but she ignored what was needed and filled his glass without question. Where was I?

After a painful reception at my father's condo in Katonah, Jenny and I left in her Saab to spend the night at the Gruen's house in Water Mill. We walked the vast Hamptons beaches alone at night with Atlantic waves crashing all around us. No words, just bonding and healing.

The following day, I rejoined the tour in Seattle, skipping the burial in Massachusetts. I don't remember much about Seattle, though programs list me dancing various roles. There was a celebration dinner at Chez Shea in the Pike Place Market for Judith Fugate, who was promoted to principal while we were there. I rejoined the tour partly because I wanted to see my friend Julie Tobiason. Julie was a member of the Pacific Northwest Ballet. She had lost her father when she was twelve, and I knew she would be a support for me. Seattle was a blur.

Life went on. At twenty-six, I married Kelly. For the ceremony, we chose a Cadbury family retreat called Wynd's Point in the Malvern Hills about three hours west of London near the border of Wales. Uncle Bruce and his family were there to help make up for the fact his brother wasn't. I gave Jenny away the following summer when she married Roland Goff. Kelly and I welcomed two sons and a daughter into the world and moved to Pound Ridge, New York, right next to Bedford. I traveled on Metro North to the city each day, retracing my father's footsteps through Grand Central Terminal. Life goes on after loss, and at times, the loss fades so completely you almost forget. At other times, it comes crashing back and the pain is alarmingly fresh.

My father follows me like a ghost. The presence isn't ominous or torturous, just there. Once, driving from Beckett to Boston with my second son, Oliver, we spotted a sign for Brimfield, Massachusetts, and I told Oliver his grandfather had lived nearby.

"You mean Grampa?" Oliver asked in a high-pitched warble from his car seat in the back. He was all of six at the time.

"No, my father. He's also your grandfather. He lived near here."

"But I never met him. What should I call him?"

"That's a very good question, Oliver. Since you already have a Grampa, how about Granddad?"

"Okay, can you show me where my granddad lived?"

"Well, let's get off here, and I'll see what I can remember. I think he lived on Elm Street."

After we exited the Mass Pike onto Route 20, I saw a vast cemetery. Oliver asked if his granddad was buried there. I didn't know the answer. I had never visited his grave. We parked on the side of the road and started to walk through rolling hills of grass, maples, oaks and weathered gray headstones that stretched as far as the eye could see. I clutched Oliver's tiny hand tightly. I wondered who needed whom at that point, but his soft little hand felt reassuring and strong. I explained to him we probably wouldn't find Granddad's grave. I'm not sure I wanted to find it, but I knew Oliver needed something to hold onto. He insisted we keep looking. We walked through acres of moss-covered slabs, fresh granite markers, real and plastic flowers and tiny American flags until I determined the search was futile. I suggested a moment of silence to remember Granddad and then a return to the car. The silence was beautiful with only sounds of rustling leaves and birds calling.

Suddenly, Oliver gasped and pointed to four large letters on a stone in the distance. He was barely reading at the time, but the four letters of his last name were clearly recognizable.

As we approached the grave, we found headstones for Howard, Thane, Margaret and Richard Bradlee. Oliver cast his big eyes up to his own father to know how to react and found tears streaming down my face.

"Are you okay, Dad?" Silence. "I didn't know grown-ups could cry." He hugged me with all the force his little arms could muster. In that moment, our roles were reversed.

Fatherhood somehow reopened the wound. I was angry Oliver would never know his grandfather. Kelly had never met him, and they would have laughed and loved and shared and bonded. I wanted to ask my dad so many questions about gardening, parenting, finances, home repairs, tomatoes, tractors, taxes, and how to make pancakes that looked exactly like Disney characters.

In 2004, my dance career was nearing an end. A friend called to let me know a plum job as artistic director of Pacific Northwest Ballet was opening up in Seattle. My memory of Seattle was neither clear nor good, so I flew across the country to see what was there, and if this far-away metropolis might hold a future for me and my young family.

Six months later, I had the job. In rapid succession, Kelly and I organized a cross-country move with three kids and a cat, a retirement, a new home and a new life.

Kelly oversaw the house hunt, narrowing it down to four. One large wooden home resembled a Swiss Chalet. It was enchanting but too expensive, so we crossed it off the list, but I couldn't stop thinking about it. Two months later, we asked our agent if it was still on the market. It was, and the owners loved the idea of selling to a young family. They had been our age with young children when they bought the house thirty-three years prior. They lopped six figures off the asking price. It was still too much, but we made a bid and bought a house.

Graham and Greta Fernald requested they give us a walk-through before handing over the keys. For two hours, Greta told us more than we ever could have known about the neighbors, light switches, dog doors, water values, wall coverings, where Graham kept his law books and where their daughter's eighth birthday party was held. Graham was near silent the entire time, dutifully following the tour. Greta's love for her home was clear.

On the front porch, before they left for their new home in Madison Park, Graham turned to me and said, "Boal. B-O-A-L." He seemed to be contemplating each letter as if holding it up to the light. "I have to ask you, I knew a boy once named Boal, Bradlee Boal. Did you know him? Is he a relation?"

After a stunned silence, I answered, "He was my father." Even Greta was silent.

Graham spoke again, "Well, isn't that something. We were at Exeter together. Lost his mother at that time, didn't he? That was hard. Then Harvard, then Harvard Law. I met his wife, too, bluest eyes. Moved to Bedford, New York, right? I knew he had two children, a girl and a boy. I suppose that's you. Is he still alive? You'll have to tell him we met. He'll remember me."

"No. He passed away almost twenty years ago."

"Oh, I'm so sorry. He was a good kid. I can still picture him."

ACKNOWLEDGMENTS

There is a short but important list of individuals—friends, coworkers and family members who persistently urged me to try my hand at writing. This book would never have reached publication without them and I remain truly grateful for their support and encouragement.

These memories were pieced together like a mosaic. Stories, like objects, were created, collected, polished and placed in different configurations until a greater whole emerged. The first piece was penned in a writing class led by author, Sidney Offit at the New School for Social Research in the mid-1980s. *Cindy Dorsey and the Burrs* was selected and read aloud by Professor Offit. Reactions were varied, but mostly heated and angry. Margo Krody, a friend and fellow member of New York City Ballet was in the class. She recalled the impact of my story years after the initial reading, and suggested I dig deeper and tell more.

Not until 2011 did I write another story, this one chronicling my visit to George Balanchine's bedside in Roosevelt Hospital. I sent the story to Wendy Perron, editor of *Dance Magazine* at the time. Wendy said, "keep writing." I did. Francis Mason published an article I wrote about Richard Rapp in *Ballet Review*, and *Dance Magazine* editor, Jennifer Stahl published two pieces, one of which (Coach) is repurposed in the book. By 2015 I had assembled about twenty short stories. The mosaic was taking shape. I sent them here and there, heard encouragement, but also rejection. Friend and former co-worker, Doug Fullington, an accomplished writer himself, was unfailingly supportive. Lia, Chad, Sarah, Oliver and Mom helped scan and assemble images and keepsakes mined from scrapbooks and albums. Twyla Tharp read an early draft and could not have been more touched by the material. Theresa Ruth Howard offered invaluable perspective. As I started to share the work with a few trusted friends, the response was warm. My kids listened dutifully. "Another story, Dad?" My late Aunt Judy offered fact-checking. I'm grateful for the dialogue with my sister and mother surrounding these tales of our shared experience. I'm also painfully aware of the reopening of wounds this work may cause. My wife, Kelly, who is renowned for her criticism laced with a healthy dose of truth serum, loved everything she read. Kelly remains my pillar of strength and my super power.

At a small fundraiser for the Joyce Theater in Manhattan, I sat next to author and editor, Leslie Tonner. After talking ballet for most of the evening we turned to writing; first hers, then mine. Leslie became the real champion of this book, enlisting husband Richard Curtis as agent, and making me write twelve more chapters. After almost a year of shopping the manuscript to different publishing houses, Leslie called to say, "Congratulations!"

ACKNOWLEDGMENTS

Richard's echo could be heard in the background. Next came
Megan Trank and the team at Beaufort Books who helped this
novice author juggle a busy day job and a first book.